IRELAND'S CALL

IRELAND'S CALL

Navigating Brexit

STEPHEN COLLINS

RED STRIPE
PRESS

Published by
Red Stripe Press
an imprint of
Orpen Press
Upper Floor, Unit B3
Hume Centre
Hume Avenue
Park West Industrial Estate
Dublin 12
Ireland

email: info@orpenpress.com

www.redstripepress.com

Hardback ISBN 978-1-78605-176-9
Paperback ISBN 978-1-78605-184-4
ePub ISBN 978-1-78605-177-6

Printed in the EU

In memory of Jean Wrigley.

Contents

Acknowledgements

I am grateful to Michael Brennan of Red Stripe Press for asking me to write an account of the Irish involvement in the historic Brexit negotiations between the European Union and the United Kingdom.

I would like to thank Eileen O'Brien of Red Stripe Press for her encouragement and advice, and Jane Rogers for the thorough and efficient way she edited the draft.

This book would not have been possible without the cooperation of a number of key figures in the process, some of whom are quoted by name and others who preferred to remain anonymous because of their current responsibilities. I am deeply grateful to all of them for taking the time to speak to me and offering their insights.

Two written sources, Michel Barnier's *My Secret Brexit Diary*, and Gavin Barwell's memoir, *Chief of Staff*, were invaluable in providing the perspectives from Brussels and London.

I would also like to thank a number of people, including Geraldine Kennedy, Joe Joyce, Maurice Manning, Ciara Meehan, Catherine Collins, William Hennigan and Mairead Mullaney, who read all or parts of the draft, spotted mistakes and made helpful suggestions. Any remaining errors, omissions or misinterpretations are my own responsibility.

I would also like to thank my family and friends for their support and encouragement during the writing of this book.

Stephen Collins

Key Actors in the Brexit Drama

The Irish side

Enda Kenny, Taoiseach March 2011–June 2017

Leo Varadkar, Taoiseach June 2017–June 2000

Micheál Martin, Taoiseach June 2000–December 2022

Charlie Flanagan, Minister for Foreign Affairs, 2015–2017

Simon Coveney, Minister for Foreign Affairs, June 2017–

Martin Fraser, cabinet secretary

John Callinan, Taoiseach's Sherpa

Rory Montgomery, second secretary of the Department of Foreign
Affairs

Declan Kelleher, Irish ambassador to the EU

Brian Murphy, chief of staff to Leo Varadkar

The UK side

Theresa May, Prime Minister 2016–2019

Boris Johnson, Prime Minister 2019–2022

Julian Smith, Government chief whip 2017–2019; Northern Secretary
2019–2020

Jeremy Heywood, cabinet secretary

Olly Robbins, May's Sherpa

Gavin Barwell, May's chief of staff

David Frost, Johnson's Sherpa

Edward Lister, Johnson's chief strategic advisor

Robin Barnett, UK Ambassador to Ireland

The EU side

Jean-Claude Juncker, president of the European Commission 2014–2019

Michel Barnier, head of the Brexit Task Force 2016–2020

Sabine Weyand, Barnier's chief of staff 2016–2019

Ursula von der Leyen, president of the European Commission 2019–

Donald Tusk, president of the European Council 2014–2019

Phil Hogan, Irish EU Commissioner 2014–2019

Maroš Šefčovič, EU chief Brexit negotiator 2021–

Chronology

2016

23 June	British people vote to leave the EU by 52 per cent to 48 per cent
28 June	European Council delivers its response
12 July	Enda Kenny travels to Berlin to seek support from Angela Merkel in Brexit talks
13 July	Theresa May becomes Prime Minister in place of David Cameron
26 July	Kenny meets May and both pledge to avoid a hard border in Ireland
27 July	Michel Barnier announced as leader of EU Task Force negotiating Brexit
4 October	Government in Dublin announces All-Ireland Civic Dialogue
5 October	May addresses Conservative Party conference, committing the UK to leave the EU single market and customs union
12 October	Barnier visits Dublin and meets Kenny

2017

17 January	Theresa May's Lancaster House speech
25 March	Rome Declaration to mark 60th anniversary of the EU
29 March	May triggers Article 50
18 April	May calls general election
29 April	European Council sets Brexit negotiating guidelines
8 June	UK general election result; May loses majority and DUP holds balance of power

14 June	Leo Varadkar replaces Enda Kenny as Taoiseach
4 October	May's disastrous conference speech, coughing fit and slogan falling down
1 December	Donald Tusk visits Dublin and declares 'Ní neart go cur le chéile'
4 December	May meets Juncker in Brussels but fails to agree joint report following intervention of DUP
8 December	EU–UK joint report agreed; the birth of the backstop

2018

28 February	Draft withdrawal agreement published by EU; May says no British prime minister could accept border in Irish Sea
22–23 March	European Council agrees guidelines for future relationship with UK
28–29 June	European Council; Varadkar meets May
6 July	May's Chequers plan for deal with EU followed by resignation of David Davis as Brexit Secretary and Boris Johnson as Foreign Secretary
20 September	European Council at Salzburg rejects May's plan
14 November	Amended Withdrawal Agreement containing UK-wide backstop published
25 November	European Council endorses Withdrawal Agreement and Political Declaration on future relationship

2019

15 January	May loses House of Commons vote on Withdrawal Agreement by a record 432 votes to 202
8 February	Varadkar hosts May at an informal dinner at Farmleigh in Dublin
12 March	May loses second vote on Withdrawal Agreement by a margin of 149
21 March	EU agrees to extend the withdrawal date from 29 March to 13 April, or 22 May if the Withdrawal Agreement is passed
4 April	Merkel visits Dublin for meeting with Varadkar and people from border areas

5 April	May writes to Tusk seeking an extension to 30 June
10 April	European Council agrees to extension until 31 October
14–19 April	Nancy Pelosi and Congress delegation visit Ireland and UK
24 May	Theresa May resigns
24 July	Boris Johnson becomes Prime Minister
30 July	Varadkar and Johnson first phone call
28 August	Johnson prorogues parliament
9 September	Johnson travels to Dublin to meet Varadkar
24 September	UK Supreme Court rules prorogation of parliament illegal
24 September	Varadkar and Johnson meet again in New York at the UN
2 October	Johnson sets our revised proposals in letter to EU
10 October	Varadkar and Johnson meet at the Wirral and agree to replace the UK-wide backstop with a border in the Irish Sea
17 October	The European Council signs off on the deal, which includes the Northern Ireland Protocol
12 December	Johnson wins UK general election with a majority of 80 seats, campaigning on the slogan 'Get Brexit Done'

2020

31 January	UK formally leaves the EU
8 February	Irish general election setback for Varadkar
2 March	Talks begin on future relationship between the EU and UK just as first Covid waves hit Europe and lockdowns begin
27 June	Formation of Fine Gael–Fianna Fáil–Green Party coalition with Micheál Martin as Taoiseach until December 2022
9 September	UK publishes Internal Market Bill setting aside key elements of the Protocol; Martin phones Johnson to protest
8 December	UK drops offending elements of Internal Market Bill after objections from the EU and US
24 December	EU–UK deal on future relationship agreed

2021

29 January	Commission President Ursula von der Leyen threatens to invoke Article 16 of the Protocol in row with UK over access to Covid vaccines; she backs down in matter of hours
1 March	Appointment of David Frost to UK cabinet as Minister with responsibility for Brexit and co-chair with Maroš Šefčovič of EU–UK partnership council
3 March	UK announces unilateral extension of Protocol grace periods for trade between Britain and Northern Ireland; EU responds with infringement legal proceedings
28 April	Arlene Foster resigns as leader of the DUP to be succeeded for brief period by Edwin Poots and then by Jeffrey Donaldson
14 May	Micheál Martin meets Boris Johnson at Chequers
11–13 June	G7 meeting in Cornwall overshadowed by Protocol row
13 October	Šefčovič offers major modification of Protocol which he says will reduce the level of checks on goods passing from Britain to Northern Ireland by 80 per cent
31 October–13 November 2021	COP summit in Glasgow; strong EU response to renewed UK threats to the Protocol
19 December	Frost resigns from cabinet and responsibility for Protocol given to the Foreign Secretary, Liz Truss

2022

14 January	Truss tells Šefčovič that key elements of the Protocol will have to go
5 May	Northern Ireland Assembly elections; DUP no longer largest party with right to nominate First Minister
6 June	Johnson survives Conservative parliamentary party vote of confidence by 211 to 148
13 June	British government publishes legislation to override the Protocol
15 June	EU announces resumption of infringement proceedings against UK
23 June	Conservative Party suffers two disastrous by-election defeats
27 June	Second stage of Northern Ireland Protocol Bill passed by Commons
7 July	Boris Johnson announces his resignation as British Prime Minister

'It is a curious reflection to inquire why Ireland should bulk so largely in our lives. How is it that the great English parties are shaken to their foundations, and even shattered, almost every generation, by contact with Irish affairs? Whence did Ireland derive its power to drive Mr. Pitt from office, to drag down Mr. Gladstone in the summit of his career, and to draw us who sit here almost to the verge of civil war, from which we were only rescued by the outbreak of the Great War. Whence does this mysterious power of Ireland come?'

Winston Churchill,
speech in support of the Anglo-Irish Treaty,
House of Commons, 15 December 1921

'Let me say very clearly: if the UK's offer is unacceptable for Ireland, it will also be unacceptable for the EU. I realise that for some British politicians this may be hard to understand. But such is the logic behind the fact that Ireland is an EU member while the UK is leaving. This is why the key to the UK's future lies, in some ways, in Dublin, at least as long as Brexit negotiations continue.'

Donald Tusk,
President of the European Council,
1 December 2017

Introduction

When the British electorate voted in June 2016 to leave the European Union, one of the unforeseen consequences was to give Ireland a pivotal role in determining the future relationship between the United Kingdom and its continental neighbours. The proponents of Brexit had never considered the impact their victory would have on Ireland, north or south, and were aghast at the central role their nearest neighbour assumed in the EU's negotiating tactics. When European Council President Donald Tusk declared bluntly in December 2018 that the UK's road to Brexit lay through Dublin there was palpable horror among British ministers.

It took years of intricate negotiations before Britain was able to leave the EU, but as part of that process the relationship between the UK and Ireland was altered in a more fundamental way than had happened at any time since the Anglo-Irish Treaty of 1921. A century after independence and the formal partition of Ireland into separate jurisdictions, the two parts of the island were united economically if not politically by the Brexit agreement, although that settlement was subsequently unilaterally set aside by the British Prime Minister, Boris Johnson.

Johnson's fall from power in July 2022, after just three years in office, was partly the result of his determination to rip up the Brexit deal he had himself negotiated. In the space of six years he brought down three prime ministers: David Cameron, Theresa May and finally himself. However, his most significant impact was to alter radically the direction the UK had taken for the previous half-century in relation to Europe.

The determination of the EU to ensure that the outcome of the negotiations with the UK on a future relationship would have to be acceptable to the Irish government was initially regarded with incredulity by the

1

proponents of Brexit. That mood gave way to frustration and even anger as the talks progressed and it became clear that the EU was prepared to accept a no-deal outcome rather than abandon the requirement that there could be no return to a hard border in Ireland.

The strong stance adopted by the EU from an early stage was due to two things. One was a hugely successful Irish diplomatic offensive to get the backing of the other member states to oppose the restoration of a hard border involving customs or security checks on the island of Ireland for fear that could reignite the violence of the Troubles. This diplomatic campaign resulted in the border issue being one of three key elements that the UK would have to deal with before talks could begin on new trading arrangements between the UK and its biggest market, the EU.

The second vital consideration was that the Irish side had strong support in Brussels for insisting that the Irish border had to be treated as a key priority in the talks. From the beginning the EU Commission and the member states were determined to preserve the single market against what was widely regarded as a British attempt to undermine it. That would necessarily involve border controls, but the question was where those controls would be. Reintroducing customs checks on the 500 kilometre-long Irish land border threatened to be a logistical nightmare with potential for smuggling on a large scale.

Even more important, the EU leaders accepted the Irish argument that creating such a border would amount to a threat to the delicate balance of the Good Friday Agreement, which had brought peace, if not political stability, to Northern Ireland. Given that the EU originated from the vision of a peaceful Europe, the potential threat to peace in Ireland arising from the reinstatement of a hard border represented a powerful emotional appeal to the member states.

From an early stage in the Brexit talks the EU insisted that there would have to be an arrangement, which later became known as the Irish backstop, to obviate the need for border controls in Ireland, whatever the outcome of the trade negotiations with the UK. The EU position, articulated with firmness and grace by its chief negotiator, Michel Barnier, confounded the Brexiteers, who were stunned and appalled in equal measure that the Irish backstop could become the central obstacle to the successful outcome of negotiations that had implications for the entire continent of Europe.

The Democratic Unionist Party in Northern Ireland was presented with a glorious opportunity to shape the outcome when it achieved the balance of power in the House of Commons after Conservative Prime Minister Theresa May called a surprise general election in May 2017. Incredibly, the DUP used its leverage to sabotage May's efforts to ensure that Northern Ireland would be treated in the same way as the rest of the UK in whatever settlement emerged. Instead it threw in its lot with the Brexiteer Tories and helped them to depose May. Her successor, Boris Johnson, then went back on his solemn pledge to the DUP and agreed a deal in the shape of a protocol that involved Northern Ireland remaining part of the EU single market, effectively putting a new border down the Irish Sea. Winning the subsequent general election on the basis of his 'oven-ready' deal, Johnson then embarked on a strategy of attempting to wriggle out of the arrangement. That process ultimately led to the publication, in June 2022, of legislation designed to set aside key elements of the Protocol.

All through the process, leading Brexiteers were convinced that the big powers in the EU, particularly Germany, would put their own national interests ahead of Ireland's and ultimately seek to cut a deal with the UK. Some senior Irish politicians, including Leo Varadkar, secretly harboured the fear that this might indeed come to pass. That it did not happen was primarily down to the German Chancellor, Angela Merkel. While she wanted an outcome which kept the UK in the closest possible relationship with the EU, her primary concern was the future of the EU itself and the protection of the single market. The UK government's approach to the entire negotiating process whittled away any sympathy she might have had for British concerns.

Some inkling of how those on the right of the Conservative Party saw the issue as it came to its conclusion was articulated by Cambridge University historian Brendan Simms in August 2019. Simms, who has written extensively on British relations with Europe, gave an address to the West Cork History Festival in August 2019 entitled 'From Backdoor to Backstop'. In it he outlined how British policy over the past five hundred years had been to keep Europe divided in order to maximise its own influence. An essential part of that policy was to prevent Ireland being used as a backdoor by continental states that wished to challenge British power.

Simms suggested that the backstop represented a modern effort by the continental powers to change the balance of power in Europe to the UK's disadvantage by forcing the British to adopt a policy on Ireland devised in Brussels and Dublin. He forecast that the EU would not have the capacity to force the UK to accept the backstop. 'If there is an intrusive border it will be North/South and not East/West,' he forecast.

Two months later Johnson did exactly what the Brexiteers believed could never happen. He agreed to a customs border down the Irish Sea which kept Northern Ireland in the EU economic zone. He agreed this with the Taoiseach Leo Varadkar rather than risk a no-deal outcome to the talks and the hugely damaging consequences that would have had for Britain. Johnson subsequently claimed that he did not realise the full implications of the deal he agreed in 2019 and attempted a variety of political manoeuvres, culminating in the Northern Ireland Bill of June 2022, designed to set it aside. The result has been to sour even further relations between the UK and its continental neighbours and to threaten European solidarity in the face of the Russian invasion of Ukraine.

This book tells the story of how the Irish government and its officials shaped the new relationship between the EU and the UK in a manner that would best serve their country's interests. In the course of the Brexit negotiations their strategy evolved from early attempts to find common ground with the UK to a hard-line stance over the backstop that resulted in chaos in the House of Commons, the sacking of one prime minister and a spectacular U-turn by her successor.

Along the way there were dizzying twists and turns, but in the end the serene determination of Barnier and his negotiating team and the dogged persistence of the Irish government prevailed in 2019 and a trade border on the island of Ireland was avoided. Instead there was an unprecedented arrangement in the shape of the Northern Ireland Protocol whereby one of the four component parts of the UK remained in the EU economic zone while the other three departed. It represented the most fundamental change in the status of Northern Ireland since the partition of the island by the Government of Ireland Act of 1920.

While the Protocol had the support, in May 2022, of a majority of members elected to the Northern Ireland Assembly, the DUP strenuously opposed it and refused to take part in a power-sharing Executive as long as it remained in its present form. Johnson cited the political stalemate in Northern Ireland as one of the reasons for unilaterally introducing the legislation to override the Protocol in June 2022. The European Commission responded by resuming infringement proceedings for earlier breaches but left the threat of stronger action for another day, depending on events. An indication of the frustration in Brussels was encapsulated in a comment from Commission President Ursula von der Leyen, who said: 'The Brexit agreement was written in English so they could understand it.'

Whatever happens to the Protocol or the entire Trade and Cooperation Agreement in the future, there is no escaping the fact that Brexit has altered the relationship between Ireland and Britain, and between the UK and the EU, in ways that will resonate for decades to come.

1

Ireland Prepares

'Our work has been taken by thousands and thousands of [migrants] crossing over into Britain.'
Elderly man in a Mayo jersey in London, explaining
why he intended to vote Leave

* * *

Taoiseach Enda Kenny was playing golf with then US Vice-President Joe Biden in Mayo on 23 June 2016, as the people of the United Kingdom went to the polls to vote on whether or not to leave the European Union. Although the two politicians were only too well aware that the British people were taking a decision on which the future of Europe would hinge, the mood on the golf course was jolly.

When they got to the last hole on the course at Castlebar Golf Club, Biden needed to hole a six-yard putt to draw the match. 'You can do it, Joe,' Kenny called out good-humouredly, and the Vice-President duly sank the putt. A little over four years later Kenny sent his golf partner a variation on the theme when the result of the 2020 US election became clear. 'We always knew you could do it Joe,' he texted the newly elected President of the United States.

Kenny's ability to strike up warm personal relations with leading politicians from other countries was one of his great skills. It was one of the qualities that enabled him to deliver a series of political achievements often underrated by the Irish public. The spectacular economic recovery that followed the financial meltdown of 2008–2010 was due in large part to Kenny's astute leadership and his ability to convey a sense of optimism about his country's prospects to the wider world. When he failed to win the expected endorsement in the general election of 2016, Biden remarked that Kenny would have won 80 per cent of the vote if he had presided over a similar recovery in the United States.

Kenny needed to deploy all his political skills when the result of the UK referendum became clear on the morning of 24 June 2016. Apart from the UK itself, Ireland was the European country that faced the biggest challenge from Brexit. That challenge combined a threat to the economic prosperity of the Republic with the potential to undermine the Good Friday Agreement, which had delivered almost two decades of relative peace. It also posed a threat to the Common Travel Area (CTA) that had bound the two countries so closely together despite the vicissitudes of history.

One of the things that stood to Kenny in the weeks and months following the referendum was that the Irish government was far better prepared for the result than was the UK itself. Intensive preparations on the Irish side for a potentially negative outcome began from the moment British Prime Minister David Cameron announced the referendum date in February 2016. Long before that, civil servants in Dublin had been weighing up the consequences of a British decision to leave the EU. Back in the summer of 2014 a team headed by the number two official in the Department of the Taoiseach, Geraldine Byrne Nason, then in charge of EU policy, prepared a ten-page document outlining the problems that would confront Ireland if the UK decided to leave.

At that stage it was becoming clear that there was a real prospect of an in/out referendum on the UK's future relationship with the EU. In fact it was the logical conclusion of a process that had been set in train by Cameron more than a decade earlier. During the Conservative Party leadership election in the autumn of 2005 he gave a commitment to Eurosceptic MP Andrew Rosindell that he would end his party's relationship with the European People's Party (EPP), the umbrella group for centre-right parties in the EU. Conservative MEP Caroline Jackson described Cameron's commitment as pathetic and forecast that it would sow the seeds of endless trouble. 'It is a stupid, stupid policy,' she said.

In hindsight Kenny saw this move by Cameron as the first and critical step in the sequence of events that led to Brexit. The two men first got to know each other when they were opposition leaders in their respective countries and Kenny warned Cameron that leaving the EPP would isolate the Conservative Party from potential allies in the EU.

The move led inexorably to Cameron's announcement in January 2013 that he would seek to reform the EU and then hold a referendum on Britain's continued membership. 'It is time for the British people to have their say. It is time to settle this European question in British politics. I say to the British people: this will be your decision.' The speech grabbed the headlines, but alarm bells did not ring in any of the corridors of power. In Brussels, the Irish Permanent Representative to the EU, Rory Montgomery, met his British counterpart, Jon Cunliffe, at a routine breakfast for the ambassadors of the member states. Ireland had just assumed the EU presidency, so Montgomery took the chair. He discussed the implications of the Cameron speech with Cunliffe but got the impression that the British diplomat was not too concerned. A UK general election was some way away and complacency was encouraged by the assumption that Cameron's coalition partners, the Liberal Democrats, would block the holding of a referendum.

The picture changed dramatically when Cameron surprised everybody by winning an overall majority in the British general election of 2015 and no longer needed the support of the Liberal Democrats to govern. The United Kingdom Independence Party (UKIP), led and dominated by Nigel Farage, a pint-drinking, blokeish, populist figure, had been campaigning to leave the EU since 1993. Farage was elected to the European Parliament in 1999 and even though UKIP did not win any seats in the House of Commons, because of the first-past-the-post electoral system, it demonstrated an ability to siphon off votes from the Conservatives. The party went on to win a significant number of seats in successive European elections, which use proportional representation. In 2004 the party won 16 per cent of the vote and twelve seats. The European Parliament gave Farage a platform that enabled him to become a national figure in Britain, and the threat he posed to the Conservatives pushed UK membership of the EU to the top of the political agenda.

The commitment to hold a referendum on the EU was repeated in the Conservative Party election manifesto of 2015 and soon after his re-election Cameron began the process of renegotiating the British terms of membership. The prospect of a British exit from the EU, or Brexit as it came to be known, received renewed and serious attention in Dublin. As negotiations began on a reform package designed to enable Cameron to persuade the British people to remain in the EU, the Irish government was keen to help in any way it could.

During their time in opposition Kenny and Cameron had built up a warm relationship that became closer once they were in power, Cameron becoming Prime Minister in 2010 and Kenny Taoiseach less than a year later. Both had an affable manner and a sunny, optimistic outlook. There was genuine rapport between them and that was deepened by the Prime Minister's historic apology for the Bloody Sunday massacre in Derry in 1972. The Good Friday Agreement of 1998 had allowed the already close ties that existed between the people of the two countries to flourish unhindered by political squabbling over Northern Ireland. The border on the island had become increasingly unobtrusive, with membership of the EU single market making it irrelevant for everything apart from security considerations. The growing warmth in relations between the two countries at all levels was reflected in the hugely successful State visit by Queen Elizabeth II and Prince Philip to Ireland in 2011 and the return visit by President Michael D. Higgins in 2014. That was one of the reasons why Kenny had no hesitation in doing everything he could within the EU to try to ensure that Cameron got an acceptable deal he could sell to his electorate.

The Taoiseach told Cameron he would work hard on five or six EU prime ministers with whom he had a strong relationship to try to persuade them to agree to the best possible deal for the UK. By this stage Kenny had built up a powerful network of allies in the EPP. During his long years as opposition leader from 2002 until 2011 he dutifully attended the EPP leaders' meetings held before every European Council meeting. Many of his Fine Gael colleagues thought this was an unnecessary diversion from Irish politics, but Kenny's diligence paid off when he became Taoiseach. By this stage he was on familiar terms with a number of prime ministers, most crucially of all German Chancellor Angela Merkel, beside whom he had been sitting at EPP leaders' meetings for nine years. Having an input into EPP decision-making was crucial given that it was the biggest political bloc in the EU. By the time he became Taoiseach Kenny was on familiar terms with most of the key figures around the table at European Council meetings.

He used those contacts to do everything he could to help Cameron win an acceptable reform package from the other EU member states. However, he often found it a hard sell when he attempted to persuade fellow EPP leaders to give Cameron's case a hearing. The Prime Minister's decision to take the Conservative Party out of the EPP still rankled with many of them. Crucially, that decision meant that Cameron never had an opportunity to build relationships with other centre-right leaders. Kenny's deep involvement in the EPP, by contrast, benefited Ireland during the financial crisis and had a significant impact on the politics of Brexit as it unfolded over the following years.

Kenny's desire to help Cameron was noted in Brussels. In an assessment by EU officials of which member states would be most supportive of the British efforts to win concessions, Ireland came out as most sympathetic to the UK, followed by the Netherlands and Denmark. This reflected the fact that, as well as relations between the two countries improving over the previous three decades as they worked together to deal with Northern Ireland, they had also become increasingly close at EU level on issues involving taxation, free trade and the single market. That closeness meant that Cameron had no difficulty in agreeing to exempt Irish citizens from his plans to impose restrictions on EU migrants claiming social welfare payments in the UK.

At a special summit in Brussels on 19 February 2016, Cameron got his deal from the other EU leaders. Its standout feature was that the UK would be granted an 'emergency brake' that would restrict EU migrants from claiming work-related welfare benefits for up to seven years. There were also changes in the child benefits payable to children in the home countries of migrants, but on the core issue of immigration the EU refused to make a major concession, given that free movement of people is one of its four basic principles. However, it was agreed to allow Britain to opt out from any references in future EU treaties to 'ever closer union'.

The following day Cameron summoned an emergency cabinet meeting at Downing Street and announced that a referendum would be held on 23 June. He told the media he would fight 'heart and soul' for Britain to remain in the EU. Buoyed by the victory of the Remain campaign in the referendum on Scottish independence two years earlier, the Prime Minister was supremely confident that he could persuade the British people to remain in the EU.

It quickly became clear that his confidence was built on shaky foundations. For a start, the influential Tory press was utterly dismissive of the deal he had obtained from the other EU leaders. Then a number of Ministers, including one of Cameron's closest allies, Michael Gove; former party leader Iain Duncan Smith; Priti Patel; and Theresa Villiers, announced they intended to campaign for a Leave vote. Most significantly of all, Boris Johnson, probably the most popular Conservative politician in the UK, who had come back into Parliament in 2014 after two terms as Mayor of London, announced he was supporting the Leave campaign. Johnson had achieved fame and notoriety early in his career by writing false stories about the EU while working as a journalist in Brussels. Far from being a hindrance his outrageous reporting propelled him to a level of public prominence on which he built during his political career. With an instinctive grasp of how to exploit media attention he projected himself as a lovable rogue and had proved during his two campaigns to be Mayor of London that he was a superb vote-getter.

He allegedly prepared two statements about his position on the referendum, one arguing for Leave and the other for Remain. He chose Leave on the basis that it would provide him with the platform to become Conservative Party leader. A string of attention-grabbing interventions ensured that he was the most effective Leave campaigner. In one he was photographed standing in front of a bus on which was emblazoned the slogan, 'We send the EU £350 million a week, let's fund our NHS instead.' During the campaign he also repeated one of his most famous lines, 'My policy on cake is pro having it and pro eating it.'

By the time the campaign got under way there was serious concern in Ireland that the UK might actually vote to leave. Irish politicians were acutely aware that their own electorate had twice voted down EU treaties, causing diplomatic embarrassment for the country. If an intrinsically pro-EU electorate like the Irish could be persuaded to vote No on the flimsiest of grounds, the chances of failure in a country with a high level of Euroscepticism in the media and political class were clearly high. Speaking at a Chatham House event in London in late 2015, Minister for Foreign Affairs Charlie Flanagan went off script to illustrate the pitfalls of referendums. He told an anecdote about a supporter who had approached him before the referendum on the Lisbon Treaty to say that he was voting No. When a shocked Flanagan asked him why, he said, 'I'm having a bad time and the wife left me and I couldn't give a damn about anything so I'm voting No.' His audience laughed, but Flanagan felt that they didn't really get the point: that referendums are not decided on logic and often have little to do with the question on the ballot paper.

Flanagan, who had first been elected to the Dáil in 1987, had ended up as Minister for Foreign Affairs at this critical juncture, despite voting against Kenny in a leadership heave in 2010. A droll, self-deprecating politician in a profession more noted for individuals with inflated egos, his calm and unflappable approach was an invaluable asset to the government in the early stages of Brexit.

During the referendum campaign Kenny, Flanagan and other senior ministers travelled to the UK to try to persuade the Irish community there to vote Remain. They were quickly disabused of any notion that Irish UK residents had the same strongly pro-EU views as their relatives at home. Young Irish people living in the UK, generally well educated and in good jobs, were strongly pro-EU, like their contemporaries at home, but older long-time emigrants were a different matter.

'We were campaigning because we were stakeholders,' recalled Flanagan. 'I did meetings in Liverpool, in Manchester and London and to be honest they didn't go that well.' A graphic illustration of that was provided at a Gaelic football match between Mayo and London in London on 29 May which was attended by the Taoiseach as part of his pro-Remain campaign. After the match the RTÉ television news interviewed a man wearing a Mayo jersey who proclaimed that he was going to vote Leave because 'Our work has been taken by thousands and thousands of [migrants] crossing over into Britain.' Flanagan recalled texting Kenny immediately afterwards to alert him. 'I got the same message from the Irish community in Manchester and Liverpool.'

That television interview with the man in the Mayo jersey shocked many people in Ireland. Senior civil servant John Callinan, who would head the Irish team during the Brexit negotiations, remembered that his wake-up call came shortly before that when he attended a meeting involving government ministers and business people to assess the consequences of a possible Leave vote. One businessman told a story about a dinner he had attended in the UK some time before with British business people involved in medium-sized enterprises. There was a good-natured conversation about the pros and cons of leaving the EU. 'At the end of the dinner the host asked for a show of hands and the result was nine to one in favour of leaving. And I remember thinking, "That's it. Game over."' Callinan had a small bet with a colleague in the Taoiseach's Department that the UK would vote to leave, but he was still shocked when it actually happened.

In the face of the negative feedback, Kenny tried to increase the volume of his support for the Remain campaign. In a major speech in Dublin in May 2016, he outlined his core message. 'First and foremost we want the UK to remain part of a strong EU and work with us to make it better. Second, Ireland will remain a committed member of the EU regardless of the outcome of the UK referendum. Third, we will preserve the strength of the British–Irish relationship that has been carefully fostered over the years.' He added that one hundred years on from the 1916 Rising the ambition must be to dismantle barriers rather than put them back up. 'We have become close. We should stay close and stay together in Europe.' At this stage Kenny was struggling to survive as leader of Fine Gael, having suffered a deeply disappointing election result in February which barely enabled him to cling on to power as leader of a minority government.

On the day of the referendum, as Kenny was hosting Biden in Mayo, the senior staff of the Taoiseach's Department went home early to get some rest before returning to Government Buildings at 3 a.m. to monitor the results. Minister for European Affairs Dara Murphy was in Luxembourg for a meeting with his EU counterparts and they gathered in the bar of the Novotel to watch the early results on Sky News. Lorcan Fullam, assistant secretary of the Department of the Taoiseach, who was with Murphy, had come armed with a spreadsheet of the UK constituencies to analyse the results as they came in. The early result from Newcastle showed a surprisingly high Leave vote, but it was the Sunderland result that came as real shock. When it came in Fullam turned to Murphy and said, 'It's over. The UK is leaving the EU.' Murphy had enough confidence in Fullam's assessment to text Kenny and say the game was up.

Large screens had been set up to transmit the television coverage in the Taoiseach's office, but by the time the officials assembled it was already clear that the British public had voted to leave the EU. Kenny kept in touch with his key officials through the night and when it was confirmed at around 5 a.m. that the result was Leave he called a cabinet meeting for 7.30 a.m.

The only silver lining that morning was that a detailed contingency plan had been drawn up and the government knew exactly what message it wanted to send out. First, it was essential that other European capitals knew that there was no question of Ireland following the British example. Ireland would not even consider exiting the EU. The second key message was that there could be no return to a hard border on the island, whatever the future relationship between the EU and the UK. The plan also spelled out the need to retain the CTA between Ireland and the UK, which, with a brief interruption during the Second World War, had remained in place since the Irish State was founded. Another priority was the protection of the economy and trade, with part of that a focus on financial stability.

In terms of an immediate response Irish officials had drawn up an hour-by-hour schedule of what would happen that morning in the event of a Leave vote. A government 'holding statement' was issued at 6 a.m.; an hour later, as the stock markets were opening, there were video conferences with Irish diplomats in Brussels, London, Belfast and Edinburgh. The Taoiseach phoned key EU leaders and spoke to opposition leaders at home before the cabinet met.

Callinan recalled that the mood that morning was grim. 'All the things we had all feared as risks if there was a No vote now became reality. No matter how well prepared you are, you still don't want that to happen. There was a realisation that this was a big moment in the country's journey and we would have to deal with it.'

He said that nobody in Government Buildings was under any illusions that Northern Ireland was going to be the dominant issue in working out the future relationship between Ireland and the UK. 'Worryingly that view wasn't reflected in London. Cameron was so confident he'd win that he wouldn't allow the civil service prepare for the Leave vote. Which meant that they weren't focusing specifically on the Northern Ireland aspect of it.' If London had ignored the issue, the

Irish government was determined to alert all the EU member states as quickly as possible to the ramifications of Brexit for the island of Ireland.

The immediate priority was to ensure that Irish concerns were conveyed to capitals across Europe. The shrewd Minister for Finance, Michael Noonan, briefed colleagues about the potential economic consequences and then uttered a prescient comment some of them would always remember. He told them Brexit was not an event but a process that would continue for many years and they had better be prepared for it. The Taoiseach then set about calling other heads of government and Charlie Flanagan was instructed to immediately start work on contacting other foreign ministers.

'We met in emergency mode in Government Buildings with most of the ministers present along with senior officials like the secretary general of the Taoiseach's Department, Martin Fraser, and assistant secretary John Callinan. I got back to my office with a list of calls I had to make,' said Flanagan. 'And of course I was touching base to state our priorities. We had them ready.' On his frequent visits to Brussels Flanagan had often pondered a remark by the renowned political scientist Basil Chubb who once described Ireland as an island behind an island. 'I remember standing in the Grand Place in Brussels and thinking that now we faced the prospect of being an island behind an island which wasn't in the European Union.'

The first call was to his opposite number in the UK, Foreign Secretary Philip Hammond. 'Now, Hammond was a really decent guy. He had not been enthusiastic about the EU earlier in his career but had come to appreciate its importance during his time as Foreign Secretary.' During the campaign Flanagan had kept in close touch with Hammond and warned him just how difficult referendums can be, but the Foreign Secretary was confident that the public would see the merits of the Remain argument. He tried to explain to Flanagan why it had all gone so wrong and then he said: 'We need your help now.'

His next calls were to Northern Ireland's First and Deputy First Ministers, Arlene Foster and Martin McGuinness. Foster was in a bind as the DUP had supported Leave while expecting Remain to win. 'Martin McGuinness of course was cock-a-hoop as he saw it as the death knell for the UK. Arlene was caught. I said to Martin McGuinness, don't rub their noses in it now, just let's see how this pans out.' But McGuinness couldn't resist calling immediately for a referendum on a united Ireland. As a former IRA leader and a Sinn Féin politician dedicated to ending Northern Ireland's membership of the United Kingdom, this was too good a point-scoring opportunity to miss.

Flanagan spoke to other Northern leaders that morning before turning his attention to Europe. 'Then I spoke to France and Germany. Frank-Walter Steinmeier was the German Foreign Minister, an SPD [Social Democratic Party] politician who went on to be President of the Federal Republic. He is a really good guy. I had had good relations with him on the Foreign Affairs Council and he was very, very angry with the British. He was so annoyed with them. The next call was French Foreign Minister Jean-Marc Ayrault. He was very supportive of Ireland.'

The next minister on Flanagan's list was Bert Koenders of the Netherlands, with whom he had a good personal relationship arising from one of the odd coincidences that happen in politics. The previous October Flanagan had hosted a lunch in Iveagh House for Dutch businessman Dr Tiede Herrema, who had been kidnapped by an IRA faction forty years earlier, and his wife, Elisabeth. Mrs Herrema asked Flanagan if he knew the Dutch Foreign Minister and he said he did but not all that well. She then told him she knew the Koenders family and had babysat Koenders when he was a child. She said, 'Next time you meet him, don't call him Minister, call him Berchie.' So when Flanagan next met Koenders the Dutch minister was astonished to be greeted with his childhood pet name. 'So we struck up a great relationship.'

Within forty-eight hours Flanagan had spoken to the foreign ministers of all twenty-six remaining EU member states. The next task was to go to them in person to cement relationships. Over the following months he trekked to every EU capital at least once and some a number of times.

At 8.15 that morning, while Flanagan was still in Government Buildings with his cabinet colleagues, David Cameron emerged from 10 Downing Street and told the assembled press that he was going to resign as British Prime Minister. It was not exactly a shock to Irish ministers and officials, but it did reinforce the point that a seismic change was taking place in British politics. The implications for Ireland had not been a factor in the referendum, but one person who did grasp them was British Cabinet Secretary Jeremy Heywood. Speaking to his wife, Suzanne, later that day as the stock market tumbled and the pound fell in value he asked her if she knew what the most difficult issue was.

'Ireland,' he told her.

'Really?' she asked.

'Absolutely. If Northern Ireland is out of the EU and Southern Ireland is in, then we'll need a hard border between them. But that would demolish the Good Friday Agreement. I don't see yet how we will solve that.'

A few hours later the Taoiseach addressed the media in Government Buildings and expressed his personal best wishes to Cameron. 'We have worked closely together at a time of unprecedented warmth in relations between our two countries. He has taken a decision this morning which he believes is in the interests of his country.'

Expressing his sorrow that the UK had voted to leave the EU he added that the British people had spoken and Ireland fully respected their decision. 'I want to assure the Irish public that we have prepared to the greatest extent possible for this eventuality.' He added that there would be no immediate change to the free flow of people, goods and services between the two islands but accepted that the Irish community in Britain would be concerned about the impact.

Kenny's priority was to make it absolutely clear to the world that Ireland would remain in the EU.

That is profoundly in our national interest. After more than forty years of membership, we have built up strong bonds of partnership with all the other member states, and with the European institutions, that will continue to serve us well. We must now begin a period of reflection and debate on how we can renew the Union of twenty-seven and equip it for the challenges ahead. There will be a discussion of the next steps at the meeting of the European Council next week. I will clearly set out our national position at that meeting, and I will ensure that our particular national interests are fully respected as we prepare to enter the next phase of negotiations.

He accepted that those talks would not begin for some months and suggested that the breathing space should be used wisely. 'I'd like to reiterate that while Ireland's future lies within the European Union,

Ireland's strong and close relationship with the UK will remain.' Balancing the two potentially contradictory imperatives of maintaining Ireland's position as a committed member of the EU while keeping a close relationship with the UK was going to be an enormous challenge.

Kenny tried to reconcile them when the European Council met in Brussels a few days later. The heads of government of all the member states, including the UK, took part in the first day's session, but on the second day the remaining twenty-seven met without Cameron present. In his contribution to that meeting Kenny told his fellow leaders about the priority he attached to protecting the peace process and the Common Travel Area between Ireland and the UK. They paid close attention, as he had been supportive of Cameron's efforts to extract the best possible deal, and the Irish had been close to the UK on a number of major issues over the previous two decades. Most other leaders favoured a tough line towards the UK, their main concern being that Brexit could lead to a break-up of the EU itself. As had become the norm at Council meetings for almost a decade the decisive contribution came from Angela Merkel. She made it clear that, like Kenny, she did not want the UK to be 'punished' for its decision, but she did insist on one specific line in the communiqué to be issued after the meeting. This would state clearly that if Britain wanted access to the EU single market in a future relationship it would have to accept the four freedoms that underpinned it: free movement of goods, capital, services and, most important of all, people.

Speaking at a press conference after the summit the Taoiseach emphasised that the central focus of the Irish government would be on protecting the peace process and the CTA with the UK, but he was also careful not to stray from Merkel's injunction that there could be no dilution of the four freedoms, including freedom of movement. 'We have an interest in having an outward-looking, strong and prosperous United Kingdom. The closer the relationship the UK is going to have with the European Union the better for us. But it is clear from the conclusions of the meeting that access to the single market is tied to the fundamental acceptance of the four freedoms which include freedom of movement of people.'

Kenny's softer line towards the UK than that of many other EU leaders was noted by some in Brussels, although his stated commitment to the four freedoms was a reassurance that Ireland had no intention of straying too far from the common position. At that stage he was clearly hoping that the UK would opt for the closest possible relationship with the EU in the future, so there would be minimum disruption in Irish–British relations.

That turned out to be a forlorn hope.

2

Brexit Means Brexit

'The closer the UK is to the EU, the better for all of us, and above all for Ireland.'

Enda Kenny 18 July 2016

* * *

Irish hopes that the UK would pursue a soft Brexit by remaining in the EU single market and Customs Union were initially raised by the election of Theresa May as the new Conservative Party leader on 11 July. After all, she had campaigned, however discreetly, for Remain and had serious experience of government as Home Secretary. The leaders of the Leave campaign, Boris Johnson and Michael Gove, had become embroiled in an act of mutual self-destruction during their botched leadership bids, which suggested that the most strident anti-EU forces were in disarray in spite of their referendum victory. When another Leave campaigner, Andrea Leadsom, the only leadership challenger left, withdrew from the race following an ill-judged comment about May not having children, it appeared that British politics might get back on an even keel.

There were soon ominous signs that such hopes were premature. Immediately on her election as Prime Minister, May declared that 'Brexit does mean Brexit.' This gnomic phrase could have meant anything, but it was a signal that a close future relationship between the UK and the EU was not very likely. Her cabinet appointments raised further doubts about the prospect of a 'soft' Brexit. The most popular Leaver of them all, Boris Johnson, was appointed to the prestigious position of Foreign Secretary, and two other leaders of the Leave campaign, David Davis and Liam Fox, were given important roles in steering the process. Davis was to head up the new Department for Exiting the European Union, which had the responsibility of working out how the UK would leave the EU. Fox was made Secretary of State for International Trade with responsibility for seeking new trade deals for the UK around the globe.

May balanced her cabinet by appointing two strong Remain figures, Philip Hammond as Chancellor of the Exchequer and Amber Rudd as Home Secretary. Still, the message to the Conservative Party was that May was aiming to achieve a decisive break with the EU. Gavin Barwell, who became her chief of staff a year later, wondered in hindsight if the way she had come to the leadership, without having to defeat a challenger in a vote, might actually have been a disadvantage. He reckoned she would have been in a much stronger position if she had defeated a Leaver like Leadsom to win the leadership.

As May was putting her cabinet together in London, Kenny set off on a round of meetings with EU leaders to drum up support and understanding for the difficulties Ireland would inevitably face. His first meeting was with the all-important German Chancellor, Angela Merkel, in Berlin on 12 July. By this stage Merkel was long established as the dominant figure in the EU. This was not simply because Germany was the largest country and the biggest contributor to the EU budget, but because she had displayed authority and political skill time and time again, particularly during the financial crisis that had threatened to undermine the Euro.

Catherine Day, who attended European Council meetings as secretary-general of the Commission, was struck by the way Merkel dominated the room at those meetings. She didn't do it by attempting to exploit her position as the leader of the biggest and most powerful economy in the EU to boss others around, but by the force of her intellect and the thoroughness with which she prepared. She was not only on top of her own brief but had a detailed grasp of the brief every other leader brought to the room. At times it was evident that she knew more about the details of an individual country's position than its own prime minister.

European Council meetings are notable for the fact that national leaders meet without officials or advisers present. The outcome of the meetings depends on the ability of each government leader to present their country's case and also on their ability to grasp the kind of compromises that might be acceptable to their colleagues. It was at times of tension and conflict that Merkel's dominance of the Council became evident. When there was an impasse she would adjourn for a short side meeting with the leader who was most out on a limb, and a way of lowering the tension was almost always found. 'Everybody in the room knew that getting Merkel onside was essential if they wanted to achieve anything,' said Day.

In an assessment of Merkel in the closing days of her term in September 2021, former EU Commission President Jean-Claude Juncker sought to explain why she was such a dominant figure in the EU for so long. 'She has listened to everyone, small, medium, big countries, she never made any distinction,' said Juncker, who as Prime Minister of Luxembourg had worked with every German chancellor since Helmut Kohl on and knew what it was like to be premier of a very small country. He also noted that she followed the domestic political debate in all EU member states far more closely than other leaders. 'That was her European political charm, that everyone had the impression that you could tell her things the way they are at home, and she wove that into the overall web of European solutions to which she contributed.'

By the time of the Brexit referendum outcome, Enda Kenny was in the enviable position of having known Merkel for more than a decade and the two of them were the longest-serving prime ministers in the EU. In many ways they were chalk and cheese. Merkel, thoughtful and reserved, led the biggest and most powerful country in the EU. Kenny, an outgoing, gregarious politician who clearly enjoyed the back-slapping side of politics, was leader of a small country on the western periphery of Europe. Membership of the same EU-wide political group, the European People's Party (EPP), was a crucial bond. Merkel issued a public message of support for Kenny during the Irish general election of 2007 when he narrowly failed to win power and she sent another supportive message during his successful 2011 campaign.

When he first took over the Taoiseach's office in February 2011, their relationship was strained for a time when Merkel joined French

President Nicolas Sarkozy in attempting to ambush Kenny at his first European Council meeting. Just a day after taking office Kenny went to that meeting seeking a reduction in the crippling interest rate Ireland was paying on the €67 billion EU/IMF bailout. Arriving at the meeting in Brussels, Kenny kissed the smiling Chancellor on both cheeks, but their exchanges behind closed doors were frosty as she pressed the Taoiseach to agree to changes in the Irish corporate tax regime in exchange for an interest rate reduction. If Merkel was cool, French President Sarkozy was hotly intemperate in his exchanges with Kenny, at times verging on the abusive. 'It was an ambush; an inexcusable attempt to take advantage of the Taoiseach's inexperience and bully him into a massive concession,' said an official who witnessed the events.

Late on the second night of the meeting, the President of the European Council, Herman Van Rompuy, called Kenny to his office and presented him with a draft of the presidency conclusions containing a reference to changes in Ireland's corporate tax regime. Kenny refused to accept it, saying that he could not go home from his first Council meeting having conceded something that would be so damaging to his country. At that stage Sarkozy and Merkel came into the room. Van Rompuy looked at them and said, 'He won't sign.' Sarkozy was furious and said that in that case Ireland would not get the interest rate reduction that had been agreed for Greece. Merkel didn't demur and the two most important EU leaders walked out of the room.

Relations between Kenny and Merkel were soon repaired as it became clear that the government he led was determined to honour the stringent terms of the bailout deal. In time Ireland got a number of interest rate reductions as a reward for complying with the bailout terms, while Greece failed to implement its commitments and lurched from one crisis to the next. Ultimately the episode redounded to Kenny's advantage as it showed Merkel that he was capable of standing up to pressure and taking tough decisions when they were required. It was clear that Brexit was going to take every ounce of political courage Kenny possessed if Ireland's interests were to be protected in the negotiations that would determine the post-Brexit European accommodation.

On 12 July 2016, the day before Theresa May was elected Prime Minister, Kenny travelled to Berlin to meet Merkel, hoping to persuade her to put Irish concerns about Brexit at the top of her agenda. Merkel, in the style to which Kenny had become accustomed, listened carefully to his arguments but did not commit herself to any course of action. The *Irish Times* reported that at a press conference after the meeting, the Chancellor 'declined to be drawn on what influence she believed Irish concerns would have on any final Brexit deal'. She contented herself with saying. 'The details will have to be clarified – we will talk about this in friendship with each other.'

The German leader said she understood Irish concerns, but added that it was impossible to give guarantees about how these concerns would influence the Brexit talks. 'Naturally it is up to the new British government when its application [to leave] is filed, but it is important that, with this application, we get clarity over what relationship Britain wants to build up with the EU because this will affect talks.' Italian Foreign Minister Paolo Gentiloni, on a visit to Dublin the same day for a meeting with Charlie Flanagan, was much more effusive in supporting Irish concerns, saying that the imposition of a hard border between the Republic and Northern Ireland would be 'very negative and dangerous'.

It was Merkel, though, who was critical to getting the Irish question to the top of the EU agenda and at this early stage it was far from obvious that Kenny's diplomatic drive would succeed. In fact, on his return home he was greeted with newspaper headlines suggesting that his backbenchers were plotting against him after the disappointing election result for Fine Gael earlier in the year.

Kenny had his first telephone conversation with Prime Minister May on the day of her elevation and described their chat in positive terms. 'We agreed to build on the close co-operation that has been developed between the Irish and British governments in recent years, including in their support of the peace process and the Good Friday Agreement, and in progressing areas of co-operation under the Ireland–UK Joint Statement.' It was a standard communiqué that said very little, but privately Kenny was worried that in their phone conversation May had given no indication at all of what her approach to Brexit was going to be.

Ever the optimist, Kenny availed of the opportunity presented by the annual MacGill Summer School at Glencolmcille in Donegal the following week to outline his hopes for a continuing close Irish–British relationship after Brexit. 'Ireland's starting point will be straightforward. A stable, prosperous, and outward-looking UK is clearly in our own interests and those of the EU as a whole. The closer the UK is to the EU, the better for all of us, and above all for Ireland.'

He added that it was obviously up to the UK to work out what kind of future it saw for itself and the nature of the relationship with the EU it wanted to achieve. 'Within the EU, Ireland will argue that the negotiations should be conducted in a positive and constructive way. But this will also depend on the UK's approach. I will be encouraging the new British Prime Minister to set realistic and achievable objectives and to build confidence in the UK's good faith.'

He made the point that the Irish and British governments, as well as the power-sharing Executive in Northern Ireland, shared the common objective of wanting to preserve the CTA and an open border on the island of Ireland. 'Ireland is in an important position given the strength of our relationship with the UK on one hand and our connectedness to the EU on the other. But my primary goal is Ireland's national interests and that goal will be foremost in any discussions: with the UK; with our EU partners; and between the EU collectively and the UK.'

The question nobody could answer at the time was how the common interests of the two countries could be accommodated in the Brexit process. At this stage Kenny envisaged that talks between the governments of Ireland and the UK would play a crucial role in determining the future relationship between the two countries. He clearly underestimated the extent to which it would be an EU/UK process with Irish interests being subsumed into the overall Brussels strategy.

Crucially, though, he showed an instinctive grasp of the need to prepare for the scale of the problem by making fundamental changes in the workings of the government machine to ensure that it was ready for one of the biggest challenges in the history of the State. One move was to establish a cabinet committee on Brexit, to be chaired by himself, that would oversee the overall government response to the negotiations at EU level and with the administrations in London and Belfast.

A key decision he made on the strong advice of his officials was to resist pressure from the Opposition and much of the media to follow the British lead and appoint a minister to deal exclusively with Brexit. 'After the appointment of David Davis, Enda Kenny was under serious pressure to appoint a Brexit minister, and he resisted, rightly in my view,' said John Callinan, the senior civil servant who led the Irish negotiating team. 'This was going to be a total government challenge rather than an issue that could be hived off to one department and, second, all the big issues were going to come to the European Council anyway so in fact the Taoiseach was the Brexit minister.'

Appointing a Brexit minister would have ignored the fundamental fact that the negotiations would be between the UK and Brussels, not between the UK and Dublin. 'From the get-go Enda saw himself as very much in charge of Brexit and he needed no persuading to take the lead,' said one senior official.

As part of that process Kenny ordered a fundamental restructuring of the Taoiseach's Department and oversaw a wide-ranging personnel and organisational shuffle. At this stage the second secretary of the department in charge of EU affairs was Rory Montgomery, a vastly experienced and widely respected diplomat who had served as the Irish Permanent Representative in Brussels during the financial crisis. He had moved from Foreign Affairs, along with the entire EU division, when its minister, Eamon Gilmore, straddled both departments as Tánaiste under the coalition deal of 2011.

Kenny decided that this arrangement needed to be reversed. At short notice Montgomery was moved back to Foreign Affairs as the second secretary in that department, and most of the EU division went with him. His place in the Taoiseach's Department was taken by John Callinan, with whom Kenny had worked closely on first taking over as Taoiseach. Callinan had accompanied Kenny to his first bruising meeting of the European Council in 2011 and the Taoiseach wanted him back in that role. For the remainder of the Brexit process Callinan would be Kenny's 'Sherpa', in EU jargon, representing him and his two successors, Leo Varadkar and Micheál Martin, in Europe. A quietly spoken Dubliner who had joined the civil service after leaving secondary school, Callinan began his career in the Revenue Commissioners before moving to the Taoiseach's Department. He worked on EU and Anglo-Irish issues before being given responsibility for the department's economic division. In the course of his career Callinan gained a reputation as a skilled negotiator with an ability to get along with politicians.

For Montgomery the transfer back to Foreign Affairs came as a shock and he felt wounded by the suddenness of the change, which was made without any consultation or discussion. It took a few weeks before the new roles and structures were defined. 'It was awkward, but in the end it actually worked out okay,' recalled Montgomery. 'In the end I was reasonably happy with the fact much of the substance of the job went back to Foreign Affairs.'

The new arrangements meant that Callinan represented Kenny at critical meetings with the EU while Montgomery ran the diplomatic effort to develop support for the Irish position across the member states. In spite of the teething problems, the Taoiseach and Minister for Foreign Affairs and their officials worked closely together in the following years. 'There were never really any disagreements on the Irish side, within the camp, about what we should be doing. It could have been difficult if the two principals had taken a different view, but they didn't,' said Montgomery.

He pointed to the active role Charlie Flanagan played in the early stages, meeting all the other EU foreign ministers within weeks of the referendum. 'In addition, we were doing the kind of detailed analysis of negotiations, the drafting and then the co-ordination of other departments. So it worked out reasonably well. It was partly because on a personal level, John Callinan and I knew each other and got on pretty well; John is not a bureaucratic turf warrior,' said Montgomery.

Another important change was that Eamonn Molloy, assistant secretary in the Taoiseach's Department, was given responsibility for Northern Ireland issues and relations with the British. Given the suspension of the Northern Executive in early 2017 and the central role the North would have in the Brexit negotiations it was another key area.

When the internal reshuffle was complete there was a clear division of responsibility. The Department of the Taoiseach would drive Brexit policy, while Foreign Affairs would implement it with outreach to EU institutions and other European capitals. The civil servant where the buck ultimately stopped was the hard-nosed secretary general of the Taoiseach's Department, Martin Fraser. He implemented the changes demanded by Kenny and stepped into the Brexit negotiations with his British opposite number, Jeremy Heywood, at critical stages in the process.

'The main thing we did fairly aggressively was gear up a massive political and diplomatic campaign to make sure that the mistake made by the British, in not paying enough attention to potential Northern

Ireland complications, was not repeated on the EU side,' said Callinan of the first months following the referendum.

> More than that, we had a big job of work to do as it was shaping up to be a negotiation about the money and citizens' rights with no focus on Ireland. There were even people who were attuned to the Border issue saying 'Sure that can only be resolved during the trade talks.' We knew that was going to be a potential disaster if we allowed it to happen. So we had a very deliberate, conscious plan to go with a massive diplomatic campaign.

Getting the Irish case out early was critical.

> It was the kind of stuff you'd expect, which was getting on planes going to meet people, getting in people's faces a little bit and making sure that the scale of what was involved for Ireland was understood. We had to explain why it was so important to deal with the Border issue rather than to leave it as part of the trade agreement when we would have no leverage. It was important to establish that early on. And to be fair, that campaign worked and maybe some individuals on the EU side probably regretted it because it sort of became this awful sore running the whole way through the Brexit process.

The nub of the diplomatic drive was to persuade the other EU states that the Irish Border issue should be dealt with as an essential component of the Withdrawal Agreement between the EU and the UK before any discussions on the future trade relationship got under way. The fear in Dublin was that if the Border was left until a trade deal between the EU and the UK was being finalised, Irish concerns might be trampled on. 'The Taoiseach gave me a very strong imprimatur to work on this diplomatic offensive which obviously included putting him and ministers into play,' said Callinan. Charlie Flanagan's blitz of meetings with other EU foreign ministers was critical in developing the momentum that pushed the Irish issue to the top of the agenda.

Charlie Flanagan stressed the commitment and skill of the Irish diplomatic team led by Rory Montgomery throughout the Brexit process:

We had Rory heading up the diplomatic effort from Dublin and we had Declan Kelleher in Brussels. Declan was due to retire but the first thing we did was to give him an extension. He was too good to let go and he was the key linkman between the government in Dublin and the Commission. We had a lot of other really talented people, Dan Mulhall in London, Anne Anderson in Washington, Michael Collins in Berlin, Bobby McDonagh in Rome and Geraldine Byrne Nason in Paris. So they were a very strong team and did a brilliant job of presenting the Irish case.

Kelleher, as the Permanent Representative to the EU, was in a pivotal role. He had been appointed to the position in 2013, having acquired a reputation as a forceful and able diplomat in his previous posting as Ambassador to China. In Beijing he learned Cantonese and made himself so invaluable that his posting was extended from the normal four years to nine. In 2012 he persuaded the Chinese authorities to accept an invitation to then Vice-President Xi Jinping to visit Ireland. The Chinese leader paid a three-day visit to the country in 2012 on a three-nation tour that also included the United States and Turkey. In Brussels Kelleher had established a wide range of contacts by the time of the Brexit vote and was on good terms with Kenny and with Ireland's EU Commissioner, Phil Hogan.

One important contact of Kelleher's in Brussels was Jeppe Tranholm-Mikkelsen, the secretary-general of the European Council whom he already knew from his time as Danish Ambassador to China. One of the features of EU affairs over the years had been an intense rivalry between the European Council, which represents the heads of government, and the European Commission, the executive body responsible for running the EU. A good relationship with both institutions was vital if Irish concerns were to be taken seriously in Brussels.

As Kenny lobbied his fellow EU leaders, Charlie Flanagan was conducting a similar campaign among the EU Foreign Ministers. 'I had to act quickly. Within 48 hours I had spoken to every foreign minister on phone, every single one of them, which was a huge undertaking. Then I departed for European capitals and the immediate priority was Germany and France, because they were the big powers,' said Flanagan.

His two-day trip to Germany was crucial. 'Steinmeier had had set aside some time for me and gave great advice on how to proceed. This was very significant because he wasn't EPP but SPD and that widened our circle of influence. Enda's relationship with Merkel was hugely significant but there was a great degree of sympathy for us in Germany with key people like MEPs David McAllister and Elmar Brok pressing our case.'

During his visit to Germany in July, Flanagan addressed the Bundestag European Affairs Committee as well as the friends of Ireland in the parliament. In August he was at the EU–ASEAN summit in Mongolia attended by foreign ministers as well as heads of government. One person everybody looked to for guidance on what was going to happen on Brexit was Angela Merkel. 'There was none of the back-slapping Irish stuff that we got from Elmar Brok or even Steinmeier about Ireland. Merkel was very direct and clinical. "Ireland, Oh yes. We are supporting you." End of conversation.'

The team in the Taoiseach's Department set out four priorities that formed the core of the government's strategy. They were: to protect the CTA; to protect the peace process by working to ensure there would be a frictionless Border on the island of Ireland; and protect trade with the UK. The fourth and overarching priority was to protect Ireland's place in the EU to make it clear to everybody that there was no question of Ireland following the British example.

Explaining the importance of the CTA to the rest of the EU was difficult. Unrestricted travel between Ireland and the UK is something that Irish people have long taken for granted, and there has been largely unrestricted movement of people in both directions for centuries. This was the natural order of things when Ireland was part of the UK, but when the twenty-six countries achieved independence as the Free State in 1922 arrangements were immediately put in place to ensure that that people from each country could continue to travel freely to the other.

The arrangement went beyond travel. People had the automatic right to live, work and claim benefits in each other's countries, just as they had done when they were part of the same state. There were some limited restrictions to free movement during the Second World War when Ireland opted to stay neutral, but they did not stop a large number of Irish people emigrating to Britain throughout the war. The CTA between Ireland and the UK was formalised in 1953 and preserving it was one of the Irish government's key priorities after the Brexit referendum. Ireland stayed outside the Schengen Area for passport-free travel (which had been established by the EU under the 1997 Amsterdam Treaty) for the simple reason that the UK had opted out. Preserving the CTA was a greater priority for Ireland than joining Schengen.

When Irish officials raised the importance of the CTA with European Commission officials after the Brexit vote there was considerable surprise in Brussels at the way the arrangement had developed, with no formal intergovernmental agreement between the two countries to spell out the detail. There is no specific law in Ireland or the UK that controls how it functions, but the two countries had over the years developed arrangements enabling people to move freely and live and work in each other's territory. The arrangement had long become an accepted part of Irish life and its potential disruption was regarded by the government as one of the main challenges of Brexit.

There was no guarantee that the problem would receive a sympathetic hearing in Brussels. In his book *Brexit and Ireland*, RTÉ's Europe correspondent Tony Connolly quoted an EU official saying in the immediate aftermath of the referendum that technically speaking Ireland could be forced to join the Schengen Area and abandon the CTA. There was also some worry about how the British might view the future of the CTA given that immigration had proved to be the key issue in the referendum.

There was considerable reassurance on that point in what was probably the first meeting of Irish and British officials after the referendum. At that meeting between civil servants from the Department of Justice and the Home Office the British officials reassured their Irish counterparts that they wanted to maintain the CTA. The Justice officials then focused on potential problems the CTA might raise for other EU countries. The CTA didn't just involve the free movement of people, it also provided for reciprocal work, pension and welfare benefit rights for the people of Ireland and the UK. One issue was whether these special arrangements could be interpreted as discriminating against EU citizens from other countries. The conclusion was that the special arrangements for UK citizens in Ireland did not prejudice any rights of EU citizens and were therefore acceptable. The key objective for the Irish side was to keep the CTA out of the negotiations on the future relationship between the EU and the UK. 'We made the argument that it didn't matter to the rest of the EU as it was not going to trammel any rights, but it was a very tricky piece of the jigsaw,' recalled Callinan.

The main argument about the need to preserve a frictionless border on the island in order to protect the peace process had more resonance in EU capitals, especially since the EU was itself founded in a Europe-wide peace process. A glossy booklet outlining the four core Irish objectives was quickly produced and widely circulated in EU capitals and Brussels as part of the diplomatic offensive. A key argument was that maintaining an open Irish Border was an essential component of the Good Friday Agreement and consequently a unique issue that went to the heart of what the EU stood for.

As the Irish campaign swung into action the British were still in the throes of setting up their structures, with David Davis at the newly established Brexit Department struggling to get his operation off the ground. Some coherence was put on the process by the appointment of the experienced civil servant Olly Robbins as head of the Department. He had been with Theresa May at the Home Office and she placed a great deal of trust in him. Robbins had been principal private secretary to Tony Blair and had continued to serve Gordon Brown in that post before moving to the Home Office. He had worked closely with cabinet secretary Jeremy Heywood and also with the UK Ambassador to the EU, Ivan Rogers. As well as taking over as permanent secretary of the Brexit Department, Robbins was attached to the Prime Minister's office as May's EU Sherpa.

On a personal level the appointment of Robbins as May's Sherpa was welcome news in Dublin as he and Callinan already knew each other.

We worked closely together in a previous chapter, when he was dealing with Northern Ireland. In the period after the Queen's visit when we were in that phase of British–Irish relations and he and I were the people tasked with driving it. So we had a good professional relationship and got on well and understood each other well, which I think mattered a lot.

An important factor in persuading the EU to take up the Irish case with such commitment was the unity displayed by almost the entire political system. The main opposition party, Fianna Fáil, gave strong backing to the government's approach. The party was kept in the loop all the way through the process, as part of the confidence and supply arrangement that gave political stability. Even Sinn Féin, which was in full-throttle opposition, did not seek to embarrass the government when there were setbacks to its strategy. This stood in stark contrast to the British parliament, where factionalism and narrow party considerations got in the way of a coherent national response all through the Brexit process.

'We were four-square behind the national effort,' said Micheál Martin. 'We made it very clear to all and sundry that this was bad news all round, for British–Irish relations, for British–European relations, and that Ireland was at one in terms of dealing with this and we were fully behind the government.'

From the beginning Martin was in touch with the Commission to say that Ireland was at one in its approach. At the leaders' meetings of the liberal ALDE group (the Alliance of Liberals and Democrats for Europe), of which Fianna Fáil was a member, Martin rubbed shoulders with some of the leading politicians in the EU, including Dutch Prime Minister Mark Rutte, Luxembourg Prime Minister Xavier Bettel and a number of EU Commissioners. 'At the very first meeting of ALDE after Brexit they expressed their concern about Northern Ireland and how Brexit would affect the peace process. I was very struck by it. Their main concern was Northern Ireland initially. Obviously, there are other concerns that they didn't want Britain to have its cake and eat it but Northern Ireland was their first concern.'

Kenny travelled to Downing Street for his first meeting with Prime Minister Theresa May at the end of July. It was May's first meeting with a foreign government leader, which she cited as testament to the importance of the relationship between the two countries. The two held a fifteen-minute discussion before joining officials for an hour-long lunch. In a foretaste of things to come May frequently deferred to her officials and gave little hint of her own views. She did confess that although she had spent years attending Council meetings in Brussels she had only just learned, to her surprise, that as Prime Minister she would be on her own in the room at European Council meetings and would not have the comfort of having officials with her. It was an early hint of just how daunting May would find those Council meetings.

The overall impression she left with the Irish side was one of extreme caution. Kenny tried to draw her out by explaining the range of Irish concerns, but May, while remaining courteous, did not engage. It was a very different atmosphere from the matey exchanges that had become the norm between Kenny and Cameron.

At a joint press conference after the lunch the Taoiseach and the British Prime Minister appeared to be on the same page. Both agreed there would be no return to a hard border on the island of Ireland and they promised to find 'creative and imaginative' ways to deal with customs checks if the necessity arose. Kenny said:

A hard border in normal circumstances means customs posts and customs checks in various places. There will be no return to the hard border between the Republic and Northern Ireland of the past, which included towers and military equipment, obviously for different reasons. So I do not favour, I do not agree to, a hard border, with a whole range of customs posts, and neither does the Prime Minister.

He went on to suggest that even if customs checks were required they would not involve physical border posts. 'There are other ways of dealing with modern technology in terms of checking trade,' he said. 'I think these are things that need to be looked at creatively and imaginatively but we are both agreed very firmly that there will be no return to a hard border as it used to be.'

May said she was committed to maintaining the strong economic relationship between the two countries, to safeguarding the Northern Ireland peace process, and to preserving the benefits of the CTA. 'There is a strong will on both sides to preserve it and so we must now focus on securing a deal that is in the interest of both of us. And alongside this, we should continue our efforts to strengthen the external borders of the Common Travel Area, for example through a common approach to the use of passenger data.'

Despite May's formal approach to the meeting, both leaders' comments after it indicated that they expected a benign outcome to the inevitable problems that the Irish Border would pose after the UK had left the EU. In hindsight their optimism was naive, but Kenny was clearly still hoping for the softest possible Brexit while May had yet to appreciate the nature and scale of the task facing her.

3

Enter Barnier

'Barnier knew Ireland, Barnier knew Dublin and Barnier knew Kenny.'
Charlie Flanagan May 2020

* * *

In the wake of the British referendum the European Commission moved quickly to prepare for the negotiations ahead. The Commission was fortunate that its president, Jean-Claude Juncker, was one of the most adroit and wily politicians in the EU, with vast experience of how the Union operated. As Prime Minister of Luxembourg he had been a member of the European Council from 1995 to 2013 and knew the leaders of almost all the member states. He put himself in pole position to become President of the Commission by defeating his French rival Michel Barnier at an EPP convention in Dublin in March 2014. Despite strong opposition from David Cameron at the European Council, his status as the favoured candidate of the EPP ensured that he was offered the post in June of that year. Kenny resisted pressure from Cameron and backed Juncker for the position.

With the EU facing a threat to its very existence, Juncker knew that it was vital to find a political figure with a serious reputation to head the Commission's negotiating team on Brexit. This was primarily to ensure that the EU would have a strong hand in the negotiations but it was also to keep the Commission in charge of the process and not allow it to be led by other EU institutions or be dictated by national considerations.

Faced with this key decision, Juncker turned to the man he had defeated in Dublin two years earlier, the French conservative politician Michel Barnier, whom he had already employed as special adviser on defence and security. Just two weeks after the UK referendum the two men travelled to Warsaw for a meeting with NATO. Barnier had been surprised when Juncker had invited him to be his defence policy adviser and he was even more surprised, but also delighted, to be asked to lead the Brexit negotiations with the UK. As someone who had long experience as a European Commissioner working at the heart of the issues that would feature in the negotiations, he relished the challenge. His answer was a unhesitating yes.

'I have to check how the idea will go down in certain quarters. Don't mention anything, we'll talk again soon,' Juncker told him with a smile. The 'certain quarters' were the German Chancellor and the French President as well as the President of the European Council, Donald Tusk. Having received the assent of the key players in the EU, Juncker then sought the approval of his Commission colleagues and Barnier's appointment was formally announced on 27 July.

From an Irish point of view Barnier turned out to be the dream candidate, although that only became clear over time. Initially there was some suspicion that he would act in the interests of the EU as a whole, which might involve Ireland being trampled on in the process. But Juncker knew what he was doing. Not only had Barnier wide experience of politics at the highest level in France and the EU, he also had an intimate knowledge of Ireland developed during his period as Regional Affairs Commissioner. In that role he had visited Northern Ireland and got to know the complexities of the situation there. During his term between 1999 and 2004 he oversaw the spending of €531 million in EU peace funding in Ireland as well as tens of millions in regional and structural payments.

His obvious regard for Ireland and his knowledge of the country soon became apparent. 'Barnier knew Ireland, Barnier knew Dublin and Barnier knew Kenny,' said Charlie Flanagan. 'So his appointment was huge because he was a friend of Ireland from day one.' However, it took some time for Barnier's commitment to defending Irish interests to become apparent. At a seminar at the Institute for International and European Affairs (IIEA), Labour Party leader Brendan Howlin expressed grave reservations about Ireland's future being entrusted to 'a Brussels fonctionnaire'. Even Taoiseach Enda Kenny, who knew Barnier reasonably well, was inclined to play down the chief negotiator's role and emphasise that final decisions would be taken by the heads of government at the European Council.

Long before his appointment, during his time as Commissioner for Financial Regulation, the British tabloid press had characterised Barnier as 'the most dangerous man in Europe'. Now they had a field day. The *Daily Express* led the charge, denouncing him as a 'Brit-bashing EU-mad French politician'. It was the opening salvo of a campaign of vilification that did not let up for the entire Brexit process. All the abuse had no obvious impact on Barnier beyond causing him some mild amusement.

Hardened in French national politics, where he had served as Foreign Minister as well as Agriculture Minister, he rarely allowed himself to get irritated in public. If anything, the criticism made him more determined to ensure that Irish and EU interests would be defended to the hilt in the negotiations. From the beginning the British hoped – and assumed – that they would be able to drive a wedge between the formal negotiating position of the EU and some of the member states. 'We have allies among the twenty-seven and we must make use of them. Our enemy is the Commission, which wants to be forgiven for making Cameron lose. Many of the twenty-seven need us,' UK Trade Secretary Liam Fox told a business meeting in London.

Britain placed a particular focus on Germany in the belief that industry, and car makers in particular, would try to force the government in Berlin to break ranks in order to protect the country's trade with the UK. This showed a complete failure to understand both Merkel's core objective of defending the integrity of the EU single market and also the wider commitment of German society and business to the European ideal. It also underestimated Barnier's skills as a negotiator, first in getting a firm commitment from the twenty-seven member states to an agreed strategy and then the determined way he went about pursuing it, keeping the twenty-seven governments and the European Parliament informed at every stage in the process. Ultimately, for the Commission and the member states the issue boiled down to the survival of the EU in the face of what was widely regarded across the continent as a British attempt to destroy it.

Barnier spent September assembling his negotiating team. Its formal title was Task Force for the Preparation and Conduct of Negotiations with the United Kingdom Under Article 50, but it was usually referred to as the Task Force. Barnier looked around for a deputy who would have the standing and the ability to lead the day-to-day negotiations. He decided that the ideal person would be German EU official Sabine Weyand, deputy director general of trade and widely regarded as one of the stars of the official world in Brussels. A native of Saarland, Weyand studied political science at the University of Freiburg and spent a year doing postgraduate research in Cambridge, where she developed a deep understanding of British politics.

Barnier broached the subject of Weyand's suitability with the abrasive secretary-general of the Commission, Martin Selmayr, another German. 'Good thinking, but she won't be coming. She is too useful here,' retorted Selmayr. In spite of the rebuff Barnier called Weyand directly and found that she was enthusiastic about taking the post. He informed her of Selmayr's opposition but told her to use her own network of contacts to get around it. Barnier had a few tense conversations with Selmayr about the issue but finally the secretary-general conceded and agreed 'to let me recruit this brilliant woman, as adept politically as she is technically'.

The other key member of Barnier's team was a young French woman, Stéphanie Riso, who had worked in the cabinets of several Commissioners on monetary and budgetary issues. 'She is a lively and direct woman who doesn't mince her words and who will be particularly useful in helping me to negotiate the explosive issue of the financial settlement with the British,' Barnier noted in his diary. Riso was familiar with Ireland from her time as deputy head of cabinet for Olli Rehn, the Finnish Commissioner who played a key role in shaping the Irish bailout programme between 2008 and 2010. 'I will have alongside me these two strong women, not at all alike, with different but complementary personalities and convictions, both of whom command great respect,' wrote Barnier. Another woman, Nina Obermaier, was given direct responsibility for Ireland and struck up a strong rapport with Irish officials. Barnier was happy that having such respected officials at the head of his team would send out a signal both inside and outside the Commission that a professional and highly competent operation was being mounted.

By the autumn Barnier had widened the team and nearly sixty officials from a variety of EU directorates had been assembled to handle the negotiations. There were two Irish members of the Task Force, Tadhg O'Briain, an energy expert, and Daniel Ferrie, who was appointed its official spokesperson. There was some concern in Ireland that there was no Irish involvement at a senior level in the Task Force. This was raised in the Dáil and in the media on a number of occasions and reflected the general anxiety in Ireland about what might happen when the big issues came to the crunch.

This anxiety manifested itself when Barnier paid his first visit to Dublin in his new role on 12 October, bringing his key officials with him. He held separate meetings with the Taoiseach, Minister for Foreign Affairs Charlie Flanagan, Minister for Justice Frances Fitzgerald and Minister for European Affairs Dara Murphy. Kenny stressed to Barnier the importance the government attached to the situation in Northern Ireland and its determination to retain the CTA between Ireland and the United Kingdom.

Talking to political correspondents afterwards, Kenny said he had emphasised to Barnier Ireland's 'unique set of priorities with regard to Brexit, and the many complex issues relating to Northern Ireland, the Common Travel Area and the depth of our economic and trade relationship with the UK.' The emphasis on the CTA indicated that there was still considerable nervousness on the part of the government in Dublin about whether the EU would accept its continuation. The news reports also emphasised that the government was keen to ensure that an Irish official was appointed to Barnier's team, a further indication of nervousness about the priority that would be given to Irish interests.

At this stage Barnier's support for Ireland and his pivotal role in deciding the EU negotiating strategy on Brexit had still not fully impinged on Irish political leaders. For instance, before meeting him in Dublin, Kenny told the Dáil, 'I will meet Michel Barnier who is coming here on behalf of the European Commission. I point out to the House that irrespective of the work that the Commission will do here, it will be the EU Council – the elected leaders and heads of government – that will oversee the political decisions arising from Brexit.'

This was hardly a resounding vote of confidence. Irish EU Commissioner Phil Hogan, who visited Dublin the following week was privately scathing about what he regarded as the government's misjudgement of the situation. By this stage Hogan had established himself as one of the most influential commissioners in Brussels. A formidable politician who had rescued Enda Keny's leadership with a masterful campaign during a no-confidence motion in 2010, the tall and imposing Hogan, known widely as 'Big Phil', had become a controversial figure during the Fine Gael–Labour government that took office in 2011. Responsible for implementing unpopular policies like the property tax and water charges, required by the EU as part of the bailout terms, he was delighted to leave domestic politics and was appointed Agriculture Commissioner in 2014. He struck up a close relationship with Juncker, who jokingly referred to him as 'Farmer Phil', and he became a key figure in pushing Irish concerns throughout the Brexit process.

'The approach here is far too focused on the Brits and we are not making the right noises to develop allies in Europe,' was his assessment in October 2016. He was aware that Barnier had been irritated by Kenny's five references during his visit to the fact that the European Council would make the final decision on the Brexit terms, which he felt was downgrading the role of the Task Force. 'Barnier is critical to getting Irish concerns into the draft negotiating document and people here had better wake up to that fact,' remarked Hogan, and he conveyed the message bluntly to the Taoiseach and his officials.

Despite the warnings from Brussels, there was still a sense on the Irish side in the final months of 2016 that maintaining good relations with the UK was the best way of protecting the country's interests. This was understandable given the need for a continued close relationship with the UK to deal with Northern Ireland, the CTA and co-operation on security and justice issues that were important to both states. One of the reasons for the Irish misjudgement was that British ministers like Philip Hammond, and senior officials, were taking a much softer line in private conversations with their Irish colleagues than the official UK government position.

The desire of the Irish side to preserve a close relationship with the British led to recurring anxiety in Brussels that Ireland might prove a stalking horse for British interests. Flanagan recalled that at this stage the EU was very sensitive about the bilateral relationship between Ireland and the UK.

The real problem in the autumn of 2016 was that it was not clear if the British were aiming for a soft or a hard Brexit and it often seemed as if they didn't know themselves. Despite the soft words in private, the fact that the three British ministers involved in the process – Johnson, Davis and Fox – were all dedicated Brexiteers was not encouraging from an Irish point of view. Even more confusing was the apparent chaos on the British side.

'It was a strange triumvirate,' said Flanagan. 'When Davis visited Dublin I asked him to explain the division of labour among the ministers and he said: "It's like this. Imagine being on a ship. Liam Fox and myself are down in the engine room shovelling coal into the furnace to keep the steamship afloat and Boris [Johnson] is sunning himself on deck."' Flanagan recalled one encounter with Johnson at a dinner for EU foreign ministers at the UN general assembly in New York in September. The other ministers attempted, without success, to penetrate Johnson's bonhomie to gain some sense of what the British really wanted. 'They were so frustrated with the bluster that the Italian Foreign Minister Gentiloni heckled Johnson while he was making a short speech. There was a real anti-British mood around the table,' said Flanagan.

A strong hint that British policy was heading in the direction of a hard Brexit came at the Conservative Party conference in Birmingham in early October. In her first address to a party conference since becoming leader Theresa May played to the gallery by delivering a rousing speech suffused with patriotic imagery. 'We have the best intelligence service in the world, a military that can project its power around the globe, and friendships, partnerships and alliances in every continent,' she proclaimed, setting the mood music for her core message, which put a little flesh on the message that 'Brexit means Brexit'.

We are going to be a fully independent sovereign country – a country that is no longer part of a political union with supra-national institutions that can override national parliaments and courts. And that means we are going, once more, to have the freedom to make our own decisions on a whole host of different matters from how we label our food to the way in which we choose to control immigration.

The clear implication of this was that she was ruling out the free movement of people as well as any future role for the European Court of Justice (ECJ). The only conclusion was that the UK would, at the very least, leave the EU single market. An important feature of the speech was May's commitment to trigger Article 50 of the Lisbon Treaty by the end of March 2017 to set in motion a two-year process for leaving the EU. The public commitment to a time frame for Article 50 prompted the EU negotiating team to start working out a detailed negotiating strategy. By contrast, May and her team of ministers were nowhere near deciding what they wanted. It soon became apparent that by setting a time frame for triggering Article 50 she had shown the EU one of the UK's few strong negotiating cards without any idea of how she intended to play it.

The content and tone of the May speech, much of it drafted by her joint chief of staff Nick Timothy, caught the Irish side by surprise. Ironically, a large team of top Irish civil servants were in London on the same day to meet their opposite numbers in the UK system. This annual get-together had begun after a 2011 bilateral agreement between David Cameron and Enda Kenny. It was one of the concrete expressions of the close and warm relationship between the two countries that had been symbolised by Queen Elizabeth's state visit to Ireland.

The meeting was held in the Foreign and Commonwealth Office on King Charles Street, near Buckingham Palace. The Irish team was led by the secretary general of the Taoiseach's Department, Martin Fraser, while his British counterpart, cabinet secretary Jeremy Heywood, led the UK delegation. The Irish Ambassador to the UK, Dan Mulhall, joined the meeting after travelling from the Conservative Party conference in Birmingham. In all about fifty civil servants from the two sides attended the meeting. The senior British officials reassured their Irish colleagues that Prime Minister May's speech should be taken with a grain of salt. 'They were asking people to make allowances for the fact that she was at her party conference,' said one Irish official. Another suggested that not every word should be taken literally as her political advisers had drafted much of the content with a party political focus.

The formal meeting between the two sets of officials was kicked off with speeches from Fraser and Heywood and was followed by contributions from the two lead negotiators at EU level, John Callinan and Olly Robbins. The meeting then broke into separate groups to deal with specific issues that were likely to arise in the Brexit talks. There were five key areas: the peace process; the Border; the CTA; police and security co-operation; and bilateral trade. The problem was that none of the officials was sure where the Brexit process would end up and on both sides there was an over-optimistic sense that the most likely outcome was a reasonably close future relationship between the EU and the departing UK.

The mood was even more relaxed and positive when they all adjourned to the Red Lion in Westminster Street to unwind over a few drinks. There was an air of camaraderie and little hint of the tension that would creep into their relationship as the Brexit process developed. 'There was a shared determination to deal with all the issues creatively and effectively to reflect the unique circumstances on the island,' said one of the Irish diplomats present.

That shared determination by officials from both countries to find solutions that would ease the pain of Brexit for Ireland continued to cause alarm at EU level. There was ongoing suspicion in Brussels that Ireland was attempting to do a bilateral deal with the UK and usurping the functions of the EU negotiating team. Barnier raised these fears during his early meetings with Kenny and that led to a degree of tension between Dublin and Brussels. 'It was a point he [Barnier] made quite bluntly,' said one Irish official. 'The Commission is your negotiator. Work out your position with us,' was Barnier's message.

It was a difficult time for the Irish as they tried to develop a strategy that would take account of the fact that Ireland stood to lose more than any other EU country. Some officials in a number of departments in Dublin were still working on the assumption that a bilateral deal with the UK would be the best way to achieve this objective, but that ran counter to the negotiating strategy being developed by Barnier and his team.

Irish officials had to walk a tightrope of exploring options with their British counterparts while staying onside with Brussels. There was a wide perception in Brussels and across many of the other twenty-six EU states that Ireland would be too sympathetic to the British 'have our cake and eat it' approach.

Tony Connolly quoted a senior British diplomat at the time conceding that Ireland was 'the weakest link', while an Irish official admitted there was a wariness among EU officials about what might transpire. 'If we came up with a bespoke solution for the Irish Border there was a fear that the Brits might then seize on it and say, "Well, you have agreed it with Ireland, now you are going to have to agree it in Dover–Calais," or wherever else they had a problem.' Hogan, who was acutely aware of these concerns, sent a firm message to the Irish government. 'You are on team EU or team UK. You had better make it clear which side you are on or it could be very damaging for the country.' Giving evidence to the Oireachtas EU Committee at the end of October he didn't put a tooth in it. 'The choice is a hard Brexit or no Brexit,' he declared; so Ireland had better be ready for a hard Brexit.

The dilemma facing the Irish side began to be picked up in the media. 'The time has come for Irish policy makers to stop dreaming of a soft Brexit and prepare for the reality that the United Kingdom is likely to crash out of the European Union in the ugliest possible fashion,' declared an *Irish Times* columnist at the end of October; and 'The biggest threat to Ireland's national interest at this stage is not that the UK is going to leave the EU but a perception across Europe that this country is too closely allied to the British.'

Charlie Flanagan kept up the diplomatic pressure to win support for the Irish position in other EU capitals. Having focused on the big powers of Germany and France and countries, like the Netherlands, Denmark and Belgium, that also stood to be affected by Brexit, Flanagan travelled to central and eastern Europe and found to his surprise that while many were not all that concerned about Brexit they were still supportive of Ireland. Poland was important as other countries such as Romania and Bulgaria tended to follow its lead. A determined effort was also made to woo Cyprus and Malta, which had close British connections, as well as forging a relationship with Portugal as another Atlantic state. The Irish diplomatic service managed to get an opinion piece about Ireland and Brexit into leading newspapers in twenty-four of the twenty-six EU states during the summer.

'But the EPP was the key. Because Enda had his EPP heads of government meetings, and I had my EPP foreign affairs meetings. And invariably there were seven or eight EPP people around the table and I could talk privately to them before the Foreign Affairs Council,' said

Flanagan. Fiannna Fáil leader Micheál Martin played his part in the campaign by taking the Irish message to ALDE meetings.

'The government kept us in the loop,' recalled Martin. 'I would meet John Callinan on a regular basis and I would ring him and other officials every now and again to say: "Look, we're going to an ALDE meeting next week. Is there any particular message you want us to give?" Enda Kenny convened meetings with party leaders and Simon Coveney kept our foreign affairs spokesperson Lisa Chambers well briefed.'

US Secretary of State John Kerry came to Ireland in October to accept the Tipperary peace prize. During his visit he met Flanagan and spoke publicly about the US commitment to the Good Friday Agreement and also to the importance of a united Europe. The government in Dublin was delighted at this strong signal of Washington's support for its Brexit priorities.

A tricky issue for the government was how to deal with Scottish First Minister Nicola Sturgeon. She came to Dublin and was anxious to enlist Irish support for her ambition to avoid Scotland leaving the EU. This was an issue the Irish did not want to get embroiled in, as it involved the sovereignty of the UK. While there was strong sympathy for the plight of Scotland being forced to leave the EU against the will of a majority of its people, interfering in the internal affairs of the UK was simply not feasible.

If Flanagan's meetings with other EU foreign ministers were encouraging, the same could not be said for his interaction with British Foreign Secretary Boris Johnson. 'I have to say around the Foreign Affairs table he was a figure of fun. People did not warm to him and he did nothing to ingratiate himself. He was provocative towards the French and the Germans and the Italians, and everyone.'

Other EU foreign ministers asked Flanagan what was happening in Britain – Johnson couldn't be bothered engaging with them.

He was acting the maggot and they didn't really talk to him. I did have meetings with him but they were shambolic. He'd say, 'Let's meet for a glass of wine and a bit of dinner later on, Charlie, you and I, man to man, and we'll sort this. What is it going to be, a hard border, a soft border? Let's work it out.' Officials were shocked at this casual approach to something so important for both countries.

Flanagan encouraged his cabinet colleagues to explore every option with their counterparts in the Northern Ireland Executive to see how a hard border could be avoided while still protecting the European single market. Mixed messages continued to come from the UK; Theresa May repeated again and again the commitment to avoiding a hard border in Ireland without going into any detail about how this might be achieved.

With the Border clearly the biggest political issue confronting Ireland, the government attempted to circumvent the political divisions in the North by embarking on an effort to get a joint approach from civic society, North and South. After intense preparations in September and October by the Taoiseach's Department and Foreign Affairs the All-Island Civic Dialogue on Brexit, as it was termed, got off the ground on 2 November.

The meeting at the Royal Hospital in Kilmainham was launched with great fanfare, and more than 250 politicians, civil servants, business people, trade unionists and civic leaders turned up. All the political parties on the island, North and South, were invited to attend. Unsurprisingly, the DUP did not even respond to the invitation, and the Ulster Unionist Party (UUP) also stayed away. Some individual unionists attended and organisations like the Ulster Farmers' Union gave some voice to the concerns of their community. The Taoiseach delivered the opening address, which was followed by two political sessions and panel discussions about the North–South and East–West implications of Brexit. During his contribution, the North's Deputy First Minister Martin McGuinness told the audience that he had been involved in some of the most important negotiations the island had seen in a hundred years, including the Good Friday and St Andrews agreements. 'What we are facing into now is just as big as that, maybe even bigger,' he said.

Despite the effort that had been put into it, the All-Island Civic Dialogue was a damp squib. Although further sectoral meetings took place over the following months, the absence of unionist participation and the growing realisation that Ireland's fate would be determined in negotiations between the EU and the UK made the effort largely irrelevant.

The same fate befell an effort by the House of Lords to make a serious contribution to the process. The House select committee on the European Union held hearings in the autumn of 2016 to examine the impact on Ireland. The committee took evidence from forty-two stakeholders including the Irish Ambassador to the UK, Dan Mulhall. There was a joint appearance by former Taoisigh John Bruton and Bertie Ahern and both spelled out the range of difficulties that Brexit had created for Ireland. The committee produced a report in December recommending that the Irish and British governments should quickly negotiate a bilateral agreement to guarantee the continuation of an open border.

While the report's recommendations were welcomed by Irish farmers, fishermen and exporters, its recommendations were quickly rejected by the government in Dublin. Minister for Finance Michael Noonan said Ireland could not do deals on the side; Taoiseach Enda Kenny was even more blunt. At an EU summit in Brussels a few days later he said that a bilateral deal with the UK was 'not available in the context of Ireland being a member of the European Union negotiating team'.

The reason the Lords report was rejected so forcibly was the continuing perception in Brussels and some EU countries that the Irish government was hedging its bets. Charlie Flanagan recalled that one of his niggling worries towards the end of 2016 was that if this perception took hold it would have the capacity to undermine EU backing for Ireland.

Alarm bells had gone off with Phil Hogan in late autumn when he heard from his contacts in Brussels that there had been a suggestion from Department of Agriculture officials in Dublin that Ireland and the UK could do a bilateral trade agreement on agriculture, as the Lords committee was suggesting. There were obvious attractions to a deal that would obviate tariffs and complicated paperwork on the movement of animals and dairy products across the Border, but it would threaten the evolving EU negotiating position.

Hogan said at the time:

I was deeply concerned. I had to put a stop to such ideas. There will be no carve-out for agriculture for any member state, including Ireland. That was one of the suggestions being put forward by the Department of Agriculture, Food and the Marine which as it happens is illegal. The Department mentioned on a number of occasions that they wanted to have a carve-out for agriculture in Ireland and effectively a bilateral arrangement with the UK. This is illegal under WTO [World Trade Organisation] rules and under EU law.

The real worry in the Department of Agriculture and among cabinet ministers was how a hard border in Ireland could be avoided once the UK left the EU. Officials in Brussels were aware that during the foot and mouth outbreak in 2001 the Irish authorities moved quickly to seal the Border to ensure the disease did not spread into the Republic. They felt that if necessary this could be done again to protect the EU single market. This was something the government in Dublin was simply unwilling to contemplate, not just because of the disruption that would inevitably arise in the economy and people's everyday lives, but more fundamentally the potential to undermine the delicate balance achieved in the Good Friday Agreement.

Rory Montgomery felt part of the problem was that some others on the Irish side did not have much EU experience. 'I think they were too quick to see things in a bilateral lens and it took a little time for them to realise this wasn't going to work. In the beginning it was very much a Northern Ireland/Irish focus. But that changed over time.' That was partly due to the fact that May stiffened her position but also because it quickly became evident in early conversations with EU officials that the notion of flexible border controls was not a runner.

> We ran into an absolute brick wall. Senior people in Brussels, not Barnier's people, were clear that if the Irish Border was effectively an EU frontier then the full rules would have to apply. That made it clear that there wasn't much point in expending a great deal of effort on looking at alternative arrangements that would operate on the island. Then May made her speech to the party conference and at Lancaster House and it was clear to see that if the British were leaving the single market in its entirety as well as the customs union then the gaps would be very substantial.

One way of getting around the Border problem was for the island of Ireland to become a single customs entity in the EU, with Northern Ireland remaining in the single market and customs union even if the rest of the UK departed. This posed as big a problem for the DUP and Brexiteer Conservatives as a hard border did for the government in Dublin and Irish nationalists in the North. Separating Northern Ireland from the rest of the UK for trade purposes was simply anathema to unionists, who would inevitably regard it as a step on the road to a united Ireland. Nonetheless, some senior British officials had privately come to the conclusion immediately after the referendum that a border in the Irish Sea rather than on the island of Ireland was the only practical way of dealing with the problem.

Even at this stage Hogan felt that a solution involving an economic border in the Irish Sea could not be ruled out, despite the apparently insuperable political difficulties. 'Moving the customs line off the island is still in the system. You're effectively saying that the four freedoms of the EU would apply on the island of Ireland and the border would be down the middle of the Irish Sea,' he said in early 2017.

4

May Closes Doors

'I was on the Irish border a month ago with Charlie [Flanagan] and I saw the threat to the peace process.'

Jean Asselborn, Foreign Minister of Luxembourg,
May 2017

* * *

Any remaining illusions that the warm relationship that had developed between Ireland and the UK since the Good Friday Agreement might cushion the impact of Brexit evaporated in early 2017. On the one hand the EU made no bones about its impatience with any attempt by the government in Dublin to indulge the notion of bilateral deals with the UK; and on the other Theresa May torpedoed any lingering hopes that she was aiming for a soft Brexit.

The impatience of Barnier's team with the Irish approach was articulated in an opinion piece written by Commissioner Phil Hogan and published in the *Irish Times* at the beginning of January. In it he argued that Ireland's strategic interests in the Brexit negotiations could be damaged by an excessive focus on the country's relationship with the UK.

There is a real risk that Ireland could allow our relationship with Europe to be defined by our relationship with the United Kingdom, which would be an enormous mistake in my view. Instead we should have the confidence and direction to recognise that post-Brexit Ireland will need to have in place a wholly different set of relationships with our EU partners – relationships which we will forge, advocate, defend and address directly and out of the shadow of our nearest neighbour.

Hogan's key point was that it was the EU-27 that would decide the UK's exit conditions and the future relationship with the departing member state. That would inevitably move the centre of power and influence on the shape of Brexit from London to Brussels. 'Unwittingly Brexit may be presenting Ireland with the chance to seize the next phase in our development and maturity as a sovereign state. It will force us to forge relations and shape our destiny within the EU without the presence of our nearest and strongest ally since 1973.'

Despite his unhappiness with the way the government in Dublin was approaching the negotiations, Hogan remained a key ally in ensuring that Irish concerns were relayed at the highest level in Brussels. Charlie Flanagan recalled that Hogan's role was crucial in ensuring that the Commission was kept fully informed about the Irish position.

'On one occasion Hogan rang me and said come out to Brussels next Tuesday and I'll organise a running buffet in the canteen in the Berlymont so that you can meet the Commissioners. I want you to meet them all and give them five minutes each, listing the Irish priorities.' Hogan had two conditions. Flanagan was to keep his phone in his pocket and stay away from the media. 'My special adviser Sarah Kavanagh and Hogan organised it so that two commissioners at a time came in to the buffet and he introduced me and I was able to brief them. When I mentioned the peace process these guys were eating out of my hand. I don't think Hogan told Barnier we were doing this. I emphasised that the Irish priority was peace.'

Flanagan said Hogan's great strength was that he understood the personal aspect of politics as well as the policy. 'Kenny had that ability too and it was essential in developing strong political support for the Irish position.' At that stage Barnier was also focused on reciprocal citizens' rights and the UK financial settlement, often casually referred to as 'the cheque'. Flanagan recalled taking to one eastern European foreign minister who said: 'I understand the peace process, and I understand the Irish priorities but tell me about the cheque. What have Czechs got to do with it?' Flanagan laughingly explained that it was the money the UK would have to pay in the divorce settlement and not the Czech Republic that was at issue.

On 17 January at Lancaster House in London Theresa May delivered a widely anticipated speech in which she said unambiguously that the UK was going to leave the EU customs union and the single market.

> I want to be clear. What I am proposing cannot mean membership of the EU's Single Market. European leaders have said many times that membership means accepting the 'four freedoms' of goods, capital, services and people. And being out of the EU but a member of the single market would mean complying with the EU's rules and regulations that implement those freedoms, without having a vote on what those rules and regulations are. It would mean accepting a role for the European Court of Justice that would see it still having direct legal authority in our country. It would to all intents and purposes mean not leaving the EU at all.

The inescapable conclusion, although it took some time for it to sink in, was that a hard Brexit was inevitable. May's tone was designed to appeal to the Leave constituency at both an emotional and a practical level. She said the Brexit referendum had not simply been a vote to leave the EU but to reorder the national story so that global Britain could re-emerge.

The silver lining for the government in Dublin was a commitment to a continuation of the CTA, which had been one of the four key objectives in its Brexit strategy. 'The family ties and bonds of affection that unite our two countries mean that there will always be a special relationship between us,' she declared, adding that 'nobody wants to return to the borders of the past.' She did not elaborate on how that was to be achieved, even though it was the core of the problem.

May did, however, have a warning for the EU. Any attempt to punish Britain for leaving would be resisted and if a poor deal was offered it would not be accepted. 'No deal for Britain is better than a bad deal for Britain,' she declared in a phrase that was to come back to haunt her.

Important sectors of the EU economy would also suffer. We are a crucial – profitable – export market for Europe's automotive industry, as well as sectors including energy, food and drink, chemicals, pharmaceuticals, and agriculture. These sectors employ millions of people around Europe. And I do not believe that the EU's leaders will seriously tell German exporters, French farmers, Spanish fishermen, the young unemployed of the Eurozone, and millions of others, that they want to make them poorer, just to punish Britain and make a political point.

This notion that the EU had as much, if not more, to lose than the UK from a bad-tempered Brexit was a mistaken article of faith that continued to inform British policy right to the end of the process. It seemed May subscribed to the illusion propagated by the Leave campaigners during the referendum that the UK could have its cake and eat it.

May's speech was acclaimed by Brexiteers and the Tory media. The *Daily Mail*'s front page, with the headline 'Steel of the New Iron Lady' alongside a picture of May and a fluttering Union flag, summed up the mood.

Watching from Brussels, Barnier was taken aback by May's performance. 'I am astounded by the sheer number of doors she is closing here, one after the other ... I am astonished at the way the Prime Minister has put all her cards on the table,' he confided in his diary.

In his analysis of the speech the *Irish Times* London correspondent Denis Staunton focused on the pledge to leave the EU customs union as pointing to the creation of a hard border in Ireland. 'Politicians in Britain and Ireland have suggested that technology might make customs checks almost invisible but no such border currently exists anywhere. Even along the border between Norway and Sweden, one of the most technologically advanced and co-operatively managed, goods must be cleared for customs and lorries are checked as they cross from one country into another.'

The following day May travelled to the Alpine resort of Davos for the World Economic Forum, where political and business leaders from across the globe gather every January to discuss the big issues of the day. Here she made a speech saying the UK was leaving the EU to take a more active role in the word. She referred again and again to the role 'global Britain' would play in the future. Enda Kenny was also in Davos and he had a short meeting with her. He publicly welcomed what he termed 'some clarity' from the Prime Minister and confirmed that Irish officials had been working on technical papers to see how a hard border could be avoided.

May came to Dublin at the end of January for the annual British–Irish summit which had been initiated by Cameron in 2011. Charlie Flanagan accompanied the Taoiseach while May was joined by Northern Ireland Secretary James Brokenshire. At their press conference after the event the two leaders said they wanted to preserve a 'seamless and friction-less' border in Ireland. The ambition was fine, but how this goal was to be achieved was not spelled out.

Miriam Lord summed up the mood in her report of the press conference in the *Irish Times*:

> Nobody rubbed anyone up the wrong way. No reports of chafing personalities in the Taoiseach's office. And a successful avoidance of rash words at the press conference that followed. This was due in part to the determination of Enda Kenny and Theresa May to use the phrase 'frictionless and seamless' as much as possible. (They managed a definite five between them and a possible half-dozen from Enda's lengthy reply in Irish to one question.) It was slightly worrying that neither side gave the slightest indication as to how this outcome might be achieved. Worse still, by the end of the press conference, it transpired their mutually desired smooth-edged Border is a conditional one. As seamless and frictionless 'as possible' according to May and 'as seamless, frictionless and as trouble-free as we can put together' according to Kenny.

Reviewing the meeting the following weekend, *Irish Times* political editor Pat Leahy was more pessimistic.

> When it comes to Brexit, it was a bad week for Ireland. It became abundantly clear that an aspiration for an essentially invisible Border is unlikely to be realised. During a series of questions in the Dáil on Tuesday, the morning after British Prime Minister Theresa May visited Dublin, Taoiseach Enda Kenny let slip an aside which perhaps

revealed as much as all the carefully nuanced diplomatic statements. 'Deputy Adams asked me about having a situation where there is no land border between the Republic and Northern Ireland. I am not sure that we are going to achieve that.'

A week later Kenny met May again, this time on the margins of an EU summit in Malta. The Prime Minister again refused to give any insight into her thinking about the form of Brexit she was contemplating, or the exact date in March on which she proposed to trigger Article 50. Speaking to journalists after the Malta meeting, Kenny warned of 'very negative consequences' if there was a return to a hard border between the Republic and Northern Ireland, although he did express confidence that the CTA would survive unchanged.

In the same week Michael Lux, a German expert in EU customs law, told a House of Commons committee that there would be no way of avoiding customs controls and expensive formalities, dismissing May's reference to a 'seamless and frictionless' border as 'nice talk'. He said that Ireland would have no choice but to have customs checks on the Border.

May's reluctance to get drawn into the detail of how a hard border could be avoided, or even into informal discussion about how the issue might be approached, frustrated the Irish side. Over time that frustration developed into irritation and even anger as she stuck rigidly to her official brief and refused to engage in a more informal manner. Looking back, Charlie Flanagan recalled the growing Irish impatience at this stage of the process. 'There was certainly no meat on the bones. She said quite clearly that she didn't want a return to the borders of the past. On further inquiry as to what that meant, detail was lacking.'

Another development in January that was to have a long-term impact on how Brexit unfolded was the suspension of the Northern Ireland Assembly. Deputy First Minister Martin McGuinness triggered the collapse by resigning from his post in the wake of a scandal arising from the way the DUP had squandered tens of millions of pounds of public money in the renewable heat incentive scheme. The suspension was to last for three years, far longer than anyone envisaged at the time, and it meant that Northern Ireland had no formal input into the Brexit process.

On 2 February the British government published a White Paper on Brexit spelling out how the EU customs union worked. It made it clear that the UK would have to leave the customs union if it wanted to conclude its own independent trade deals around the world. The White Paper stated the objective of a new customs arrangement that would enable UK–EU trade to be 'as frictionless as possible'. It referred to a number of ways of achieving an 'associative arrangement'. The problem was that nobody, including the British themselves, could say what an 'associative arrangement' might entail.

The accumulating evidence that the UK was heading for a hard Brexit prompted a stiffening of position on the Irish side. The notion that the two countries could find common ground to avert the most damaging impact of Brexit was fading fast. The hardening Irish position was reflected in a speech Kenny delivered at the Institute for International and European Affairs in Dublin in the middle of February.

> It is a matter of vital national interest for Ireland that we do not return to the days of a hard border that we knew only too well. Or indeed create a new one in the future. This is a political matter, not a legal or technical matter. It will have to be solved by political leadership. Brexit is a British policy, not an Irish policy or an EU policy. I continue to believe it is bad for Britain, for Ireland and for Europe … Let me make one thing absolutely clear. Ireland will be on the EU side of the table when the negotiations begin. We will be one of the twenty-seven.

Phil Hogan's warnings had clearly been heeded.

Meanwhile, the Irish diplomatic effort to highlight the need to avoid a hard border to protect the Good Friday Agreement continued. Flanagan recalled how a campaign to inform EU foreign ministers about the importance of the issue developed in the early months of 2017. 'I decided to bring foreign ministers over to the Border. Get them to walk the Border and see the problem at first hand.'

Peter Sheridan, the chief executive of Co-operation Ireland, proved to be a crucial link in setting up meetings for visiting dignitaries with local farmers, business people and victims of the Troubles. 'We had foreign ministers from Denmark and Belgium coming over and we even had the Luxembourg minister. It became apparent that these guys were really engaged by the issue and once they had seen it for themselves they became strong supporters of the Irish position,' said Flanagan. 'It worked very well because the ministers loved their field trip to the Irish border. We didn't have the local politicians to any great extent but got them to meet local people who would be most affected.' He recalled that at one EU foreign ministers' meeting, the Luxembourger Jean Asselborn, the longest-serving member of the Foreign Affairs Council, started the meeting by saying, 'I was on the Irish border a month ago with Charlie and I saw the threat to the peace process.'

The campaign was widened to involve other countries which might have an influence on the UK. Australian Foreign Minister Julie Bishop was invited to Ireland to talk about the historic connection between the two countries. She met Flanagan and the two ministers discussed the implications. Speaking to the media, she did not overtly criticise the UK but she emphasised the importance of the EU for her country's trade. 'Many Australian firms have accessed the EU via Britain. With the uncertainty surrounding what a post-Brexit Britain will look like, I believe Australian firms will look to Ireland to fulfil that role,' she said. The New Zealand Foreign Minister Murray McCully also visited Ireland and met Flanagan at Iveagh House. He confined his public statements to backing the Irish bid to host the Rugby World Cup, but his visit was portrayed by the hosts as a more general expression of support for the country's Brexit campaign.

The big international challenge, though, was to get support from the United States. Historically American pressure had always been a key strategic objective in Irish attempts to put pressure on British governments. It had played an important role during the War of Independence in forcing the British to the negotiation table. In more recent times Ronald Reagan's intervention with Margaret Thatcher had been pivotal in securing the 1985 Anglo-Irish Agreement, while Bill Clinton had played a leading role in creating the Good Friday Agreement.

At this critical juncture for Ireland Donald Trump was the newly elected President. In the light of his strong support for Brexit and his hostility to the EU it appeared there was little prospect of American support for Ireland this time around. Trump appeared to be unreservedly on the side of the UK in the Brexit process.

Flanagan recalled that after the 'shock and horror' in Ireland at the election of Trump there was a fear in Dublin that the massive political capital the country had built up in Washington over the decades might evaporate. There was also domestic pressure on the Taoiseach to demonstrate the government's rejection of Trump's policies by refusing to present the President with a bowl of shamrock on St Patrick's Day, something which had become an annual event over previous decades.

Even before his inauguration Trump's transition team had made it clear to the outgoing Irish Ambassador to the USA, Anne Anderson, that the President would be inviting the Taoiseach for the St Patrick's Day event. When Anderson met Trump at a pre-inauguration event for some 150 ambassadors and diplomats he reportedly told her: 'I love Ireland! I love Ireland! I love Ireland!' At the same event Vice-President Mike Pence, who was introduced on stage as the grandson of an Irish immigrant, reminisced about cutting turf when he visited relatives in Doonbeg, County Clare, not far from the golf course Trump would later own. Kenny and his officials had no doubt that he should go to Washington whatever the political ramifications at home.

Theresa May was the first foreign dignitary Trump received after his inauguration at the end of January. It was a signal that the UK was intent on pursuing a free trade agreement with the USA as soon as its departure from the EU was complete. It was against this background that Charlie Flanagan went to the US capital to see what could be salvaged from Ireland's previously excellent relationship with the White House.

In the event he was pleasantly surprised to find that a number of the leading figures in the Trump administration were extremely well disposed to Ireland, whatever their views about the EU. 'It was chaotic in Washington. But the one thing that was evident was the Irish connection because it seemed that every staffer we met in the corridors of Washington was Irish.' The number of self-declared Irish-Americans included the President's chief of staff Mike Mulvaney, his national security chief Mike Flynn, special adviser Kellyanne Conway, press spokesman Sean Spicer, and his chief strategist and adviser Steve Bannon. Many of these people would leave or be fired in the following years, but a strong Irish-American contingent survived in the Trump administration to the end.

Flanagan met Flynn, who expressed strong US support for the peace process and the Good Friday Agreement. This proved to be the key argument in winning the backing of the Trump team for Irish concerns. 'We realised immediately that the peace process button was the one to push. Once you make them aware that the Good Friday Agreement could be endangered by the restoration of a hard border they were then completely onside,' said Flanagan.

He also found to his surprise that Irish-Americans of all political hues also rallied to his support. 'Some of the Irish republican groups in America with whom I had a frosty enough relationship like the Ancient Order of Hibernians and more radical Sinn Féin supporters wanted me to brief them and made it clear they were on my side.'

At the next council of EU foreign ministers Flanagan briefed his colleagues on Brexit and his US trip. He advised them all to get over to Washington as quickly as possible to explain the EU position. After the meeting EU High Commissioner for Foreign Affairs Federica Mogherini approached Flanagan to tell him that his advice had been noted, but EU countries simply did not have the contacts in the White House to arrange such meetings. 'So Ireland's influence in Washington is real,' Flanagan recalled.

In spite of the importance of the political link, never mind the significance of US investment in Ireland, there was considerable opposition to Kenny's decision to go to the White House in March. At the end of January a range of political figures were calling on him to boycott the event. Labour leader Brendan Howlin claimed the Taoiseach's presence in the White House would present Ireland as a 'supine supporter' of Trumpism, while the Green Party and a variety of hard left TDs objected to the visit. Independent cabinet minister Katherine Zappone distanced herself from Kenny by saying the invitation should be kept under review, and junior minister John Halligan was even more forthright, saying that Kenny should not go.

Kenny ignored the objectors and followed his instinct, backed by advice from his senior officials and colleagues. Flanagan summed up the official mood by publicly declaring: 'For me it's a no-brainer. Enda Kenny has been invited. It is essential that he avails of an opportunity early in the administration to reinforce the important links between Ireland and America.' Fianna Fáil leader Micheál Martin took the same pragmatic approach, saying it was important for the country that Kenny should go to Washington.

When the Taoiseach arrived in the US capital for St Patrick's week he managed to pull off the difficult feat of publicly differing from Trump on the important issue of immigration while maintaining the level of bonhomie appropriate to the occasion. He told a nodding, smiling President that St Patrick was an immigrant – the patron saint of immigrants, in fact. 'Ireland came to America because – deprived of liberty, opportunity, safety and even food itself – we believed.'

The Irish media was generally scornful of Kenny's skilful tightrope act but the speech received widespread acclaim in the international press. Such highly regarded liberal voices as the *New York Times* and historian Simon Schama expressed gratitude that Kenny had spoken up for decent American values to a president committed to overturning them.

Right through the early months of 2017, as the government wrestled with Brexit, the focus of Irish politics was elsewhere: on the question of Kenny's leadership. With elements of Fine Gael and much of the media baying for blood there had been some doubt about whether he would survive long enough to make it to St Patrick's Day in the White House. Things got so bad in February that parliamentary party chairman Martin Heydon emailed all TDs and senators to say that he was 'greatly concerned that the Taoiseach and leader of our party is not being shown the respect his service and his office deserve'. He went on to say that in the interests of common decency members should refrain from further public attacks on the party leader. The belated acclaim at home for the stand Kenny took against Trump shored up his leadership for a time and he was given the space by his TDs to see out the Brexit process until the UK triggered Article 50.

Just before he went to Washington Kenny had another meeting with Theresa May on the margins of a European Council meeting in Brussels. Irish frustration at May's approach evolved into barely suppressed anger when Kenny asked her for an indication about when in March she intended to trigger Article 50. He was hoping for some guidance as he was heading straight from Brussels to the United States and needed to know whether he would have to respond during his trip. Giving nothing at all away, May coolly replied with a smile that it would be before the end of March – which everybody knew already. Kenny felt insulted but didn't let that show in his press conference afterwards, saying simply that the EU stood ready to respond whenever the British made their move. 'We're their closest ally, their nearest neighbour, the country most affected by Brexit and yet she couldn't even tell him,' said one Irish official, giving vent to Irish frustration with May.

The British had still not made their move when EU leaders, minus the British, met in Rome on 25 March to mark the sixtieth anniversary of the signing in the Italian capital of the treaty that established the EEC and set the European project on a firm footing. EU Council President Donald Tusk made a forceful speech defending the concept of a united Europe.

Today in Rome we are renewing the unique alliance of free nations that was initiated sixty years ago by our great predecessors. Europe as a political entity will either be united, or will not be at all. Only a united Europe can be a sovereign Europe in relation to the rest of the world. And only a sovereign Europe guarantees independence for its nations, guarantees freedom for its citizens.

Tusk's ringing defence of the EU convinced the Irish delegation that they could rely on his strong support in the difficult negotiations ahead. 'The event itself was all very ceremonial. You had six speeches from six men and it had the capacity to be a boring occasion. But Tusk won the room because he gave a rousing and intensely personal speech charting his personal life journey to the age of sixty, alongside that of the EU. He just blew away the room,' recalled John Callinan.

Tusk spoke about living in communist Poland and looking out in admiration at the evolution of the EU, which had everything the people of his country wanted but could not have. 'So it was this immensely personal, powerful expression of embracing the European Union and everything it stood for. The other side of the coin was his horror that one of its biggest and most powerful members would choose to leave and turn its back on it. He took it very personally.'

Tusk's personal abhorrence of the UK decision to leave the EU was to surface at regular intervals during the Brexit process in unvarnished public comments. It earned him the enmity of Tory Brexiteers and the

British media but was another source of reassurance for the Irish negoti-
ators that they would not be abandoned. The President of the European
Council was just as committed to defending the country's interests as
Commission President Jean-Claude Juncker and chief negotiator Michel
Barnier.

By this stage it was becoming clear to the government in Dublin
and to EU officials in Brussels that May's central focus was on British
politics, specifically on preserving her leadership of the Conservative
Party against the machinations of the Brexiteers. All the issues facing
the UK, including the question of the Irish Border, were being viewed
through this prism.

The task facing Irish officials in the early months of 2017 was to
ensure that the country's concerns would be regarded as a priority by
EU negotiators. Ireland's Permanent Representative to the EU Declan
Kelleher had a series of meetings with the Barnier Task Force at the
European Commission's headquarters in the Berlaymont Building
in Brussels. The Task Force had begun intensive work the previous
October to prepare for the negotiations ahead. It was a stark contrast
to the shambolic preparation in the UK where the absence of clearly
defined goals hampered preparation.

One thing Kelleher stressed in his meetings with the Task Force
and his fellow EU ambassadors was that the Irish Border represented
a unique challenge and that finding an acceptable solution to it had no
implications for borders anywhere else in the EU. The point he made
again and again was that an open border was an essential element of
the peace process that had been supported so strongly by the EU. The
Spanish, French and others needed to be persuaded that finding arrangements to deal with the unique circumstances of Northern Ireland did
not have implications for other internationally recognised borders.

Dara Murphy, on a St Patrick's Day visit to Spain, was told bluntly
of the Madrid government's concerns that any provisions for seamless
entry of Northern Ireland into the EU at a future date had implications
for Catalonian independence. The Spanish were not prepared to sign up
to any provision that did not ring-fence Northern Ireland to ensure that
it would not have knock-on effects for Spain or any other EU country.
Murphy reported back to Kenny, who raised the issue with Spanish
Prime Minister Mariano Rajoy and Donald Tusk at an EPP gathering in

Malta. After some discussions about how Spanish concerns, including the problem of Gibraltar, could be reflected in the Irish provision, they decided that it would be best to deal with it in a separate protocol when the time came. The Spanish experience and other meetings he had around the EU convinced Murphy that protecting the peace process was the strongest card to play in the campaign to get special treatment for Ireland on the border issue.

A glossy brochure produced by the government in Dublin in early 2017 made the case on its opening page:

> The Good Friday Agreement of 1998 (also known as the Belfast Agreement) remains the foundation of the Northern Ireland peace process and brought to an end more than 30 years of violent conflict. British and Irish common membership of the EU was a significant enabling factor in securing peace and the European Union has played an important role in consolidating that peace and supporting reconciliation. Protecting the gains of the Peace Process and reflecting the unique circumstances of Northern Ireland throughout the Brexit process are clearly in the interests of both the EU-27 and the UK.

This was the core argument deployed by Kelleher in his dealings with the Task Force. While other countries also made their concerns known to the Task Force, by far the most active representations were made by Ireland. As well as frequent communications from Kelleher and his officials in the Permanent Representation, Barnier and his team also heard from a variety of the Irish organisations representing a range of interests from farming and fishing to business. They also met opposition parties and listened carefully to Fianna Fáil, on whose support the government in Dublin relied for its confidence and supply arrangement.

It meant that by the time Theresa May triggered Article 50 the Task Force was fully up to speed on the Irish situation. 'Sabine Weyand and her team had explored the issue in minute detail and by the time the Brexit talks actually started they knew far more about the implications of a hard border for Ireland than their British counterparts,' said one Irish official.

By the spring of 2017 the Irish focus was clear. After the disappointing meetings between Kenny and May and the lack of clarity about the British strategy, a decision was taken in Dublin to abandon attempts to find mutually acceptable Anglo-Irish technical solutions to the problem posed by the Border. The Irish approach had changed from an early willingness to examine possible technical solutions to insisting that it would ultimately come down to political decisions. By March 2017, Barnier and his Task Force were at one with the Irish in deciding to challenge the British to come up with a political solution to the border issue.

5

The Unity Declaration

'I want to reassure the Irish people that in these negotiations, Ireland's interests will be the European Union's interests.'
Michel Barnier, addressing a joint sitting of the Dáil
and Seanad, 11 May 2017

* * *

On 29 March 2017 Theresa May made the move everybody had been waiting for – triggering Article 50 of the Lisbon Treaty. Tim Barrow, who had replaced Ivan Rogers as UK Permanent Representative to the EU, handed the Prime Minister's six-page letter to European Council President Donald Tusk. In the letter May insisted that she wanted to negotiate the UK's divorce and its future trading relationship with the EU within the two-year period specified by the Lisbon Treaty. She went on to make a key demand. 'We believe it is necessary to agree the terms of our future partnership alongside those of our withdrawal from the EU.'

This was immediately rejected by German Chancellor Angela Merkel, who said the talks would first have to clarify how the commitments, rights and duties which the UK had entered into over its forty-four-year membership could be unravelled. 'It is only if we have sorted that out that we can next – and I hope soon – talk about our future relationship.' The idea that the terms of the future relationship could be negotiated in parallel with the divorce settlement was just the first in a series of miscalculations the British made during the process.

May compounded her error by not only suggesting that the UK could live with a breakdown of talks on trade but by issuing a veiled threat to disrupt the security and counterterrorism co-operation in which the UK, as a member of the US-backed Five Eyes system, plays a key part. 'We should work together to minimise disruption and give as much certainty as possible. Weakening our co-operation for the prosperity and protection of our citizens would be a costly mistake,' she said.

Irish Times London editor Denis Staunton neatly summed up May's tactical error:

> As she starts the clock on two years of negotiations, May remains transfixed by the threat from her right flank and its supporters in the press. But when she lifts her gaze she may see the peril her chosen strategy poses to the integrity of the UK as she takes it on a lonely journey out of the EU, drunk on a notion of sovereignty and all puffed up with no place to go.

The obvious dangers of May's strategy were also noted by none other than her cabinet secretary Jeremy Heywood. In a joint memoir published after his tragically early death from cancer, his wife, Suzanne, noted her husband's view, in January 2017, that the Prime Minister's commitment to rule out any new barriers within the UK was going to be a problem.

> The political rationale for this new pledge was clear. A hard border between Northern Ireland and the Republic would jeopardise the Good Friday Agreement and a border in the Irish Sea separating Northern Ireland from the rest of the UK would be unacceptable to Unionists. But though understandable, it further narrowed the UK's leave options. If borders weren't allowed, it wasn't clear how any differences in product regulation or tariffs between Britain and Europe would be managed – or indeed how any of this could be reconciled with the Prime Minister's desire, which she also expressed in her speech, for 'tariff-free' and 'frictionless' trade with Europe.

From an Irish point of view, May's letter, which outlined the seven principles on which the UK would conduct negotiations, contained one important point of reassurance. Principle five in her letter stated:

> In particular, we must pay attention to the UK's unique relationship with the Republic of Ireland and the importance of the peace process in Northern Ireland. The Republic of Ireland is the only EU member state with a land border with the United Kingdom. We want to avoid a return to a hard border between our two countries, to be able to maintain the Common Travel Area between us, and to make sure that the UK's withdrawal from the EU does not harm the Republic of Ireland. We also have an important responsibility to make sure that nothing is done to jeopardise the peace process in Northern Ireland, and to continue to uphold the Belfast Agreement.

Despite their frustrations at May's refusal to spell out how she proposed to avoid a hard border, Irish officials had managed to come to a mutually agreed form of words with their British counterparts about the relationship between the two countries after the UK's departure from the EU. That formula, which was adopted in May's letter, was an important step for Ireland.

The next big question was how the EU's formal response would deal with Irish concerns. The answer arrived two days later when Donald Tusk outlined the EU position in the Draft Negotiating Guidelines. From an Irish point of view the guidelines could not have been better. The political campaign waged by Kenny, his ministers and senior officials had persuaded Tusk and the European Council to back the strategy being followed by Barnier and his Task Force. Irish concerns would be central to the talks on the UK Withdrawal Agreement. The Border was listed as one of the three core issues that would have to be settled before talks on the future relationship began, the others being the UK financial settlement and citizens' rights.

The EU Draft Negotiating Guidelines were set out in a relatively brief statement of principles, running to twenty-six paragraphs. Paragraph 11, dealing with the Irish position, read:

The Union has consistently supported the goal of peace and reconciliation enshrined in the Good Friday Agreement, and continuing to
support and protect the achievements, benefits and commitments of
the Peace Process will remain of paramount importance. In view of
the unique circumstances on the island of Ireland, flexible and imaginative solutions will be required, including with the aim of avoiding
a hard border, while respecting the integrity of the Union legal order.
In this context, the union should also recognise existing bilateral
agreements and arrangements between the United Kingdom and
Ireland which are compatible with EU law.

The elevation of the Irish Border issue to a central plank of the EU's
negotiating position was a considerable achievement for Kenny and his
team. The Conservative Party and the British press had been obsessing
about the cost of the financial settlement and whether it would be as
high as €100 million, as suggested by the *Financial Times*, or little or
nothing, as advocated by Brexiteers. As in the referendum campaign,
little attention had been paid to the impact on Ireland. The EU commitment to avoiding a hard border as one of its three core issues therefore
came as a considerable surprise to the British side.

Flanagan expressed delight that the first phase of the Brexit campaign
had led to such a firm commitment. He publicly hailed the document,
which, he said, was 'as good as could have been hoped for' from an
Irish perspective, and he paid tribute to the work of diplomats and officials over the previous months. He also pointed to the references in the
statements and speeches of Prime Minister May as evidence that the
Irish position would receive special attention in the Brexit negotiations
to come.

With tensions between the Irish and British governments rising,
John Callinan found himself the subject of a potentially embarrassing
front page story in the *Irish Times*. Just before Easter he gave a talk at a
trade union conference organised by Impact and SIPTU (the Services,
Industrial and Professional Trade Union) about the challenge Brexit
would pose for the Irish food sector. During his speech Callinan
commented on the divisions and confusion he had detected on the
British side. 'I see signs in the contacts that we're having, both at EU
level and with the UK, of a gradual realisation that Brexit in many

ways is an act of great self-harm, and that the focus now is on mini-mising that self-harm.' He went on to highlight the internal divisions on the British side just weeks ahead of the start of formal negotia-tions with the EU, saying that it was clear there was no single, settled position in London. 'Even within the British government, there are very different views,' he said.

In April 2021 Callinan looked back at this episode with some amuse-ment, but it wasn't funny at the time. 'The journalist reported what I had said quite fairly and there was no breach of Chatham House rules or anything like that but I was surprised when I saw it on the front page of the paper. I had to get on to Olly Robbins and give him a heads-up immediately as I knew it would not go down well in London so soon after Article 50.'

On 26 April, just days before the crucial European Council meeting to approve the Draft Negotiating Guidelines, EU Commission President Jean-Claude Juncker and his Brexit negotiator Michel Barnier travelled to London to meet May and her Brexit negotiator, David Davis, over dinner at Number 10. Barnier noted in his diary that the meeting was cordial and helpful, although Juncker had frankly pointed out the distance between the two sides. 'My sense is that the British are talking amongst themselves, as they did throughout the referendum campaign, and that they are underestimating the legal complexity of this divorce and of its many consequences.'

An account of the meeting in the *Frankfurter Allgemeine* gave a much more negative perspective on the dinner. It quoted Juncker as telling May at the end: 'I'm leaving Downing Street ten times more sceptical than before.' The report said May had told Juncker and Barnier that the UK did not legally owe any money to the EU, that the issue of citizens' rights could be sorted out at the next summit in June and that a free trade deal could be negotiated in two years.

Merkel responded by issuing a public warning that Britain should have no illusions about its status after it left the EU – that of a 'third country' which could not enjoy the rights of EU membership. The message was reinforced in a letter sent by Donald Tusk to EU leaders in advance of the European Council meeting, in which he emphasised that 'before discussing our future, we must first sort out our past.' The issues he identified for immediate priority were citizens' rights, the final obligations of the EU and 'finally, in order to protect the peace and reconciliation process described by the Good Friday Agreement, we should aim to avoid a hard border between the Republic of Ireland and Northern Ireland.'

In the days before the summit the Irish side began, at Kenny's insistence, a frenetic campaign to get another important objective agreed by EU leaders. He wanted them to publicly commit that in the event of a united Ireland ever coming about Northern Ireland would be automatically readmitted into the EU.

Kenny had been persuaded in the wake of the Brexit referendum by SDLP MP Mark Durkan, one of the negotiators of the Good Friday Agreement, that this issue needed to be addressed by the EU as part of the Brexit process. Durkan suggested that the precedent of East Germany automatically becoming part of the EU after the unification of the country in 1990 should be applied to the Irish case. He feared that after Brexit Northern Ireland would be treated like a newly applying member state if there was ever a vote for a united Ireland and there was even a remote prospect that the Republic might be forced to leave the EU to enable unity. The prospect of the EU blocking Irish unity at some future date seemed far-fetched, but Kenny decided that the issue needed to be clarified.

Some officials in the Department of Foreign Affairs regarded the Kenny approach as unnecessary and even dangerous as it would inevitably stoke unionist hostility and encourage an even more hard-line British stance. The domestic political argument in favour of it was that it would ensure that the government was not outflanked by Sinn Féin, which was campaigning for 'special status' for Northern Ireland.

The Taoiseach publicly raised the East German example at the MacGill Summer School in July 2016 and he continued to pursue it behind the scenes. A memo drafted in the Department of the Taoiseach in October 2016 spelled out the German parallel and drew attention to the role Ireland had played during its EU presidency in 1990. At that time Taoiseach Charles Haughey and Minister for Foreign Affairs Gerard Collins played an important role in facilitating Germany unity, despite the objections of Margaret Thatcher and François Mitterrand. 'A point we need to focus on is the gratitude that Germany at the time felt it owed to Ireland for pushing German unity within the EU. Kohl certainly had that sense of gratitude.'

The British insisted in the wake of the referendum that the German precedent would automatically apply if there was ever a vote for Irish unity, so there was no need to make any special provision for such an eventuality. This view was shared by leading EU officials, but Kenny nonetheless decided to push for a reference to it in European Council conclusions. John Callinan and Declan Kelleher decided that the best tactic would be to wait until shortly before the crucial 29 April EU summit to spring the Irish request. They let it be known that it was something Kenny really wanted, despite the initially negative reaction from European Council officials.

If EU officials were sceptical, the British were furious when Kenny formally sought the inclusion of the unity clause in the Council conclusions. 'We did spring this very late,' recalled John Callinan. 'The way Brussels usually works is that these things are in draft conclusions or draft minutes and they're going around for weeks. We sprang this only a few days before the meeting.' Initially the unity clause was a wordy document but Callinan and Kelleher decided that it needed to be pared back as it would be easier to get agreement on a short statement than on a long and wordy formula. The original draft was reduced to two sentences, with an adjustment to ensure that one of the sentences would not be dropped: a semicolon instead of a full stop at the halfway point. The Irish text read:

> The European Council acknowledges that the Good Friday Agreement provides for an agreed mechanism whereby a united Ireland may be brought about by peaceful and democratic means; and, in this regard the European Council acknowledges that, in accordance with international law, the entire territory of such a united Ireland would be part of the European Union.

When they learned of the move the British sprang into action to try to block it. 'They were very alarmed and they went on a full-court press to try and stop us,' recalled Callinan. 'Their argument was that at this point an election had been called in the UK and they asked if, at the very least, could we not leave it until the next summit in June. We decided that having to stop at that stage would make us look weak and we also felt we needed to deal with the genuine concern on the part of several member states that to back down would suggest we were too close to the British.'

It was not only the British who had worries about the new paragraph, which became known in the talks as 'the Kenny text'. On the morning of the Council meeting Kelleher received a phone call from his French counterpart, Pierre Sellal, to say that French lawyers were worried it might create a dangerous precedent because European Council declarations carry legal weight. Sellal wanted to know what kind of united Ireland was involved.

A hastily convened meeting involving Kelleher, Sellal and the European Council secretary-general, Jeppe Tranholm-Mikkelsen, took place in the Irish delegation room in the Europa Building in Brussels where the summit was due to begin a few hours later. Kelleher explained that the only scenario envisaged was the one catered for in the Good Friday Agreement, which specified that a referendum on the future status of Northern Ireland could be called by the British Secretary of State if he or she concluded that a majority of people in the region favoured change. The wording of the Council declaration referred to 'such a united Ireland' and not to any situation brought about without the consent of both parts of the island. Sellal took the explanation to French President François Hollande and he dropped his objections.

When the summit began Tusk put the Draft Negotiating Guidelines to the twenty-seven EU heads of government and they were agreed without debate in less than two minutes. Kenny then put his case for the unity clause to his fellow leaders and they accepted it without demur. In her post-summit press conference Merkel said she had never seen such unity of purpose at a European Council meeting.

The outcome was a stunning diplomatic triumph for Ireland. At a personal level it was an important victory for Kenny. He knew it would be the last major moment of his leadership and his success in getting the importance of the Irish Border recognised in the guidelines with the addition of the unity clause was the icing on the cake for him. As he left the European Council building that Saturday afternoon in Brussels Kenny punched the air in a gesture combining triumph and relief that he had achieved something important for his country.

At the press conference following the summit Kenny stressed that agreement on the unity declaration did not involve any early moves towards a united Ireland.

> In my view, the conditions do not exist now for a border poll. The value of today's decision is that if at some time in the future that action is taken, a referendum is triggered and a decision made by the people of Northern Ireland, that not only will both governments recognise it, but that the European Council will recognise the entire island of Ireland then as being part of the EU, without Northern Ireland having to reapply.

'I think the full significance of the unity declaration was never fully recognised,' recalled Callinan:

> At one level it was a statement of the glaringly obvious but it was very important for Enda Kenny to deliver in the final days of his leadership. More significantly, though, as well has having a legal standing the clause served an important political purpose. Until it happened I had not fully appreciated how much this was going to be seen by the other member states, by my Sherpa colleagues and other prime ministers, as evidence that the Irish were not the British poodles. It actually and unexpectedly became a very significant moment in the journey. Because that suspicion, that somehow we would be batting for the Brits or be too accommodating to them, was quite strong.

The outcome of the summit was that the Council agreed on three major issues that would have to be settled to the satisfaction of the EU before the UK divorce could become effective and the talks moved on to the nature of the future relationship. Those issues were the scale of the UK financial settlement; mutually agreed recognition of citizens' rights; and measures to ensure the avoidance of a hard border on the island of Ireland.

One senior EU official involved in drafting the negotiating guidelines confessed later that one of the reasons the Irish border issue had been accepted as one of the three core issues was that most other EU governments had no idea that it had the potential to become a major stumbling block to an agreement with the UK on a future relationship.

However, as the agreement on the guidelines required unanimity once it was included there was no way of removing it without Irish consent.

During the summit the EU's chief negotiator, Michel Barnier, told the national leaders he hoped to see sufficient progress on these issues so that they could start talks on Britain's future relationship with the EU by October, in a little over six months. A more realistic assessment was made by a senior Irish official. 'We have won the first lineout but the rest of the match is still ahead of us. But it was important to get a good start.'

Two major political events, one in Ireland and the other in the UK, intervened before the next phase in the Brexit process could begin. In the UK Theresa May called a general election on 18 April, setting 8 June as polling day. In Ireland Enda Kenny decided it was time to step down as Taoiseach. Ever since the deeply disappointing outcome of the general election in February 2016 the Fine Gael knives had been out for Kenny and, even as he gloried in the outcome of the Brussels summit, journalists were asking him when he intended to step down.

The Irish diplomatic campaign on the importance of the Border continued following that crucial European Council meeting. Michel Barnier came to Ireland in May, after Article 50 had been triggered while the British general election campaign was in full swing. Flanagan recalled Barnier's visit to the Lough Egish co-op and a dairy farm in Monaghan.

> Barnier showed a side of himself that people hadn't really appreciated. We went into a field of cattle near Lough Egish and one journalist said, 'Oh, Mr Barnier, mind your shoes, mind your shoes.'

> 'Don't tell a sheep farmer from Savoy to mind his shoes. You'd think I didn't know anything about farming,' was his response and of course the local IFA fellows were delighted. They immediately saw him in a different light. He also gave them loads of time and they were delighted to find that the EU Brexit negotiator was on their wavelength.

Ireland's EU Commissioner, Phil Hogan, accompanied Barnier on his visit to Monaghan along with Flanagan and local minister Heather Humphreys. Frank McNally of the *Irish Times* captured the mood.

When Mr Flanagan called Mr Barnier's a 'field trip', he wasn't exaggerating. The Brexit negotiator has probably never seen so many fields in a single place before, and got a closer look at them later during a private visit to one of Monaghan's 4,565 farms, which at a typical 23.5 hectares, are much smaller than the national average.

As to the big picture of how he could reconcile the apparently irreconcilable problem of Brexit and the Border, all he would say is that he came to the problem, not as a technocrat from Brussels but as a politician who had once represented a small rural county exactly like this one.

When it was suggested to him that the task of marrying a hard Brexit to a soft Border was impossible, he responded philosophically: 'There is always a road.'

In his Brexit diary Barnier recalled his trip to Monaghan with affection. The experience of standing alongside 'Big Phil' Hogan on a small country road where the Border was marked with nothing more than a yellow line down the middle made a lasting impression. 'Here in Ireland where I am put in mind of Sorj Chalandon's powerful novel *Return to Killybegs* it is difficult not to be touched by the sensitivities and emotions of those who speak to me and the memories that remind me of tragedies past.'

As time went on Barnier's emotional commitment to Ireland became a powerful influence on the entire Brexit process. Flanagan recalled that Barnier's stress on his attachment to Ireland sometimes irritated his lead official Sabine Weyand. 'She was also well disposed towards us but oftentimes at meetings Barnier would talk about his love for Ireland and Sabine would intervene to say "Get on with it, there is a bigger picture here."'

During his visit Barnier addressed a joint sitting of the Dáil and Seanad, noting that this honour was usually reserved for important heads of government. 'I am all the more humbled by this but the invitation clearly demonstrates the gravity of the situation in which Brexit places Ireland and the sensitivity of the debate for the citizens of this country,' he wrote in his diary.

In his address he spelled out his support for the Irish position. 'Today, in front of these two Houses, I want to reassure the Irish people that in these negotiations, Ireland's interests will be the European Union's interests. We are in these negotiations together and a united EU will be there for Ireland.'

With his ambitions for the Brexit negotiation terms achieved, Kenny decided it was time to go. Before leaving Brussels on 29 April he told reporters that he would speak to his party soon now that the Brexit guidelines had been agreed by European leaders. He didn't wait long and he announced his departure to his party's TDs and senators on 17 May. Fine Gael had two weeks to elect a new leader and it was no secret that it would be a two-horse race between Leo Varadkar and Simon Coveney. In fact the race was over before it began as Varadkar had recruited the bulk of the parliamentary party to his cause and, crucially, had the backing of Phil Hogan who advised him on tactics and lobbied TDs and senators on his behalf. The parliamentary party had 65 per cent of the votes in an electoral college system, so Varadkar began with an unassailable lead. Coveney managed an impressive two to one victory among the party membership but it was not enough to close the gap.

Varadkar's elevation to the party leadership and the Taoiseach's office made headlines around the world. As an openly gay man and the son of an Indian immigrant he was seen as a representative of the new liberal, open-minded Ireland that had been reflected in the referendum on marriage equality. Just thirty-eight years old and only ten years in the Dáil, Varadkar was the youngest politician ever to be Taoiseach. He had a very different political style from Kenny; while he was uncomfortable with the back-slapping side of politics he was an adroit media performer and his cool, calm approach to politics appeared to resonate with the changing mood of the electorate. Because of his ability to perform in front of the television cameras he was regarded by most Fine Gael TDs as the leader who could save their seats and reverse the slump in the party's fortunes that had taken them unawares in 2016. Privately Varadkar had been highly critical of the way Kenny had fought the 2016 general election campaign and the majority of his TDs were convinced that he would make a much better job of it next time around.

Varadkar appointed his rival Simon Coveney to the position of Minister for Foreign Affairs and Trade in place of Charlie Flanagan, who was moved to the Department of Justice. While the new Taoiseach kept responsibility for steering the country's Brexit strategy in his own department, Coveney insisted on a prominent role in the evolving drama. Brexit was by far the most important issue facing the new Taoiseach and Minister for Foreign Affairs but they had the advantage of inheriting the team of able and experienced officials in their respective departments who had steered the strategy so well to date.

Varadkar dropped Dara Murphy as Minister for European Affairs and replaced him with the young Meath TD Helen McEntee, who had been in the Dáil for only four years. McEntee became a familiar face on Irish television screens during the rest of the Brexit process as she stood beside the Taoiseach after EU meetings. More important, she proved to be an able communicator of the government position in media interviews at home and abroad.

In a move designed to keep himself up to speed with opinion in Northern Ireland, Varadkar appointed Jim D'Arcy from Louth as a special adviser. A blunt-speaking former senator and county councillor, D'Arcy had a detailed knowledge of the Northern political scene and knew leading politicians on both sides of the sectarian divide. A strong critic of Sinn Féin during his time in the Seanad, D'Arcy nonetheless knew many leading party members and his fluency in the Irish language gave him credibility with nationalists. He also developed good relations with leading DUP politicians, including Arlene Foster and Jeffrey Donaldson, which enabled him to keep abreast of the mood in the party and report back to the Taoiseach.

The changing of the guard in the Irish political leadership took place at a time of political convulsion in the UK following Theresa May's surprise decision to dissolve parliament less than three weeks after triggering Article 50. The reason she gave for the move was the need for a big majority in the House of Commons to give her a strong mandate to pursue the kind of Brexit she wanted.

Claiming that the will of the British people to leave the EU was being frustrated by the Labour Party, the Liberal Democrats and the Scottish Nationalists, she declared: 'Britain is leaving the European Union and there can be no turning back. Every vote for the Conservatives will make it harder for opposition politicians who want to stop me from getting the job done. Every vote for the Conservatives will make me stronger when I negotiate for Britain with prime ministers, presidents and chancellors of the European Union.'

Government officials in Dublin were privately hopeful that the outcome of the election would provide May with the stronger majority she sought and enable her to bring more flexibility into her negotiation stance. One source suggested that she had been 'held to ransom' by some of the hard Brexiteers in her party and that a large majority would strengthen her hand to adopt a more moderate position.

Charlie Flanagan reflected this view in an RTÉ interview. He said that a stronger majority for May could provide her with greater flexibility to negotiate and this provided grounds for optimism. 'We could be looking towards a less hard Brexit than that was anticipated after the referendum,' he suggested hopefully.

Initially May seemed to have everything going for her, with Labour leader Jeremy Corbyn trailing far behind her in the opinion polls. An average of the first three polls put the Conservatives on 46 per cent of the vote with Labour far back on 25 per cent and the Liberal Democrats on 11 per cent. However, May proved to be an ineffective campaigner while Corbyn and Labour gradually developed momentum as the long campaign wore on. What had seemed a sure thing turned into a disastrous gamble by the time election day arrived. Instead of extending her seventeen-seat majority May lost thirteen seats while Labour gained thirty. With 318 seats the Conservatives were the biggest party in the House of Commons but no longer had a majority in the 650-member chamber.

Facing a hung parliament, May turned to the DUP with their ten seats to prop up her government. A deal that involved extra spending of £1 billion sterling was negotiated by the DUP as the price of their support. Now that the DUP had a pivotal position in holding the balance of power in the Commons, political leaders in the UK and Ireland paid more attention to the leverage the DUP had over the Brexit process. The DUP had been the only major party in Northern Ireland to campaign for a Leave vote in the 2016 referendum; and the fact that a majority of people in the region had voted Remain did not alter the party's position.

The *Irish Times* in an editorial analysing the UK election result said voters had rejected a hard Brexit and suggested the key role in which the DUP now found itself 'should help ensure a more favourable Brexit for Northern Ireland and, by extension, the island as a whole.' More presciently, it also forecast that 'the convulsions set off by Brexit may be just beginning.'

The DUP had been given an unexpected opportunity to exert a serious influence over the UK approach to Brexit. Given the EU's firm commitment to the government in Dublin that the border issue would have to be dealt with as part of the Withdrawal Agreement, it meant that Ireland was now central to the negotiating positions of both sides. Finding a resolution to the border conundrum was going to have a critical bearing on the future relationship between the UK and the EU.

6

Leo Takes the Helm

'Boris asked me to give you this.'
A comedian handing Theresa May a mock P45
during her keynote speech to the Conservative Party
conference, 9 October 2017

* * *

Leo Varadkar was elected Taoiseach by the Dáil on 14 June 2017, just as the Brexit negotiations were about to kick off. Announcing his cabinet to the Dáil he emphasised that Ireland would remain at the heart of Europe, whatever happened. In his first day in office the new Taoiseach spoke to the two most powerful leaders in the EU, Angela Merkel and French President Emmanuel Macron, and he also had a phone conversation with Theresa May, who was engaged in talks with the DUP about her government's programme. Brexit was the main issue in all these conversations.

A few days later Varadkar and May met face to face in Downing Street and they appeared to get off to a good start. The *Irish Times* London editor Denis Staunton reported that the Taoiseach beamed as he walked into the oak-panelled state dining room in 10 Downing Street for a joint press conference with the Prime Minister. 'It's my first time in this building, so there's a little thrill in it as well. As we spoke on the way in, I was reminded of that famous scene in *Love, Actually* where

Hugh Grant does his dance down the stairs,' the Taoiseach remarked. Some people at home cringed at the naivety of the remark but it reflected Varadkar's sense of elation at becoming his country's leader.

'The contrast between the two leaders was cruel,' wrote Staunton:

Varadkar full of wide-eyed optimism at the start of his ascendancy, May looking exhausted and hunted as she faces the possibility of being bundled out of Downing Street at any moment ... She has lost her majority in parliament, her authority over her party and her popularity in the country. All the Taoiseach has to worry about is Shane Ross and Máire Whelan.

Officials on both side were conscious in advance of the meeting that neither May nor Varadkar was very good at small talk. That was to prove a problem in the months ahead but the first meeting went reasonably well; 'the Taoiseach's cool indifference chiming more easily with the prime minister's natural reserve than did the rowdy bonhomie of his predecessor', was Staunton's assessment.

Gavin Barwell, a former minister who lost his seat in the election, took over as May's chief of staff following the departure of Nick Timothy and Fiona Hill, who were blamed for the disastrous decision to go to the country. Barwell noted that the key figures with whom Downing Street would be dealing in the Brexit negotiations were Juncker, Barnier and Tusk in Brussels, while the important national leaders were Merkel, Macron and Varadkar. 'Varadkar was the youngest ever Taoiseach, of mixed Irish/Indian heritage and the first ever Irish minister to come out as gay, in many ways the embodiment of the new socially liberal Ireland. He and Theresa didn't immediately hit it off, but their relationship improved over time.'

Arriving in Brussels two days later for his first EU summit Varadkar reiterated the line Kenny had been taking since the UK vote to leave a year earlier:

Our objective is a very clear one and it's a very simple one: that there should not be an economic border between Northern Ireland and the Republic of Ireland. Part of the reason why we have a successful peace process, and the reason for the improvement in the economies north and south is that there is no economic border, and that remains our objective.

That first summit was a potentially daunting situation for Varadkar. 'I remember saying to him when he became Taoiseach that when you walk into that room, it's like nothing you've ever done before,' recalled John Callinan, who was now acting as EU Sherpa for his fourth Taoiseach, having done the job for Bertie Ahern, Enda Kenny and Brian Cowen. 'It's so different from a ministerial council where you have a structured agenda and three or four officials lined up behind you. At the European Council, it's just the leaders on their own along with Tusk and Juncker so the dynamic is very different.'

In the event Varadkar adapted quickly and appeared to enjoy his first EU summit as much as he had the visit to Downing Street. The free-flowing format suited his ability to think on his feet. He said after his first European Council meeting:

The Council of Ministers tends to be people reading out statements to one another – this is very different. It's people talking about a document in front of them and making changes to the document, changing the language and wording and the meaning without reference to officials or advisers.

So I really felt that the elected politicians were in control – which isn't the way you necessarily feel all the time in politics. There are also very frank exchanges as well between heads of government. People don't speak in riddles. People were very frank in terms of their views on things and where there were differences of opinion, there were differences of opinion.

May was not nearly as comfortable being left to argue the UK's case without officials present. In part this was because of her buttoned-down personality but she also had to contend with the fact that she was in an extremely isolated position; many of the other leaders saw her as being on a mission to undermine the EU. Barnier noted that the British had initially hoped the Prime Minister could start discussing Brexit at the Council meeting, but May realised that was not possible as the only channel of communication on the issue was with him. 'And so, this evening after her presentation, none of the other 27 heads of state or government made a response, and Donald Tusk suspends the session to allow her to leave the dinner.'

Initially Merkel had made a strong effort to try and get close to May, partly because the Chancellor wanted to persuade the British to remain as close as possible to the EU but also from a sense of female solidarity. 'Merkel saw an opportunity to develop that relationship in a way that could have an influence on the outcome but it never happened and I remember Merkel, after the UK general election, being scathing about her and how she ran her campaign,' said one Irish official. 'Merkel knew everything and the machine around her was phenomenal. She was very well briefed on the position of all the other leaders as the machine around her was exceptionally good.'

The other problem that bedevilled the entire process was that every approach taken by the British was largely informed by domestic politics. 'May was negotiating all the time, it's just that most of the time she was negotiating with different parts of her own party and government. Added to that she was not the kind of politician who reacted instinctively. She was quite formal and reserved and then of course she was the Prime Minister taking the UK out of the EU so there was no way to be clubby and chummy with the other leaders,' added the senior official.

The widely held belief in the UK, particularly in the Tory press, that Brexit would lead to a break-up of the EU was reflected in a screaming headline in the account of the summit in the London *Daily Express*: 'EU on the verge of CIVIL WAR'. This assessment was not simply wrong, it had the effect of drawing the other twenty-seven member states closer together. Donald Tusk summed up the feeling of the EU leaders in wake of the summit: 'We have managed to maintain the political unity of the EU in the face of multiple threats and challenges. Never have I had such a strong belief that it [the EU] is going in a better direction.'

The formal negotiations about the UK withdrawal had begun with a fanfare on 19 June, just before the summit, when David Davis and a team of his officials arrived in Brussels to begin negotiations with Barnier and the key members of his Task Force. The two sides agreed on the structure of the negotiations, dates and the priorities for the talks. They agreed to establish two technical working groups, one on citizens' rights, and one on a UK financial settlement, and a separate 'dialogue' on Ireland and the border issues with the ambition of agreeing on these issues by October.

During lunch, which was also attended by Juncker, Barnier put a direct question to Davis. 'Can you confirm that the United Kingdom wants to leave the European Union and also wants to leave the single market and the customs union?' Davis answered 'Yes' to the three-fold question. This confirmed what Barnier already knew. The British were determined to go for a hard Brexit.

Significantly it was agreed that the dialogue on the border issue would be managed by Barnier's deputy, Sabine Weyand, and Olly Robbins, the permanent secretary at the Department for Exiting the EU and May's Sherpa. Robbins was highly regarded by both Barnier and Callinan for his ability and his knowledge of how the EU worked, but these very things made him suspect in the eyes of Tory Brexiteers. The appointment of the top officials to deal with the Irish portfolio was a measure of how centrally both sides saw the issue, a point acknowledged by Barnier and Davis when they addressed the media after the meeting. In a harbinger of things to come the negotiators revealed that the Irish Border was the issue which consumed most of their time at this first meeting and they agreed that it was technically most difficult.

Although both men gave an upbeat assessment, describing the talks as positive and useful, there was no disguising the difficulties ahead. Davis confirmed acceptance of the EU position that talks on the future relationship, notably trade, would only begin when sufficient progress had been made on the three core issues of citizens' rights, the 'divorce bill' and the Irish Border. Barnier, in a clear dig at Theresa May, insisted that 'a fair deal is possible and far better than no deal'.

Simon Coveney met Barnier in Luxembourg the following day and said he had been left in no doubt that Ireland's interests would be protected. 'For the EU-27's part, we have set out our position plainly and in this position there is a strong acknowledgement of Ireland's unique concerns and priorities, including on: protecting both the Good Friday Agreement in all its parts and the gains of the peace process; avoiding a hard Border on the island of Ireland, and maintaining the Common Travel Area. In short, there is no doubt that Ireland's interests are the EU's interests.'

With Brexit negotiations under way the Conservative government finally concluded a confidence and supply arrangement with the DUP. Most attention was focused on the allocation of the extra £1 billion to Northern Ireland to cement the deal but there were mixed views about what impact the arrangement would have on the British negotiating stance. Initially there was optimism in Irish government circles that the DUP might push May in the direction of a soft Brexit. This was reflected in comments from Coveney, who said an 'enhanced Northern Ireland voice' could be beneficial in relation to the final Brexit deal. He was in for a rude awakening over the following years as far as the DUP was concerned.

One indication of the British mood was a remark by Boris Johnson in the House of Commons in early July suggesting that if European leaders expected the UK to pay an exit tax they could 'go whistle'. Asked for his response by a journalist in Brussels Barnier replied, 'I am not hearing any whistling. Just the clock ticking.'

By the end of July the increasing confidence of the government in Dublin that Ireland would remain at the centre of the EU Brexit strategy was reflected in a more robust attitude to the UK. The row kicked off when the London *Times* reported that the Irish government was proposing an economic border in the Irish Sea as a way of avoiding a border on the island of Ireland. While there had not been a formal proposal on that score from the government, officials had let their British counterparts know that it was the favoured approach.

The response from the British was emphatic. A statement from David Davis's department declared: 'As we have always been clear our guiding principle will be to ensure that, as we leave the EU, no new barriers to living and doing business within the UK are created. Therefore we cannot create a border between Northern Ireland and Great Britain.'

If the British were emphatic, Northern unionists were furious. DUP deputy leader Nigel Dodds, who led the party's Westminster MPs, said he would use the party's leverage with the Conservative government to put an end to such talk:

The DUP will not tolerate a border in the Irish Sea after Brexit that makes it difficult to live, work and travel between different parts of the United Kingdom. The Prime Minister has already reiterated this.

At Westminster we will continue to use the influence of our ten MPs to ensure that respect for the territorial integrity of the UK remains at the core of the negotiations process.

Ian Paisley Junior tweeted: 'One of two things will now happen. A very hard border or Ireland will wise up and leave the EU.'

Varadkar entered the fray, taking a tough line on the responsibility of the British to sort out the border issue. Briefing political journalists on his priorities ahead of the summer holidays, he abandoned conciliatory language about co-operating with the British government to ease the problem. He made it clear that the work undertaken by the Revenue Commissioners to look into technological solutions, such as electronic monitoring of an open border, had come to an end.

'What we are not going to do is design a border for the Brexiteers because they're the ones who want a border. It is up to them to say what it is, how it is would work.' He went on to say that while there was a political border between the Republic and Northern Ireland there was not an economic one and he didn't want to see one. 'It's the UK, it's Britain that has decided to leave and if they want to put forward smart solutions, technological solutions for a border of the future, and all of that, that's up to them.'

The Taoiseach's blunt comments made headlines at home and in the UK. 'Varadkar's rocket is the most forthright statement of the Irish Government's position since the Brexit vote,' concluded *Irish Times* political editor Pat Leahy. 'It also marks a significant shift away from the essentially collaborative stance adopted by the Irish towards the British since the referendum. It will give relations between Dublin and London a jolt of the type not seen for many years.' He added that Varadkar's intervention was simply the public expression of a private frustration with the British that had been growing for the past year.

This prompted the British media to start turning their guns on Varadkar. He was depicted as having adopted a new and more hostile attitude to the UK than his predecessor. The Tory media appeared to be reflecting a co-ordinated briefing campaign from senior government sources in London. This caused considerable puzzlement among officials in Dublin, who felt there had been no particular change in the Irish position. 'There may have been a change in tone from Leo but there was no change in the approach,' said one senior official, who made the point that the Taoiseach was repeating the line adopted by Enda Kenny in his speech to the IIEA in March.

What did become clear as Varadkar settled into office was that there was a lack of rapport between himself and May. While Kenny had not managed to get past her official reserve, his natural ebullience ensured that their meetings ticked along. By contrast Varadkar's cool confidence and May refusal to stray from her official brief meant there were no meaningful exchanges between the two leaders when they met in the autumn of 2017.

'The personal chemistry wasn't great and there's no getting away from that,' said one official. 'Part of it was that they were just very different people but there would be gaps in the conversation. It's hard to describe but they didn't click at all.' He recalled one summit in Brussels where Varadkar attempted to break the ice before the real business began. 'He noticed that she was wearing a bracelet and said, "That's a beautiful bracelet you have on," expecting her to say thank you or some such but she just said nothing.'

Varadkar himself recalled that he never managed to get May to engage in a personal sense:

She's a very good woman. We never had a row or anything but anytime you met her or spoke to her on the phone she kind of stuck to the script. So even though we had a number of meetings with our teams we never had that meeting where the deal gets done, where you have that conversation without officials where you can say, 'If I were to say this, what would you do?' Unfortunately we never were able to have that meeting with Theresa even though I did try it on occasion. She was in a very difficult situation as she was trying to manage a divided party back home.

That September, in Florence, May delivered what was flagged as a major speech in which she adopted a conciliatory tone on the big issues of citizens' rights, the financial settlement and the Irish Border, without spelling out how agreement could be reached. She also called for a transition period after the March 2019 deadline for the conclusion of Brexit. 'The problem with the British approach was that policy changes were announced in a series of speeches; it did not evolve through serious negotiation so we could not be sure what exactly they were proposing,' said one senior EU official.

The EU position in the autumn of 2017 was developed in lockstep with Irish concerns. Declan Kelleher and Emer Deane, his deputy at the Permanent Representation, were given access to a room in the Berlaymont adjacent to where the talks between the Task Force and UK negotiators were in progress. At intervals during the talks Sabine Weyand or one of her team would brief the Irish officials on the state of play and consult about what was acceptable or feasible.

In the build-up to the European Council meeting in October, which was supposed to finalise the terms of the Withdrawal Agreement, it became clear that the Irish Border was proving to be the most intractable issue in the negotiations. The UK was still sticking to the belief that technical fixes could solve the problem. A twenty-eight-page British position paper on Northern Ireland on 16 August referred to technical solutions that would make the land border as seamless and as friction-less as possible through streamlined customs arrangements, waiving the need for entry and exit declarations, exempting small businesses and expanding trusted trader schemes.

As far as the EU was concerned, one big problem with this was that the UK appeared to be proposing a full resolution of the border issue through untried technology. It also raised suspicions in Brussels that the British were trying to use the Irish issue as a way of getting a favourable trade deal at a future date.

The EU's formal response came on 6 September. It took the form of six guiding principles. One of them stated bluntly: 'The onus to propose solutions which overcome the challenges created on the island of Ireland by the United Kingdom's withdrawal from the European Union, and its decision to leave the customs union and the internal market, remains on the United Kingdom.'

This formed the background to the EU October summit which would determine whether sufficient progress had been made on the With-drawal Agreement to move on to talks on the future relationship. Before the summit May suffered a political disaster at home when her leader's address to the annual conference of the Conference Party on 4 October turned into a shambles.

She went into the conference hoping to recover some of the ground she had lost with her party as a result of the ill-timed general election. However, her speech turned into a public relations disaster when a comedian managed to get himself on the stage and handed her a fake P45, saying 'Boris asked me to give you this.' The shock triggered a coughing fit and her voice began to go. To cap it all, the letters on the conference slogan behind her started to fall down. 'The fact that it was not her fault was irrelevant; she was beginning to get a reputation for being unlucky in a profession where the prevailing view is that you make your own luck,' recalled Barwell.

Watching the catalogue of disasters from Brussels, Barnier noted. 'I don't want to laugh at this, let alone mock her for it. She is a courageous and tenacious woman surrounded by a great many men who are more interested in their personal fortunes than in the future of their country.' The immediate reaction of rebel Conservative MPs was to threaten a motion of no confidence in her leadership. That did not happen, but her political standing took a knock from which it never recovered. It focused the attention of British politics on the future of her leadership rather than the negotiations with the EU on the Withdrawal Agreement.

There had been a general expectation in June that 'sufficient progress' on the Withdrawal Agreement could be made by the time of the October summit, but that had not happened. While the main British focus was still on the scale of the financial divorce settlement the Irish border issue was already proving to be more difficult. British cabinet secretary Jeremy Heywood had grasped the nature of the problem from the beginning. He now told his wife it was clear that the EU and the Republic of Ireland were going to stand side by side, which meant that 'unless a solution was found to the border issue that the Irish would accept, Britain wouldn't be allowed to move forward.' It took time for that penny to drop with his political masters.

Still, Varadkar was in a reasonably upbeat mood at the end of the summit, refusing to concede in public that the negotiations were becoming bogged down, even though officials privately briefed the media that the two sides were still far apart. Speaking at a post-summit press conference, Varadkar suggested 'sufficient progress' could be made by the December summit to enable the talks to move on to the second phase governing trade and the future relationship between the

EU and the UK. 'I've no crystal ball so it's impossible for me to predict the future but I'd have a degree of confidence that we'll be able to get to the point of sufficient progress by December. It's not that everything has to be agreed ... we just need to make sufficient progress and I think that's possible.'

He even had some positive things to say about Britain and how much Ireland would miss the influence of its closest neighbour in the EU. 'I have to say that once again that I am going to miss the United Kingdom when they leave the European Union. She [May] made some very strong interventions on digital tax.' The Taoiseach also said that May had used very positive language about the unique situation facing Ireland. 'She stayed with that language in relation to the Border; she said that the United Kingdom wouldn't accept a physical border on the island of Ireland ... but once again we need to see that backed up by detail.'

EU Council President Donald Tusk was a little more downbeat, saying that there would need to be a more positive narrative to reach a Brexit deal in December. This sentiment was echoed by European Commission President Jean-Claude Juncker: 'We have some details but we don't have all the details we need.'

Varadkar's optimistic mood didn't last long. The EU Task Force produced a paper on 8 November that was designed to clarify the border issue. A key paragraph read:

It consequently seems essential for the UK to commit to ensuring that a hard border on the island of Ireland is avoided, including by ensuring no emergence of regulatory divergence from those rules of the internal market and the customs union which are (or may be in the future) necessary for meaningful North–South co-operation, the all-island economy and the protection of the Good Friday Agreement.

In simple terms, what this meant was that in order to avoid a hard border, and protect North–South co-operation and the all-island economy, Northern Ireland, would to all intents and purposes remain in the single market for goods and in the EU Customs Union. The British were stunned by the scope of the paragraph and its implications for the future relationship between the EU and UK. It challenged the assumption that the UK could leave the single market and customs union and still avoid a hard border in Ireland.

David Davis denounced the 8 November paper in these words: 'We recognise the need for specific solutions for the unique circumstances of Northern Ireland but it cannot amount to creating a new border inside the UK.' On 15 November, there was a stormy meeting in Brussels between Task Force and British officials. Both sides were angry over the other's perception of the issue, with the British still insisting that the border problem could only be solved in the future trade talks.

This clear difference of opinion soured the next meeting between Varadkar and May, which took place on the fringes of an informal EU summit in Gothenburg, Sweden in early November. The abiding memory Irish officials have of that meeting is that the two leaders and their officials were jammed into a small portacabin with hardly room to move. Varadkar tried without success to get May to engage about how a frictionless Irish Border might work and how it would relate to the customs partnership with the EU now being proposed by the British.

'There were only about six of us in the room and Leo was probing her on what practical arrangement the British were proposing to avoid a hard border. All she would say was "we'll find a way" and Leo found this very frustrating.' This frustration was clear when he met the media afterwards. 'What we want to take off the table, before we even talk about trade, is any idea that there would be a hard border, a physical border, or a border resembling the past ... Then we'd be happy to move on to phase two.'

Describing the meeting as forthright, he added, 'Nothing changed today. But what was useful were the frank exchanges. Each clearly understands the other's position.' At the heart of the deadlock was the Irish and EU insistence that the UK explain how it could preserve a soft, frictionless border between Northern Ireland and the Republic, while the UK insisted that the issue could not be tackled until the EU agreed to move to discussion of phase two issues, particularly trade.

The Taoiseach said it was up to May to put meat on proposals that the UK had already made on establishing a customs partnership union with the EU. 'The UK side has put forward a proposal that there be a customs partnership union between the UK and EU. We would like to tease out what that means.'

A 'customs partnership' was one of the solutions the British had suggested for the post-Brexit world. Under this arrangement the UK would continue to act as the external border of the EU and track goods that were to be re-exported to the bloc. EU tariffs and standards would be applied to those, while tariffs and standards set by London would apply to goods circulating only in the UK.

Varadkar insisted this was a circle that could not be squared. 'It is hard to understand how that would work, how they would contain within their jurisdiction goods and services brought in from third countries, and then, secondly, how we could have fair competition on that basis if they were concluding agreements, let's say, for instance, with South America on agricultural products.' He repeated his insistence that the UK 'can't have its cake and eat it'. The Taoiseach said he remained an optimist about the December time frame for the conclusion of sufficient progress on phase-one divorce talks. 'I think it is certainly possible ... but if we have to wait until the New Year, or wait for further concessions, then so be it. But I think it would be in all our interests to proceed to phase two in December.'

Varadkar's blunt talking in public fuelled the developing British narrative that he had upended Kenny's Brexit strategy and was taking a more aggressive line. This view was not shared by the Irish officials who served both leaders. According to one of the Irish negotiators:

Nothing could be further from the truth. I mean nothing changed in the policy. What changed was the personality and the style of the leader. Leo had a much more blunt and direct communications style. That was perceived by some people as a toughening of the stance and a toughening of the position. It actually suited him to have this view that everything has changed and you have this tough guy taking a harder line but it wasn't really the case. It was true at a smaller level in that his demeanour generally was more direct and more hardball. Enda would be softer and more pleasant but that was the height of it.

True or not, the perception that Varadkar was adopting a more aggressive line took hold on the British side. In large part this was because the emergence of the Irish Border as a serious obstacle to the future relationship between the UK and the EU had come as a shock to London. British fury about the way the talks on the Withdrawal Agreement were going was reflected in renewed attacks on Varadkar in the British media. An editorial in the *Sun*, the biggest-selling British tabloid, proclaimed that Ireland's 'naive young prime minister should shut his gob and grow up'. Saying that a hard Brexit would be catastrophic for Ireland, it added that 'Varadkar's rookie diplomacy, puerile insults and threats to veto trade negotiations are bringing it ever closer.'

A similar view, generally expressed in more sedate tones, was echoed across the Tory press. Another trope was that the EU was using Ireland as a pawn to get the better of the UK. The *Spectator* magazine devoted its cover to the topic with the headline 'Divide and Rule: How the EU used Ireland to take control of Brexit' over a caricature of Barnier and Juncker drawing a border down the Irish Sea while May and her officials attempt to draw it across the English Channel.

The British couldn't make up their minds whether it was the Irish using the EU or the other way around and they continued to miss the point that the member states had decided from the beginning that they were going to stick together. That meant sticking by Ireland. On 24 November Theresa May met Donald Tusk in Brussels. He said there was 'active interest' from member states in achieving sufficient progress but warned her of his concern about Ireland. 'The Irish Taoiseach was being tougher in private than he was in public, and if he wasn't satisfied others wouldn't be,' Tusk told her. The secretary-general of the Council, Jeppe Tranholm-Mikkelsen, spelled it out for her in blunt terms, saying the UK's 'imaginative solutions' had not convinced the EU or the Irish. Any solution would have to do more than give a general commitment that there would be no return to a hard border. It had to be something that spelled out what would happen if the border issue was not sorted out satisfactorily in the overall EU–UK future relationship.

The talks between the EU Task Force and British officials on how to avoid a hard border entered a critical phase in the closing days of November. Although there was no public signal from either side about the progress of the talks, the DUP was sufficiently alarmed by the prospect of UK concessions to warn Theresa May that any move which affected Northern Ireland's relationship with the rest of the UK risked losing the party's support for her minority government.

DUP leader Arlene Foster went public to say she had made it clear to the British government that there could be 'no arrangements agreed that compromise the integrity of the UK single market and place barriers, real or perceived, to the free movement of goods, services and capital between Northern Ireland and the rest of the United Kingdom'. DUP MP Sammy Wilson said he was seeking clarification from the British government on reports that the Prime Minister was preparing to make concessions to the EU on the Border. 'If there is any hint that in order to placate Dublin and the EU they're prepared to have Northern Ireland treated differently than the rest of the UK then they can't rely on our vote.'

Coveney made the immediate riposte that the Irish government simply could not accept the re-emergence of a border on the island. There was support for the Irish position from an unexpected source, the Exiting the European Union Committee of the House of Commons, which comprised MPs from the government and opposition parties. It produced a report saying it could not see how Britain's commitment to keeping the Border open could be reconciled with its policy of leaving the customs union. Hilary Benn, the Labour MP who chaired the committee, said:

Our report concludes that we cannot at present see how leaving the customs union and the single market can be reconciled with there being no border or infrastructure. Even by their own admission, the government's proposals are untested and speculative, so it has yet to set out how no border can in practice be maintained with the UK outside the single market and the customs union.

At the end of November, May briefed her ministers on her strategy in the talks with the EU. Boris Johnson was the most negative, arguing that accepting any role for the ECJ was 'wrong in principle and will go down badly'. Other leading ministers, including Philip Hammond and David Davis, took a different view – they said that enough progress had to be made to generate the momentum for an agreement.

The EU then came forward with a revised text on Northern Ireland which went much further than the British were expecting. It suggested that if the Irish Border problem was not solved by a deal on the future trading relationship, a provision in the Withdrawal Agreement to ensure there was no economic border would come into play. 'The prime minister was hugely frustrated when Olly [Robbins] told her about this text. She was exasperated at being asked to make commitments about what we would do if we couldn't reach an agreement about our future relationship before we even had a chance to talk about it,' wrote Barwell. His assessment was that the plan would left the UK with two unpalatable options: either the entire UK stayed in the customs union and followed some single market rules; or Northern Ireland would have to do so, which would mean a partial border in the UK.

7

The Backstop Is Born

'There cannot be any border controls between Northern and southern Ireland, there cannot be border controls between Northern Ireland and the UK, but there can between UK and the EU. So our primary school students can see that there is a riddle to be solved.'

Austrian Chancellor Christian Kern,
15 December 2017

* * *

The Irish position received a massive shot in the arm on 1 December when Donald Tusk visited Dublin for talks with the Taoiseach and senior officials. He didn't confine himself to private assurances that Ireland would get the full backing of EU institutions and the member states in resisting a hard border, he loudly proclaimed his views in public.

After his meeting with Varadkar, Tusk told a press conference that it was no secret they had discussed Brexit, with a special focus on the Border between Ireland and Northern Ireland. 'I came to Dublin to reassure the Taoiseach and all the Irish people that the EU is fully behind you and your request that there should be no hard border on the island of Ireland after Brexit. The Irish request is the EU's request. Or as the Irish proverb goes: "Ní neart go cur le chéile" [There is no strength without unity].'

He repeated the point that had been made by a number of EU leaders since the Brexit referendum. 'It is the UK that started Brexit and now it is their responsibility to propose a credible commitment to do what is necessary to avoid a hard border.' Tusk went on to say that he had asked May to put a final offer on the table by 4 December so that an assessment could be made at the European Council meeting later in the month as to whether 'sufficient progress' had been made to allow the sides move on to the trade talks.

He then revealed that he had promised to consult Varadkar before agreeing to allow the talks to move on. 'Let me say very clearly: if the UK's offer is unacceptable for Ireland, it will also be unacceptable for the EU. I realise that for some British politicians this may be hard to understand. But such is the logic behind the fact that Ireland is an EU member while the UK is leaving. This is why the key to the UK's future lies, in some ways, in Dublin, at least as long as Brexit negotiations continue.'

The impact of Tusk's remarks cannot be overstated. His use of the Irish language to emphasise the solidarity of the EU with Ireland really buoyed Irish ministers and officials, but the really devastating line for the British was the assertion that the key to the future of the UK's relationship with Europe lay in Dublin. That was music to Irish ears but was regarded by the British as a profound insult.

Brian Murphy, Varadkar's chief of staff, recalled that the issue only crystallised for the British on the evening that Tusk met Varadkar and declared that the road to Brexit was through Dublin. 'That was an extraordinary moment. It came after a really positive meeting and we were helped because the British tabloids went after Tusk which infuriated him. He just wasn't having it.'

Gavin Barwell wrote later that as if things had not been difficult enough in Downing Street Tusk's remark about the key to the UK's future lying in Dublin ramped up the tension. 'It is difficult to think of anything more inflammatory he could have said as far as the DUP were concerned and it wasn't the only time he made such remarks. Maybe they were slips of the tongue, maybe they were gestures of solidarity to a fellow EU member or maybe, as a Pole, he had a natural sympathy for a country having to deal with a larger neighbour.'

Tusk's ringing support for Ireland was delivered on a Friday, just days in advance of a crucial lunchtime meeting between Jean-Claude

Juncker and Theresa May which was due to take place in Brussels the following Monday, 4 December. This was now the deadline for a deal on the Withdrawal Agreement and EU and UK negotiators worked furiously over the weekend to finalise its provisions. By this stage almost everything had been agreed apart from an acceptable formula to prevent a hard border on the island of Ireland. Irish officials worked closely with the EU team over that weekend as successive drafts were considered and modified. The Irish ambition was to ensure that there would be no regulatory divergence in Northern Ireland from the rules of the single market. This was ultimately accepted by both sides along with a sop to the British, a stipulation that technological solutions to the border could not be ruled out of any trade agreement if they could be shown to work.

John Callinan recalled that the Irish side was heavily involved in the drafting of that crucial part of the report. 'So we were working through the weekend on the drafting and there was a triangle between Dublin, London and Brussels working on the management of the border issue and ultimately the thing was done and agreed.' The Irish side understood the agreement to mean that the border issue would either be resolved through agreement on an acceptable EU–UK future relationship or through mutually agreed special arrangements for the Irish situation. Crucially, there was a fallback final option which was to become known as the 'backstop'. This was that in the absence of either of those agreed arrangements Northern Ireland would remain fully aligned with the EU. After a great deal of haggling, the expression 'no regulatory divergence' between North and South was replaced in the text by the phrase 'continuing regulatory alignment.'

Over that weekend May had the frustrating task of getting all her ministers and the DUP onside with a formula that would also keep the Irish government and the EU happy. 'Theresa's frustration wasn't helped by the fact that Leo Varadkar studiously avoided taking her calls that weekend, something that I can't remember any other head of government doing,' Barwell recalled.

Nonetheless, by Sunday night the plan with the backstop commitment was agreed at official level but May needed to square it off with a number of people in the London political system. The Irish were told late on Sunday night that most of the relevant people were on board but that one or two were away and it would be Monday morning before they could confirm.

There was now a strong mood of optimism in Dublin, and Coveney reflected this in an interview on RTÉ's *Morning Ireland* on Monday morning. When the cabinet met, shortly after nine o'clock, there had been no final decision in London, but before it ended in mid-morning confirmation arrived from Downing Street that the deal was agreed.

Everything appeared to be in place to allow Juncker and May to unveil the agreement after their lunchtime meeting in Brussels. There was jubilation in Dublin and arrangements were put in place for a press conference to be hosted by Varadkar and Coveney. However, the carefully laid plans were thrown into disarray by a tweet in mid-morning from RTÉ's well-informed Brussels correspondent, Tony Connolly, which spooked the DUP. Connolly tweeted that the deal contained a core commitment to no regulatory divergence between North and South, whatever happened in the future. While the actual phrase in the final draft of the agreed report referred to 'continued regulatory alignment' the tweet prompted the DUP to demand that May reject the deal.

There was astonishment in Dublin that the British did not have the DUP on board, given that the government in London was reliant on them for support. 'As far as we were concerned the thing was done and agreed and we assumed May had prepared the ground,' said Callinan. Brian Murphy recalled that it was one of the most dramatic moments in the entire process.

> We were actually briefing the opposition parties on the deal as word came through. Mary Lou [McDonald] was sitting in the room and being briefed when we learned that there was a problem in Brussels. I have to say, to be fair to Mary Lou and others, they didn't try and exploit the situation for their own advantage. There was certainly a feeling of collegiality around Brexit on that day. They didn't say 'You were fooled by these people and you should have been prepared for perfidious Albion.' Fianna Fáil wouldn't have done that but you thought the Shinners might.

Once the cat was out of the bag there were contacts between May in Brussels and Arlene Foster in Belfast but they didn't solve the problem.

Foster went public to insist that Northern Ireland must leave the EU on the same terms as the rest of the UK. 'We will not accept any form of regulatory divergence which separates Northern Ireland economically or politically from the rest of the United Kingdom,' she said in a public statement.

'What followed was one of the worst days of my time as chief of staff,' recalled Barwell. He and the party's chief whip, Julian Smith, were bombarded with messages from Conservative MPs who either supported the DUP or were worried that the party would withdraw from the confidence and supply arrangement and collapse the government. 'Julian called the Prime Minister to inform her it was too dangerous to proceed. She called Arlene from Brussels but was unable to talk her around and had to return to London without an agreement.'

In Dublin the planned press conference featuring Varadkar and Coveney was put back a number of times until it became clear that May would be unable to proceed with the deal for fear of losing DUP support. In Brussels Juncker and May had to publicly admit that their efforts had failed and it looked as if the carefully worded Withdrawal Agreement had turned to ashes.

A stunned Varadkar finally gave a press conference in Dublin to say he been told as late as that morning that a deal had been struck which would ensure that there would be no hard Border on the island of Ireland, adding, 'We don't want an Irish Sea border any more than we want one between Newry and Dublin.' Despite the failure to agree on the day he remained optimistic. 'I acknowledge that Theresa May is negotiating in good faith. My position is unequivocal. Ireland wants to proceed to phase two. We cannot agree unless there are firm guarantees on the lack of a hard border in any circumstances. I still hope this matter can be concluded in the coming days.' When asked by a reporter about the difference between the terms 'no regulatory divergence' and 'regulatory alignment' he said the two things meant the same thing and he was happy to accept either.

Reflecting the frustration that May had not got the DUP's support before going to Brussels he said it was never the Irish government's role to ensure the DUP was onside. 'We engaged in negotiations in good faith with EU and UK. We agreed a text this morning, we believe it stands, but we believe the Prime Minister needs more time.'

Juncker, ever the shrewd negotiator, kept the door to an agreement open by praising May, saying she was a tough negotiator who had defended the UK's point of view, but adding that despite everybody's best efforts it had not been possible to reach agreement on the day. 'We stand ready to resume the negotiations. I have to say we are narrowing our positions and I'm still confident that we can reach sufficient progress before the European Council on 15 December.' May also sounded positive in spite of the spectacular failure to achieve the expected agreement. She insisted that both sides felt they had had a constructive meeting and wanted to move forward together. 'We will reconvene before the end of the week. We will conclude this positively,' she maintained.

The following day there was a decisive shift in the British position. May indicated that she was prepared to rescue the deal by promising that any 'regulatory alignment' with the EU would apply to the whole of the UK, not just Northern Ireland. This idea had surfaced during the autumn but had been dropped because neither side was particularly comfortable with it. It re-emerged in the wake of the DUP rejection of 'regulatory alignment' on the island of Ireland and initially May appeared to have a substantial majority of MPs on her side. In the immediate aftermath of the breakdown, she faced universal hostility from MPs to any deal that would treat Northern Ireland differently from the rest of the UK.

Brexit Secretary David Davis then told the House of Commons that the assumption in the talks with the EU had been that everything that had been talked about would apply to the whole of the UK, not simply to Northern Ireland. This was far from the truth, but MPs were suddenly confronted with the notion that a promise to ensure regulatory alignment between the two parts of Ireland had been expanded to include the entire UK. Although Labour denounced the shambolic nature of the Conservative government's handling of the Brexit negotiations, all parties agreed that any regulatory alignment should be UK-wide and nobody spoke in favour of any special regime for Northern Ireland. Opposition MPs focused on blaming the Prime Minister for the breakdown in Brussels.

In case anybody was in any doubt Arlene Foster again spelled out her party's bottom line: 'When we looked at the wording and had seen the import of all that, we knew we couldn't sign up to anything that was in that text that would allow a border to develop in the Irish Sea,' she told RTÉ. The DUP's leader at Westminster, Nigel Dodds, unsurprisingly laid the blame for the fiasco at the door of the government in Dublin. 'It should come as no surprise that Dublin and the Irish government wish to advance their interests. The aggressive and anti-unionist way in which they have gone about doing so is disgraceful. It has set back Anglo-Irish relations and damaged the relationships built up within Northern Ireland in relation to the devolution settlement. That damage will take a long time to repair.'

The immediate focus of the EU negotiating team and the Irish was to get back to work on the text to see if the agreement could be rescued. 'We spent about three days effectively going back around the track again to see how the difficulty could be overcome. Ireland and the EU made clear that we were not amending a comma of the vital paragraph. We were open to tweaks in other parts of the text or to things that could be added in to offer comfort but the fundamental thing was not to change it. So that was done and over the next few days we found a formula for agreement,' said Callinan.

The day after the Brussels debacle the British team engaged in intense negotiations with the DUP to see what potential amendments to the section of the joint report on Northern Ireland would be acceptable. Barwell recalled that May first apologised to Foster before having a positive phone conversation with Varadkar.

He explained that he couldn't agree to the key part of the text being watered down. He didn't want to be remembered as the Taoiseach who agreed to the reintroduction of a border between North and South, but he understood that she needed to secure some changes. He also promised to be the UK's best friend in the second phase of the negotiations; after all, the east–west trading relationship was more important than the north–south one. Rather cheekily, given his refusal to take her calls over the weekend, he suggested they should talk more.

The two leaders agreed to a joint statement which read: 'The Taoiseach reiterated the firm Irish position regarding the text as outlined by him on Monday. They agreed to speak again over the coming days.' A statement from Downing Street said the two leaders had agreed on the paramount importance of no hard border or physical infrastructure at the border between Ireland and Northern Ireland.

'The Prime Minister said she recognised the significance of this issue to the people of Northern Ireland and Ireland and how this remained a joint priority for both governments, and the EU, to resolve.' The statement went on to say that both governments would work hard to find a specific solution to the unique circumstances in Northern Ireland that respected the integrity of the UK, the European Union and the Belfast Agreement. 'We are committed to moving together to achieve a positive result on this as well as restoring devolved government to Northern Ireland. Both leaders looked forward to continuing relations as close neighbours and allies as the negotiations progress.'

As the rest of Europe looked on in bemusement Dutch Prime Minister Mark Rutte came to Dublin to talk to Varadkar and expressed support for the Irish position. Varadkar told journalists after his meeting with Rutte that May was now going to bring forward some new text to add to the deal to assuage the concerns of the DUP, but he insisted that the substance and meaning of the deal must not be altered.

An opinion poll in the *Irish Times* on 7 December showed that the public were firmly on Varadkar's side. Almost 70 per cent of voters said he should veto a deal that did not meet the Irish demands. Despite the fact that his government had been embroiled in a lengthy controversy about the treatment of Garda whistleblower Maurice McCabe, which had led to the resignation of Tánaiste and Minister for Justice Frances Fitzgerald, both Fine Gael and the Taoiseach were close to record levels of support. 'Battling the Brits' was clearly a popular strategy regardless of the dangers involved.

On Thursday Varadkar and May had another fifteen-minute conversation to discuss a new text tabled by the British side to reassure unionists. Both leaders also spoke to Juncker during the day but May had great difficulty getting Foster on board as the DUP leader sought yet more changes to the text. Finally, late on the Thursday night, May told Foster there was no more time left for any further changes and she was going ahead with the new text. May then cleared it with Varadkar. 'We woke the Taoiseach, who, to our surprise, agreed to one final change, and President Juncker, who agreed to meet for an early breakfast,' recalled Barwell. May boarded an RAF plane in the middle of the night and headed back to Brussels for her breakfast meeting with Juncker.

A flavour of the tension of that week is captured in Suzanne Heywood's recollections. She recorded in her diary that on 8 December 2017, the EU had decided that enough progress had been made to allow the next stage of negotiations to begin the following month.

> The joint report includes the idea of an Irish backstop. It meant that if the border question could not be solved through a trade or technology arrangements the whole of the UK would have to remain aligned to the rules of the EU single market and customs union. The backstop was something that Downing Street knew Brexiteers would hate – but without it Brussels would have refused to allow the UK to move on to the next stage in the talks.

She noted that her husband, Jeremy, the UK cabinet secretary, had received his third dose of immunotherapy to treat his cancer that week.

> It has been a difficult week, Jeremy told me. He'd spent hours on the phone to Martin Fraser, secretary general to the Irish government, after the DUP had rejected the original version of the backstop which had only included Northern Ireland. It had taken days of negotiation before they'd found an acceptable compromise – broadening it to include the whole of the UK – though the DUP still didn't like it. 'Difficult' to Jeremy meant 'horrendous' in anybody else's vocabulary.

The final draft of the joint report contained ninety-six provisions, fourteen of them referring to Ireland. The crucial ones were paragraphs 49 and 50 which spelled out the scope of the regulatory alignment required to ensure there would be no hard border on the island.

Paragraph 49 read:

> The United Kingdom remains committed to protecting North–South co-operation and to its guarantee of avoiding a hard border. Any future arrangements must be compatible with these overarching requirements. The United Kingdom's intention is to achieve these

objectives through the overall EU–UK relationship. Should this not be possible, the United Kingdom will propose specific solutions to address the unique circumstances of the island of Ireland. In the absence of agreed solutions, the United Kingdom will maintain full alignment with those rules of the Internal Market and the Customs Union which, now or in the future, support North–South co-operation, the all-island economy and the protection of the 1998 Agreement.

Paragraph 50, which was cobbled together to meet the DUP's concerns, read:

In the absence of agreed solutions, as set out in the previous paragraph, the United Kingdom will ensure that no new regulatory barriers develop between Northern Ireland and the rest of the United Kingdom, unless, consistent with the 1998 Agreement, the Northern Ireland Executive and Assembly agree that distinct arrangements are appropriate for Northern Ireland. In all circumstances, the United Kingdom will continue to ensure the same unfettered access for Northern Ireland's businesses to the whole of the United Kingdom internal market.

The political dynamite for Theresa May was the commitment in paragraph 49 that if no solutions were agreed on the unique circumstances of the island of Ireland, the UK would stay aligned with the rules of the internal market and the customs union. This quickly became known in British politics as the 'backstop' and over time was to prove a millstone around May's neck.

British Conservative commentator Roderick Crawford reflected later in a detailed paper for the Policy Exchange think tank that this was a turning point in the entire process.

Getting these UK concessions was a diplomatic triumph for Ireland and the Commission: failing to secure adequate reciprocal concessions was a staggering failure for the UK. The negotiations that led to this largely occurred behind closed doors between August 2017 and December 2017 when the UK's negotiating position collapsed under pressure to gain EU approval to move on to phase two of the talks. The UK's failures began even earlier. After the Joint Report, the pass had been sold.

Rory Montgomery has a similar assessment.

So basically, the whole approach was established on the EU side in the autumn of 2017 and the British essentially accepted it ... So the basic parameters of the approach were set out from the beginning. They were implemented very well by Barnier and his team. If it had been a more formidable British Prime Minister than Theresa May or if Theresa May had won a good majority in the election of 2017 and had not been dependant on the DUP there might have been a different course of events, but who knows.

After their breakfast meeting in Brussels May and Juncker held a joint press conference at which they announced that the withdrawal deal had been agreed and had reached the threshold of sufficient progress in the areas of citizens' rights, the financial divorce settlement and Irish-specific issues. This meant that the talks could now move on to the next phase, which involved working out a framework for the future relationship between the EU and UK. From an Irish point of view the deal was a triumph. The commitment to a frictionless border had been formally enshrined in the agreement, with both sides signing up to regulatory alignment as a last resort if the talks on a future relationship did not work out. The fact that the alignment would involve the whole of the UK, not just Northern Ireland, appeared to be a bonus as it suggested that a soft Brexit, the goal of the Irish government, was now a real possibility. In order to assuage the concerns of the DUP, the British pledged that Northern Ireland would not be treated differently from the rest of the UK.

In hindsight Rory Montgomery believes the British misjudged the situation because the backstop was listed as only the third option, in the event that agreement on a new EU–UK relationship or special arrangements failed to deal with it.

Frankly nobody on the EU side, certainly in the Commission, ever believed that options one or two were a runner. And so the reality was that what was seen as the backstop was never, in reality, the backstop at all. It was the view on the EU side, and on the Commission side in particular, that this was what was going to be necessary. But the British put a lot of faith in the fact that they were able to point rhetorically to the statement in the joint declaration that this was only option three. And we did it ourselves too in an attempt to offer reassurance without really believing it.

At a press conference on the morning of 8 December Varadkar maintained that the government had achieved all it had set out to do in phase one of the negotiations.

> If you see the language that is there in the paragraphs, it talks about a commitment to avoiding a hard border, there being no physical infrastructure, no associated checks and controls, and that commitment is overarching and stands in all circumstances, so the strongest commitment that exists in this document is that political commitment that there be no hard border.

When asked if the deal meant Britain was heading for a soft Brexit, with close ties to the European single market and customs union, Varadkar was coy, saying that everybody would have to get away from the binary idea of a soft or hard Brexit. 'We're actually now getting into the detail. And I think as we get into the detail more and more, the British public and British people will come to understand why it makes sense actually that we have very similar or almost identical rules and regulations when it comes to trade. That's what facilitates free trade, that we do have the same standards.' Privately Irish officials were confident that the deal meant that the new relationship between the UK and the EU would be as close as possible to the status quo.

Varadkar was at pains to stress that the Irish government recognised the concerns of the unionist community; there was no 'question of us exploiting Brexit as a means of moving to a united Ireland without consent', but he pointedly said that the nationalist community in Northern Ireland would 'never again be left behind by an Irish government'. That direct appeal to nationalist sentiment surprised a lot of people. 'When Leo led off that press conference with the famous line about never leaving Northern nationalists behind it caused some raised eyebrows. It sounded strident and clearly wasn't a civil service line but it was very deliberate on his part even if not everybody thought it was wise,' said one Irish official later.

Officials were also worried that arising from the same press conference Varadkar was widely quoted as describing the commitment to avoid a hard border on the island of Ireland as 'politically bulletproof'. They felt that this could in time turn out to be a hostage to fortune. In contrast to the remark about not leaving Northern nationalists behind, the 'bulletproof' claim was not a deliberate statement on his part but arose casually in response to a question from RTÉ's political correspondent Martina Fitzgerald. She asked him if he believed the deal was 'politically bulletproof' and he responded simply 'Yes'. Many of the newspaper headlines the following day used the 'bulletproof' line.

At a joint press conference in Brussels May and Juncker expressed relief that the joint report had been agreed, and Juncker said the Commission was satisfied that sufficient progress had been achieved in each of the three priority areas of citizens' rights, the dialogue on Ireland/Northern Ireland, and the financial settlement.

May told journalists that if it did not prove possible for the UK to reach agreement on regulatory alignment with the EU, 'we will look to the unique circumstances of Northern Ireland.' She said the deal would ensure 'no hard border' in Ireland and added that it was a 'significant improvement' which had required give and take on both sides and that she would continue to govern in the interests of Northern Ireland and uphold the Belfast Agreement.

Arlene Foster claimed that the deal copper-fastened the arrangement that Northern Ireland would the leave the EU – including the single market and customs union – with the rest of the UK. She was adamant there would be no border in the middle of the Irish Sea. DUP Brexit spokesman Sammy Wilson MP told the *Irish Times* that the party had got assurances in the document 'that we will be leaving the customs union and the EU along with the United Kingdom, we have assurances on that and we will have totally unfettered access to the UK's internal market'.

An Irish official recalled that during that negotiation the UK side asked for and received agreement from the EU about language that specified that Northern Ireland would have unfettered access to the

British market. 'The key point, though, was that the unfettered access provision did not apply the other way around to British goods coming into Northern Ireland. The wording on that score referred to "as frictionless as possible" or words to that effect.'

Looking back, he recalled the relief all round that the deal was agreed, even if there had been a serious wobble. But the wobble was a harbinger of things to come.

> We knew it was not going to be plain sailing in the next phase. A lot of what the Brits were trying to do was kind of fudge and keep it vague and to be fair we all know the Good Friday Agreement is a masterpiece of constructive ambiguity but you can't really do things that way with the EU. So, this document was published, and even from the day it was published, it was sort of in trouble. And this was treated as kind of told you so evidence from those who said they [the British] won't honour what they've agreed, they won't stick to it.

A week later EU leaders gathered in Brussels for their regular European Council meeting and agreed that 'sufficient progress' had been made on citizens' rights, the UK financial divorce settlement and the Irish border to allow the talks on the future relationship to proceed. The relief at having got over the first hurdle did not blind them to the difficulties ahead. It was clear to almost everybody involved that the British had given contradictory assurances – to leave the single market and the custom unions but to maintain the existing frictionless border arrangements.

The position was summed up by Austrian Chancellor Christian Kern, who said that even a primary school student could see that the first phase deal on the Irish Border would come back to disrupt the talks because it was impossible for Britain to leave the single market while avoiding a hard border on the island of Ireland. 'There cannot be any border controls between Northern and southern Ireland, there cannot be border controls between Northern Ireland and the UK, but there can between UK and the EU. So our primary school students can see that there is a riddle to be solved.'

Other leaders pointed to the difficulties in more diplomatic terms. Juncker warned that the hardest decisions were still to come as the

UK confronted the reality of extricating itself from the single market and customs union. Merkel cautioned that there was not a great deal of time to sort out the many problems. 'We made clear that Theresa May has made an offer that should allow us to say that we have seen sufficient progress,' she told reporters. 'Nevertheless, there are still a lot of problems to solve. And time is of the essence.' In theory there were just three months to sort out a deal on the future relationship before the twelve-month transition period in advance of the UK's exit began.

There was great relief in the UK government that the joint report had finally been agreed, but some apprehension about how it would play out. 'It appeared that the gamble had paid off, but appearances can be deceptive,' recalled Barwell. 'Our hopes that there might be some flexibility in the language were ultimately dashed, and the DUP were never really reconciled to what we had signed up to. If the EU's legal inability to agree the future relationship until after we had left made the backstop inevitable, paragraph 49 of the joint report was key to its development and to our failure to secure parliamentary support for the deal Theresa negotiated.'

The issues that needed to be confronted by the EU and UK negotiating teams were difficult enough, but they were exacerbated to an extraordinary degree by the divisions in the British cabinet and the Conservative Party. May faced a monumental challenge in attempting to develop a coherent line that could bring her feuding ministers and MPs together while simultaneously negotiating with the EU. At the heart of her difficulties was the Irish backstop.

During the fraught negotiations between the fourth and eighth of December there was a dawning realisation all round that Ireland could be the stumbling block to a harmonious future relationship between the EU and the UK. When the withdrawal deal was finally concluded Sabine Weyand turned to John Callinan and said: 'This will come back to haunt us, you know.' She never said a truer word.

8

Ireland First

'If, in London, someone assumes that the negotiations will deal with other issues first, before moving to the Irish issue, my response would be: Ireland first.'

Donald Tusk, 8 March 2018

* * *

Following the high-wire drama of December 2017, in the early months of 2018 the UK government and the EU wrestled with the practical details of how to give legal effect to the principles of the agreed joint report, particularly the Irish backstop. It was the rock on which Theresa May perished after more than a year of constant drama that threw the British political system into chaos.

The Prime Minister's problems began in January when officials gave her an economic analysis of the impact on the UK of a variety of options for a future relationship with the EU. The bottom line was that there was no version of Brexit that would be as good for the UK as staying in the EU, and the more distant the relationship the bigger the economic hit. Brexiteers in the cabinet regarded this as another version of 'Project Fear', while for the Remainers it was a reminder that they were engaged in devising a policy that would make the UK worse off.

'As usual the prime minister found herself somewhere between these two extremes: she accepted that a distant relationship would have an economic cost but questioned some of the assumptions and the way the analysis was presented,' noted Barwell.

As far as the Irish Border was concerned, customs and regulatory alignment remained the core of the problem. Boris Johnson was the most hard-line of the British cabinet Brexiteers on the issue. He claimed the Irish Border was 'the tail wagging the Brexit dog', and he opposed any hybrid option on customs to try to square the circle, flatly denying there was any problem in the first place. Others who understood the issues better took a very different view. When May met Merkel at a security conference in Munich the Chancellor's EU Sherpa Uwe Corsepius observed: 'If you want a close relationship [with the EU] Ireland will be a small problem but if you want a Canada-style relationship it will be a big problem.'

By this stage the Irish were happy that they had succeeded in getting May and the key people around her to appreciate the political and societal risks of a hard border. They felt that May was genuinely concerned about the prospects of a serious deterioration in Northern Ireland and was determined to avoid it. 'Given the kind of decent human being she is, we felt that if we could frame the message properly she would understand it and that is in fact what happened,' said Callinan. 'I think we saw a certain point along the way where something changed. They were now very structured with all of their speeches and they'd always be in touch in advance about what she was going to say in relation to the North and the Border. It was very carefully pre-planned and there was a marked change in the way she spoke about the North. That was a big plus.'

As the British struggled to work out a negotiating position EU officials got on with figuring out the kind of transition period that would kick in after a final agreement was completed and the UK left the EU at the end of March 2019. There had been some suggestions from the British that the transition period should be as long as four years, but the EU foreign ministers agreed on a relatively short transition of twenty-one months, which would end on 31 December 2000. During that transition all the rights and obligations of membership would continue to apply to the UK although it would not participate in decision-making during the period.

More critically, the Commission worked on producing a legal text to give practical effect to the outline of the Withdrawal Agreement concluded in December 2017. When the draft legal text was published at the end of February 2018, a political storm ensued. The 120-page report contained 168 articles and two protocols translating into legal terms all the issues that had been agreed in December. The most important ones concerned UK's financial settlement, citizens' rights and the future of the Border between Northern Ireland and the Republic. To deal with the Border the draft proposed a 'common regulatory area' for the island of Ireland in the event that no agreement proved possible on trade between the EU and the UK; in other words, a backstop.

The first page of the document spelled out the approach. 'With respect to the Draft Protocol on Ireland/Northern Ireland the negotiators agree that a legally operative version of the "backstop" solution for the border between Northern Ireland and Ireland, in line with paragraph 49 of the Joint Report, should be agreed as part of the legal text of the Withdrawal Agreement, to apply unless and until another solution is found.'

The commitment to include the backstop in the legal text of the Withdrawal Agreement was exactly what the Irish negotiators wanted. The document also spelled out that the common regulatory framework would involve an 'area without internal borders in which the free movement of goods is ensured', covering customs, VAT, energy, agriculture, goods and other sectors, across the island of Ireland. 'The territory of Northern Ireland ... shall be considered to be part of the customs territory of the Union,' it said. In a nod to British concerns it also mentioned that other options, including technological solutions for a virtual border, would continue to be explored, but it gave no commitment on this point.

The proposal caused immediate outrage in the Conservative Party and the DUP. May told the House of Commons that no British prime minister could agree to it as it would effectively keep Northern Ireland under EU customs rules and put the EU–UK border in the Irish Sea. Speaking at Prime Minister's Questions, May said she would be making her opposition to it 'crystal clear' to the EU Commission. 'The draft legal text the Commission have published would, if implemented, undermine the UK common market and threaten the constitutional integrity of the UK by creating a customs and regulatory border down the Irish Sea, and no UK prime minister could ever agree to it,' she said.

Boris Johnson suggested the row over the Border was being used to keep the UK inside the customs union. It was no surprise that the

DUP Westminster leader Nigel Dodds expressed amazement that the EU thought the arrangement 'could possibly fly with either us or the British government'. He told the BBC, 'We did not leave the European Union to oversee the breakup of the United Kingdom.' Simon Coveney attempted to cool the atmosphere by saying the backstop was 'very much a default and would only apply should it prove necessary'.

Barwell gives a flavour of the reaction on the British side.

> The EU had translated the Northern Ireland section of the joint report into a legally operative backstop that essentially kept Northern Ireland in the customs union and parts of the single market. It would create a border in our country, breaking up the UK single market, and it was contrary to the spirit of the Good Friday Agreement, an east–west border was just as offensive to unionists as a north–south one was to nationalists. So we found ourselves facing two challenges: what kind of future relationship did we want and what was our counter proposal to the backstop?

Rory Montgomery gives a different perspective, suggesting that the legal text was the logical outcome of the whole approach established on the EU side of the autumn of 2017 and accepted by the British.

> It found realization in the Commission's draft protocol of the end of February 2018 which occurred during the Beast from the East, I remember, because we were all basically snowed in. That's when Theresa May said no British government could possibly accept what was being proposed but in a way what was being proposed was nothing that she hadn't effectively agreed to in December 2017. But I think she did not fully understand the consequences of what she was doing.

While the backstop was the main item of contention between the two sides, another issue that was to remain a sore point through the following years was the role of the ECJ. The draft document outlined how disputes over the operation of the Brexit agreement in future years would be settled by a joint committee made up of representatives from both sides, but it proposed that this committee would be able to refer to the ECJ for a binding ruling – and the EU court would have the power to levy a fine or suspend parts of the Brexit treaty.

Barnier insisted that the text was no surprise as it was simply a legally worded assessment of what had been agreed in negotiations to date. He called on the UK to come up with alternatives if it was unhappy. He stressed that the document was a draft and would be circulated among the EU-27 and the European Parliament's Brexit steering group for revision and agreement before being placed on the negotiating table.

A few days later, on 2 March, Theresa May delivered a more considered response in a significant speech in the Mansion House in London. She adopted a conciliatory tone which was clearly designed to lower the temperature. While it fell far short of spelling out the detailed negotiating position desired by the EU, it represented an important step back from the hard-line speech she had delivered at Lancaster House a year earlier in which she promised to leave the single market, the customs union and the jurisdiction of the ECJ.

On the Irish Border issue she vowed not to allow Brexit to set back the peace process in Northern Ireland and to work with the EU to ensure that a hard border on the island of Ireland could be avoided. She committed her government to finding a solution to the dilemma around Britain quitting the EU's single market and customs union in March 2019 without imposing restrictions on the Irish Border.

May insisted that her government had been clear all along that the UK did not want a hard border in Ireland and had ruled out any physical infrastructure or any Border-related checks and controls. However, she added:

> But it is not good enough to say, 'We won't introduce a hard border; if the EU forces Ireland to do it, that's down to them.' We chose to leave; we have a responsibility to help find a solution. But we can't do it on our own. It is for all of us to work together. As Prime Minister of the whole United Kingdom, I am not going to let our departure from the European Union do anything to set back the historic progress that we have made in Northern Ireland – nor will I allow anything that would damage the integrity of our precious Union.

Her remarks were interpreted as a rebuke to hard Brexiteers in her own party, including Jacob Rees-Mogg, who had argued that the Border was a problem for Ireland and the EU to sort out, not Britain.

The thrust of her speech was an acceptance of the case for a softer Brexit than she had argued for up to then. She acknowledged that Britain faced hard choices about its future relationship with the EU and that leaving the single market would affect British business. This was a far cry from her earlier claims that Britain could have exactly the same benefits in trade with the EU after Brexit as it had as a member state. Now she admitted that 'life is going to be different. In certain ways, our access to each other's markets will be less than it is now.'

She also acknowledged that, even after Britain left the jurisdiction of the ECJ, it would still be affected by the court's rulings, not least because the ECJ determined whether agreements the EU had struck were legal under the EU's own law. She said that if Britain entered into a free trade agreement with the EU it would have to make binding commitments to ensure fair competition, possibly by adhering to the EU's rules on competition and state aid.

The Prime Minister emphasised that after Brexit, parliament would be able to decide how far Britain's regulatory regime should diverge from the EU's. But she suggested that regulations for goods were likely to remain the same, partly because most EU regulations are themselves determined by international standards. Even on the free movement of people, May called for discussions on how British and European citizens could continue to live and work in each other's countries. May's softer tone arose from the realisation that before she could start negotiating Britain's future economic relationship with the EU she would have to agree the terms of a transition arrangement after Brexit. Before the EU would agree to that the UK would have to sign off on a legal text embodying the joint report agreed the previous December.

Barwell, who drafted the speech, wrote later (in 2021) that he was proud to have been involved in spelling out hard truths. 'I wish the government had said these things in the summer of 2016 but better late than never – and if some of them seem obvious now, I can tell you that we were conscious of the risk we were taking in saying them so bluntly.'

Varadkar welcomed May's change of tone but expressed concern that she had still not fully recognised the implications of leaving the

EU customs union and single market. He called for more detailed and realistic proposals from the UK, given the time constraints on an agreement with the EU in order to meet the deadline for British withdrawal in March 2019.

Barnier also welcomed May's speech for its clarity in confirming that the UK would leave the single market and the customs union, but privately he noted that her offer amounted to an attempt to cherry pick both. 'Rather than reacting aggressively or negatively we choose to push the Prime Minister to the brink and remind her of the tight corner she has backed herself into.'

While May's speech fell far short of a detailed negotiating position it was an important moment in Britain's internal debate as it indicated that the Prime Minister was inching towards a relatively soft Brexit. She attempted to reassure the Brexiteers in her party by stressing that parliament could choose to put more distance between Britain and the European Union at any time after Brexit. While her cabinet had agreed to the speech, the faultlines in the Conservative Party were becoming ever more obvious. To them the Irish backstop was an affront on all levels. For a start it gave the Irish government a power the Brexiteers had never remotely contemplated during the referendum campaign. To add insult to injury they regarded the strong and unexpected EU commitment to the Irish case as an attempt to use the issue as leverage for the softest possible Brexit.

That EU commitment was in evidence the following week on 8 March when Donald Tusk came to Dublin to update Varadkar on the latest developments. Asked about suggestions from the UK that the future trade relationship could be dealt with in advance of agreement on how to avoid a hard border, he said that while the EU must respect the UK position it also expected the UK to propose a specific and realistic solution to the problem.

'As long as the UK doesn't present such a solution, it is very difficult to imagine substantive progress in the Brexit negotiations If in London, someone assumes that the negotiations will deal with other issues, forst, before moving on to the Irish issue, my response would be Ireland first.' c

At this stage Barnier met the two biggest Northern Ireland parties and got an inkling of how difficult it would be to find a solution acceptable to both. The Sinn Féin delegation comprised party leader Mary Lou McDonald, Northern First Minister Michelle O'Neill and party MEP Martina Anderson. They welcomed the draft treaty and the proposal to include Northern Ireland in the customs union, but they wanted the EU to go further and declare 'special status' for the region. They had folders with 'Special Status' written on the covers in big letters for the benefit of photographers. Barnier made it clear he was not going down that road but at their subsequent press conference the Sinn Féin leaders announced that 'special status' for the North had been discussed. 'When it comes to the Irish question, it's difficult to stick to the facts alone!' Barnier noted in his diary.

His meeting with the DUP was much more difficult. The delegation was headed by party leader Arlene Foster and included MEP Diane Dodds, and her husband, Nigel, deputy leader and MP. 'Strangely it is not the DUP leader who speaks up but Diane Dodds. It is not easy to know where power lies in the party,' noted Barnier. He said that on several occasions he and Weyand tried to make them focus on facts and truth but instead they claimed that 'we are puppets of the Dublin government which they hate and we want to create a border between Northern Ireland and the rest of the United Kingdom so that there isn't one across the middle of the island.' After a tense forty minutes Barnier got Dodds to agree that there was already practical regulatory alignment between the North and the rest of Ireland in agriculture, animal disease prevention, and controls at ports and airports for products coming from Britain. 'It is the UK's decision to leave the single market that has created the problem. Help us to find concrete solutions to this problem,' urged Barnier, but he was wasting his breath.

The following week, in the run-up to the March European Council meeting, Barnier briefed the ambassadors of the twenty-seven EU states. He told them that May needed to conclude an agreement on the transition period in order to reassure British business and that represented 'a window of opportunity' to make progress on some of the major issues. 'However, not everything will be settled since there will remain points of real divergence on the governance of this agreement, on the role of the EU Court of Justice and especially on Ireland and Northern Ireland.'

Declan Kelleher told the meeting that the withdrawal treaty would have to provide concrete and operational solutions to avoid a hard border in Ireland and he emphasised that the British needed to understand this. Barnier said that British attempts at cherry picking would have to be resisted. He quoted Luxembourg Prime Minister Xavier Bettel, who had said a few days earlier: 'Before, they were in and had many opt-outs. Now they want to be out with many opt-ins.'

On St Patrick's Day Barnier was warmly welcomed at the official Irish reception in Brussels. He found the occasion moving and it prompted him to reflect in his diary: 'I have a great fondness for Ireland and the Irish people. The French have always had a special affection for the country.' He remembered de Gaulle's last visit abroad when he went to Ireland for a long stay after he resigned as President in 1969.

It was back to serious business at the European Council on 23 March when he joined the twenty-seven heads of government to report progress on the negotiations. He told the leaders that they appeared to be on the road to an orderly rather than a disorderly British withdrawal, but he warned that there were two points of serious divergence which should not be underestimated. One was the opposition of the Conservative Party base to any role for the ECJ in the governance of the Withdrawal Agreement; the other was the Irish question. He pointed out that the unity of the EU-27 had forced May to enter discussions on the basis of the Irish protocol, even though just a few weeks earlier she had said that no British prime minister could possibly accept it.

At the meeting President Macron and Dutch Prime Minister Mark Rutte took the floor to express their solidarity with Leo Varadkar and their support for the Irish position. They were followed by fifteen more heads of government expressing the same view and backing the work of Barnier and his team. Rutte's support was very important for the Irish government as there had an assumption in London that the Dutch would be an ally of the UK in the Brexit talks. Rutte had visited Dublin before Christmas 2017 to show his solidarity, and the country's energetic ambassador in Dublin, Peter Kok, co-ordinated a common approach from other leading EU ambassadors in Ireland.

In early 2018 the second biggest ship in the Dutch navy, the 16,500-tonne *Johan de Witt*, visited Dublin. In a speech at a reception on board Kok declared humorously, 'The Netherlands has promised its full support to Ireland in the Brexit talks. And here we are with a warship!'

In the run-up to the European Council meeting in March the British cabinet met to try to agree a united position on the legal text for the financial settlement, citizens' rights and the implementation period in an attempt to influence the EU guidelines for negotiations on the future relationship. Davis made a strong argument as to why an implementation period was necessary but Johnson insisted that the UK would be a vassal state as long as they were in it.

The outcome of the Council meeting was much as the British had expected, although May was disappointed that it was nowhere near her favoured option – a bespoke model somewhere between the single market/customs union and a standard free trade agreement. 'If we wanted to shift them we needed to present a compelling alternative vision for our future relationship,' noted Barwell. The problem for the British was that ministers could not agree on what kind of future relationship they wanted. Johnson, in typical fashion, declared, 'the Northern Ireland issue is a gnat'.

The stalemate meant that the British were unable to come up with a counter-proposal to the EU on the backstop. 'The only viable alternative was to propose the whole of the UK being in a customs union with the EU in the backstop. This was far from ideal, it was better than a border within our own country, but the (cabinet) committee couldn't agree on that either. I was in despair. We had now used up thirteen of the twenty-four months of the Article 50 period and we couldn't agree on what kind of customs arrangement we wanted,' wrote Barwell.

As the British struggled to agree what they wanted, the EU held to its clear negotiating strategy. Barnier visited Ireland at the end of April and in Dublin consulted with Sabine Weyand and Nina Obermaier, 'the members of my team who with great tenacity have led the difficult discussions with the British on the Irish question while maintaining a daily privileged link with the Irish government'.

Barnier had hoped to fulfil an old dream and retrace the footsteps of his hero, Charles de Gaulle, who came to Kerry the day after he resigned as French President in 1969, but he didn't have time to do it on that occasion. Instead he met Varadkar and Coveney at the Dundalk Institute for Technology, where he addressed a meeting of the All-Ireland Civic Dialogue. In his speech he emphasised that without an Irish border backstop there would be no Withdrawal Agreement. 'The backstop is not about moving British red lines, it is a consequence of those red lines,' he noted in his diary. He went on with a succinct outline of the need for a backstop. 'Since we do not want a physical border on the island of Ireland and since the UK has agreed to respect Ireland's position in the single market, goods entering Northern Ireland which may end up in France, Belgium or Poland must comply with the rules of the single market and the EU customs code.'

After his speech in Dundalk, Barnier travelled to Northern Ireland, where he met a number of community, business and political leaders. He found there was a broad understanding of the EU position, apart from within the DUP. 'The tragedy is that the DUP, which represents just over 30 per cent of the electorate in Northern Ireland, is holding to ransom not just all the other players but the whole of British political life, just because its ten MPs provide Theresa May with the votes needed for her majority in the House of Commons.'

This assessment was only half the story. At this stage a number of British cabinet ministers, and Johnson in particular, had a deep-seated objection to the backstop, while the Brexiteers on the Conservative back benches were equally adamant that it was unacceptable. While May had come to accept the reality that some form of backstop would have to be put in place, she had to first convince her cabinet that it was necessary and then try to convince her party to support it.

Throughout June 2018, May and her cabinet wrestled with devising a counter-proposal to the EU on the backstop and agreeing a White Paper that would outline the British approach to the future relationship. What May came up with was a proposal that the whole of the UK should remain in the EU customs union and aligned to single market regulations for a limited period. A four-page document published on 7 June suggested that the arrangement would last for just a year after the transition period that would follow Brexit. 'The UK is clear that the temporary customs arrangement, should it be needed, should be time limited, and that it will be only in place until the future customs arrangement can be introduced,' said the document. In March both sides had agreed that the backstop should apply 'unless and until another solution is found' to avoid a hard border in Ireland, and May claimed the new proposal was consistent with that commitment.

The planned publication of the document on 7 June was delayed for 24 hours by a dispute between the Prime Minister and her Brexit Secretary, David Davis, who insisted that it should specify the date on which the backstop would end. May held separate meetings with Davis and two other Brexiteer ministers, Foreign Secretary Boris Johnson and International Trade Secretary Liam Fox to try to persuade them to agree to her plan.

Gavin Barwell recalled those fraught meetings between May and her senior ministers. The plan had been to publish the document a day earlier but it was more extensive than Davis had realised and he threatened to resign. 'The conversation with Boris was probably the worst meeting of her premiership,' recalled Barwell. 'He was so rude that I came close to interrupting him and asking him to leave. He said we'd made a mistake in signing up to the joint report. Why had we agreed to all this mumbo jumbo about Northern Ireland?'

Davis was more frustrated than angry that the proposal included a commitment to continued alignment on regulation as well as customs, which represented a change to the plan he had signed up to. 'He wanted to stick with what we had originally agreed but the Prime Minister was clear from a recent conversation with Leo Varadkar that publishing a counter-proposal that only dealt with customs and not regulation would make us look ridiculous. She was only prepared to make a small drafting change. To my surprise David backed down.'

That evening Olly Robbins flew to Brussels to have dinner with Barnier. He outlined May's struggles to develop a coherent British position in the face of conflicting advice from her ministers. 'Listening to Olly Robbins, I get a clear sense of both Theresa May's tenacity and the difficulties in which she finds herself,' Barnier confided in his diary. 'For her this is not really a negotiation with the European Union but a far more intense negotiation, on an almost hourly basis, with her own ministers and her own majority. And all the while the clock is ticking.'

The following day Barnier gave a negative response to the British proposal, telling journalists that the backstop being proposed by the EU was 'devised for the specific situation of Northern Ireland'. He went on to say, 'Our backstop cannot apply to the whole UK.' He also insisted that the backstop could not be a temporary, time-limited option. However, the Irish reaction was more positive; Coveney described the

British backstop proposal as a step forward as it addressed two key issues, customs and regulatory alignment.

That full proposal in the shape of a British government White Paper had been expected in time for the European Council at the end of June but it became clear that the deadline would not be met. Varadkar expressed disappointment at the delay. 'So, two years after the referendum, less than a year from Brexit, we still don't know how they see that new relationship and that is a real problem,' he said.

On 8 June Varadkar made an attempt to reach out to unionists by visiting the Orange Order headquarters in Belfast, the first time a leader from the Republic had ever done so. He was welcomed by the Grand Master Edward Stevenson and, according to the *Belfast Telegraph*, there was even some applause from onlookers. The visit had been arranged after contacts between Varadkar's Northern adviser Jim D'Arcy and the secretary of the Order, Reverend Mervyn Gibson. The Taoiseach also visited Ian Paisley's widow, Eileen, during his trip to the North.

The British were still working on their detailed proposal when the European Council met on 28 June. Barnier addressed the twenty-seven leaders, telling them that Ireland remained 'the most difficult and explosive issue'. He said that in the absence of a customs union Political Declaration between the EU and the UK an offer had been made to integrate Northern Ireland into the EU customs territory, which was an exceptional departure from the principles that underpinned the Union. 'This is not enough to avoid controls on goods, though. That would require regulatory alignment in Northern Ireland with our rules and standards for goods and agricultural products and the introduction of technical controls to monitor this alignment.'

Barnier went on to tell the EU leaders that in order to mollify the DUP and her Tory critics, May would argue in a White Paper for a common UK-wide solution and seek access to the single market for goods. 'This strategy would isolate the Irish issue in the negotiations and ultimately instrumentalise it for the benefit of the entire UK,' he warned. 'This of course would be the à la carte single market we do not want and would amount to cherry picking on a grand scale. But above all the British want to postpone any solution on Ireland until discussions on the future relationship begin. For us the risk is clear: the entire future negotiation could end up being a hostage to the Irish question.' After Barnier's presentation several EU leaders expressed both solidarity with Ireland and concern about a no-deal outcome.

Speaking to the media, Mark Rutte said: 'I believe the first, second, third priority now is to solve this issue of the Irish Border. When that is solved then some of the other issues will be easier to discuss.' Juncker publicly reiterated the point Barnier had made at the Council meeting. 'I wouldn't like us to be in a situation where the last remaining problem would be the Irish one. I don't like that.'

At this stage May had decided to bring matters to a head with her ministers by organising an 'away day' for the cabinet at the Prime Minister's official country residence at Chequers in early July. In the meantime she asked Olly Robbins and his team to analyse four options: a no-deal Brexit; a Canada-style free trade agreement; the bespoke model May herself favoured; and full membership of the single market and customs union. In the following weeks Robbins and his team had a number of meetings with May to define what exactly she wanted to propose.

The core of her plan was a free trade area for goods between the UK and the EU with no customs or regulatory checks at the UK–EU border. The idea was that this would solve the Irish border issue and allow the UK to have an independent trading policy. In return for the benefit of having frictionless trade with the EU, the May proposal involved four key commitments. The first was ongoing harmonisation with EU rules on a range of goods and agricultural products, which would remove the need for regulatory checks at the UK-EU border. The second was a deal on customs to remove the need for customs checks at the border. The third was harmonisation of rules on state aid rules and environmental standards. The last was accepting a role for the ECJ as the ultimate arbiter in dispute resolution.

May faced two massive obstacles. The first was getting her cabinet to agree on a proposal that represented a significant climb-down from the position she had held when Article 50 had been triggered more than a year earlier. The second, and even bigger, obstacle was persuading the EU to agree to something that had the potential to undermine its very existence.

9

The Rocky Road to Salzburg

'We have wrapped a suicide vest around the British constitution – and handed the detonator to Michel Barnier.'

Boris Johnson, 9 September 2018

* * *

The British cabinet travelled to the Prime Minister's country residence at Chequers on 6 July for a day-long meeting designed to get May's ministers to come together once and for all to back her Brexit strategy. Her plan essentially involved full regulatory alignment with Europe for goods and agricultural products, with Britain and the EU being treated as a single customs territory. On the morning of the meeting the media quoted a government source as saying that any minister who 'can't face making the right decision for the country' would have to immediately forfeit their official car and get a taxi to bring them back the sixty-four kilometres to central London. To prevent leaks ministers were instructed to leave their mobile phones outside the door of the meeting room.

'As I made my way to Chequers I had no idea how the day would pan out,' recalled Barwell. 'It could be the breakthrough moment when the government finally settled on what it wanted or it could lead to the end of Theresa's premiership.' A clear majority of the cabinet favoured May's plan for a frictionless trade arrangement with the EU, but a powerful minority, including David Davis and Boris Johnson, were deeply unhappy with it.

At a briefing by officials before the cabinet meeting began Johnson was in fighting form, delivering a stream of negative comments on the plan. He suggested that 'the coffin lid has pinged off' the earlier hybrid plan favoured by May and that 'a certain amount of turd-polishing has gone on.' Liz Truss asked if there was a Plan B but given that they had not yet agreed on Plan A, it appeared to be an idle question.

When the formal cabinet meeting began, Deputy Prime Minister and May loyalist David Lidington spoke first. He backed the plan because frictionless trade with the EU was good for the economy and it also addressed the Northern Ireland issue, which was crucial for the future of the United Kingdom. May then called on Davis to speak, even though she expected him to oppose the plan. He did so, but in a respectful and nuanced fashion, acknowledging that there was a complex balance of judgements to be made about what was feasible in the negotiations with the EU, about the parliamentary arithmetic and about public opinion. He feared that the UK would be pushed into further concessions.

Johnson took a more subdued line than he had at the pre-cabinet discussions but said he was sad that the UK would be locked into the EU regulatory framework. Other ministers then pitched in, taking predictable positions for and against. An exception was Michael Gove, and his contribution was regarded as the decisive one, give his prominence in the Leave campaign. He said the government needed to acknowledge that it had shifted its position and, while he didn't feel joyous about it, he understood the reasons for it and supported it. Liam Fox also fell in line, saying the plan was at the limit of being able to be reconciled with the government's promises.

When other ministers had made their contributions May summed up. She said there was a clear majority for the plan and she agreed some minor changes to reflect the mood of the meeting. She did acknowledge that it had taken a long time to get to this point but now that the cabinet had an agreed plan, collective responsibility would apply and ministers should speak with one voice to support it. After the meeting May invited the ministers to stay for dinner and they settled down for an enjoyable evening, toasting each other and agreeing to write joint op-eds promoting the compromise. It seemed that frustration had been replaced by euphoria.

Barwell, on whose memoir the foregoing account is based, was delighted with the outcome but he remained nervous because of a brief conversation with a visibly deflated Davis who had expected more support for his position. Barwell also had a serious reservation about the outcome. 'There was one thing that was clear from this mammoth meeting, but it was left unsaid. Some ministers said that if the EU rejected the Chequers proposals they wanted to go back to a more distant model, while others said they would then support membership of the single market and customs union. It was clear that if Plan A didn't work, the May government would never be able to agree Plan B.'

Observing the events of the day from Brussels, Barnier called it 'The Battle of Chequers'. He noted in his diary that it was a battle on two fronts. 'The first one is the war Theresa May is waging against some of her ministers ... The second battle, of course, is the one on the horizon with the European Union.' He observed that, cornered by her hardliners, May was trying to preserve her red lines while asking Europe to change its rules and accept an à la carte single market for goods and a customs union in which the UK would enjoy the benefits while retaining the freedom to do its own trade deals.

In spite of his negative private assessment Barnier issued a restrained tweet saying the discussion at Chequers about the future relationship was welcome but he awaited the White Paper with interest to see if its proposals were operable and realistic in the light of the European Council's guidelines.

The government in Dublin welcomed the Chequers agreement and said that it would be considered by EU ministers at a meeting in Brussels on 20 July. However, the government statement emphasised the importance of the backstop. 'While our preference is still for an overall EU–UK relationship which would resolve all issues, it remains essential that a backstop is agreed which provides certainty that in any circumstances, and, no matter what the outcome of the negotiations on the EU–UK future relationship, a hard border will be avoided,' it said, calling for the negotiations to be intensified. 'Time is short.'

The difficulties facing May in selling the outcome to her own party were illustrated by an analysis produced for the backbench Brexiteer

European Research Group (ERG). The main spokesman for this hard-line caucus of over a hundred Tory MPs was Jacob Rees-Mogg, whose polite, fogeyish mannerisms – coating a bitterly anti-EU message – had made him something of a media celebrity. 'These proposals ... lead directly to a worst-of-all-worlds, "black hole" Brexit where the UK is stuck permanently as a vassal state in the EU's legal and regulatory tar pit, still has to obey EU laws and ECJ rulings across vast areas, cannot develop an effective international trade policy or adapt our economy to take advantage of the freedom of Brexit, and has lost its vote and treaty veto rights as an EU member state,' he said.

On the day after the Chequers meeting May phoned Varadkar to brief him on the outcome. The Taoiseach told her he welcomed the fact that the UK government had reached a position where it would put forward detailed proposals for the future EU–UK relationship post-Brexit. He added that he was looking forward to seeing greater detail on those proposals in the period ahead and hoped they would be a helpful input to the negotiation process. Varadkar noted that time was running out and the government would engage constructively with the Barnier Task Force and the other EU member states in the weeks ahead. He also made clear that the government was open to proposals that met the Irish aims of avoiding a hard border and maintaining free trade with the UK, while respecting the EU single market and customs union. The two leaders agreed that they and their officials would maintain close contact.

Simon Coveney also welcomed the fact that the UK government was finalising specific proposals for the future EU–UK relationship.

> Ireland's position is that we want to see the closest possible relation-ship between the EU and the UK. On the backstop for the border, our position remains clear. While our preference is still for an overall EU–UK relationship which would resolve all issues, it remains essen-tial that a backstop is agreed which provides certainty that in any circumstances, and no matter what the outcome of the negotiations on the EU–UK future relationship, a hard border will be avoided.

Before their respective bosses spoke, Barwell called Brian Murphy, his counterpart in Dublin, to brief him on what had been agreed at Chequers.

Murphy gave the outcome a cautious welcome. He said that the Irish government would study the White Paper and listen to whether ministers stuck to the Prime Minister's line over the coming days; but he also remarked that in the past when the Prime Minister tried to move things forward, others in her own party had pushed back.

Murphy's assessment proved spot on. The following day David Davis resigned from the cabinet. He rang May to say he had thought long and hard and had come to the conclusion that he couldn't live with the policy endorsed at Chequers. In his resignation letter he acknowledged 'it is possible that you are right and I am wrong'. His resignation was followed by that of Steve Baker, who went on to become a leading light in the ERG, but the big news was the resignation of the biggest beast from the Leave campaign, Boris Johnson. The Foreign Secretary's departure was a huge blow to May and her government as he became the focus of the opposition to the Prime Minister within the Conservative Party and he commanded enormous media attention. 'At a time when we should have been straining every sinew to sell the proposals to the EU we were instead engaged in a desperate effort to sell them to the Conservative Party,' noted Barwell.

Barnier was in New York when Johnson and Davis resigned. He noted in his diary that throughout the one and a half years of the Brexit negotiations to date he had not once met the British Foreign Secretary. 'Boris Johnson has treated this negotiation from a strictly domestic point of view and only according to the logic of the Battle of Brexit which he himself led.'

The Irish response to the cabinet resignations was restrained. Coveney said the focus of the government in Dublin was on the direction of policy in the UK and he welcomed the fact that May had repositioned her government's approach. He said this was a case of the Prime Minister 'showing her authority and I think many people have been impressed by that and now obviously there's some kick-back which isn't surprising'. He went on to say that what had emerged from the Chequers meeting was 'not the finished article' but it did provide the basis for serious negotiation which needed to proceed at pace to meet an October deadline for reaching an exit deal.

The Irish government welcomed the publication of the detailed British White Paper a few days later. 'We will consult with our EU lead negotiator Michel Barnier and his team and our other EU partners,' it said in a statement, but it reiterated that the Withdrawal Agreement had to contain a legally operable backstop. Coveney said the White Paper signalled a much softer Brexit. 'We always believed it would be necessary for the British Prime Minister to stamp her authority to actually get a clear British negotiating position. She's done that in the last week,' he said.

Barnier took a decidedly more sceptical view of the White Paper. While it was a little more realistic than earlier British proposals, he said, it was still unacceptable and represented a generalised attempt to cherry pick the benefits of the EU to give the UK a clear competitive advantage in a range of areas.

The challenge facing May at this stage was summed up by her chief of staff who wrote later that if the EU had welcomed the Chequers plan it would have been easier to convince MPs who wanted a close relationship that the government was on the right track. Had the Conservative Party closed ranks behind her it would have been easier to persuade the EU to compromise. 'Trying to do both at the same time was almost impossible.'

During the summer of 2018 May went on a campaign to try and persuade EU leaders to take her plan seriously. The Danish Prime Minister Lars Rasmussen told her he hoped Chequers would be a turning point, but it was up to Barnier to make the call. When she asked him to try to persuade Barnier of its merits, Rasmussen told her that Denmark would be supportive, but she needed to be realistic. The EU-27 had to stick together.

A meeting with President Macron at his official summer residence in August was cordial, but he asked detailed questions about the alternative to the Irish backstop, the proposed customs arrangements and what it would mean for the UK's ability to do trade deals. On the backstop she asked him how he would feel if goods had to be checked between Corsica and mainland France. He replied that he could see the desirability of finding a solution that preserved the integrity of the UK as well as the single market and the invisible border on the island of Ireland.

Back in the UK the pressure on May was unrelenting. Boris Johnson wrote a comment piece for the *Mail on Sunday* in which he described the

Chequers plan as a humiliation for Britain comparable to a seven-stone weakling being comically bent out of shape by a five-hundred-pound gorilla. 'And the reason is simple: Northern Ireland, and the insanity of the so-called backstop. We have opened ourselves to perpetual political blackmail. We have wrapped a suicide vest around the British constitution – and handed the detonator to Michel Barnier. We have given him a jemmy with which Brussels can choose – at any time – to crack apart the union between Great Britain and Northern Ireland.'

Simon Coveney was one of many Irish and British politicians who criticised Johnson's comments. 'I think they are ill judged and will offend a lot of people,' he said. But, of course, offending those who disagreed with his views was precisely what Johnson was aiming to do.

May continued her campaign to get EU leaders to understand the British position. Merkel told her she understood why Barnier was taking a tough line but the Prime Minister took some comfort from the Chancellor's comment that the issue could not be left to Barnier alone. Juncker delivered a state of the union address to the European Parliament on 12 September that welcomed the Chequers commitment to a free trade area between the EU and the UK but also contained a warning. 'If you leave the Union, you are no longer part of our single market and certainly not only in the parts of it you chose.'

Juncker insisted that it was Brexit, not the EU, that was creating the border challenge in Ireland. 'The European Commission, this parliament and all other twenty-six member states will always show loyalty and solidarity with Ireland when it comes to the Irish Border. This is why we want to find a creative solution that prevents a hard border in Northern Ireland. But we will equally be very outspoken should the British government walk away from its responsibilities under the Good Friday Agreement.'

On 18 September Barwell and Olly Robbins flew to Dublin to have dinner with their Irish counterparts Brian Murphy and John Callinan. 'Though the company was good the message was less encouraging,' recalled Barwell. 'Chequers might work for Ireland but we shouldn't expect them to speak up for it.'

Murphy later recalled that there were some points in the process where the team around May misjudged the situation. 'They would say to us, "You have an important role to play at this particular summit and it would be very helpful of the Taoiseach could pave the way for a breakthrough." The problem was that their own behaviour made that impossible.'

This was never more apparent than at a special European Council meeting in Salzburg in late September which cruelly exposed the gulf in understanding between the British and EU positions. In the run-up to the meeting the British media built it up as a critical moment in which May would throw down the gauntlet to the twenty-seven EU leaders demanding that they support the Chequers plan as the basis for a deal. On the morning of the meeting an opinion piece by May outlining the British position was placed in leading newspapers in most of the EU states, including the influential German daily Die Welt. Many of the EU leaders were irritated by what they regarded as an attempt to go over the heads of the Barnier team; but what they found really flabbergasting was that when May addressed them after the traditional leaders' dinner shortly before midnight she did little more than read the article out loud. She presented the Chequers plan not as a first step towards a deal but as a take it or leave it offer. Specifically she insisted that a border in the Irish Sea was simply not acceptable. The other leaders were taken aback at May's presentation and the absence of any new proposals, but they held their fire for the moment.

When Varadkar met May after breakfast the following morning he told her that the UK needed to put detailed proposals on the backstop on the table He warned that time was short and they needed to get down to discussions on a legal text. The Taoiseach told May his objective remained the same: to achieve a legally operable and robust backstop within the Withdrawal Agreement, that ensured no hard border on the island of Ireland. She said that she did not believe it would be possible to come up with a solution in time for the October deadline.

Afterwards Irish sources described the meeting as useful. The British side said it had been 'relatively warm' as well as 'frank'. However, as the day unfolded and the European Council got down to business it became clear that the reality was very different. 'The dawning truth later was that, in a premiership littered with missteps, May had made one of her worst errors of judgment as the two leaders met in a private room in Salzburg's Mozarteum University,' was the verdict of the *Guardian* newspaper report under the headline 'Macron Puts the Boot in After

May's Breakfast Blunder'. According to the paper's correspondent Daniel Boffey:

> For weeks the working assumption in Brussels had been that, on the Irish issue at least, a major step forward would be made by the next leaders' summit in October. But the Prime Minister dropped a bombshell over coffee with Varadkar. She did not believe it would be possible for her government and Brussels to come to a solution by then. Six months after promising to come up with a fix that would avoid a hard Irish Border in all possible circumstances, she appeared to be stalling for time again.

After her breakfast with Varadkar, May attended the European Council and spoke to some of the leaders, including Angela Merkel, before leaving to let the twenty-seven get down to business and discuss the Chequers proposal. The session began over lunch with Barnier's outline of why border checks between Britain and Northern Ireland were essential to preserve the integrity of the single market. He also gave an uncompromising assessment of how the Chequers plan would give the UK a serious competitive advantage over the EU.

Merkel was next to speak and as usual she summed up the mood around the table. 'This negotiation will largely determine the future of our relationship with the United Kingdom. Some of us are more lenient, others firmer. We need to be united, cordial and clear. On Ireland I will follow what Leo says.' She added that on the future relationship there were some points of agreement but the internal market could not be compromised.

After her contribution others referred to the need for unity and solidarity. 'I am struck by the justified confidence all of them have in their colleague, the Irish Prime Minister Leo Varadkar,' noted Barnier. 'On Ireland it is up to Leo to give the green light,' was the consensus.

The most hard-line position was taken by French President Emmanuel Macron, who went public after the meeting to dismiss the British plan and denounce the Tory Brexiteers. 'Those who told us that they could easily do without Europe, that everything would go well, that it is easy and would gain them a lot of money are liars,' he proclaimed at his post-Council press conference.

European Council President Donald Tusk was equally firm. 'Everybody shared the view that while there are positive elements in the Chequers proposal, the suggested framework for economic co-operation will not work, not least because it risks undermining the single market.' Watching him on television in the British delegation room May's team were dumbstruck – a brief conversation between him and the Prime Minister had led them to expect that he would strike a more positive note. 'This was political dynamite,' recalled Barwell, 'and it was grossly discourteous of him not to tell the Prime Minister what he was going to say.' May recast her post-summit comments in the light of Tusk's remarks and walked into the British press conference 'bristling with anger'. Tusk added petrol to the flames by posting a photograph on Instagram of him serving May a slice of cake with the caption: 'A piece of cake perhaps? Sorry no cherries.'

Brian Murphy recalled:

Salzburg was one of the points where things went very badly wrong, where the British misjudged it. Before the meeting started EU leaders were clearly sending out a vibe suggesting they were not very happy with May's opinion piece but she then read out the whole thing to them. Afterwards Tusk tweeted the cake picture with the message you can have the cake but not the cherries. She was furious about it – she went and berated him – but I think it was simply water off a duck's back as far as he was concerned.

A senior official remarked:

May felt she was ambushed and had been kicked around but how she thought it was clever to have an op-ed in the leading EU newspapers on the day of the meeting is strange. The British might have thought they were being reasonable and constructive but the way it was written with an eye to the home audience made it slippery, at best, and at worst, offensive.

And then when she got into the room for what was meant to be her big moment she basically read the article and failed to connect with any of them. It was an absolute disaster. The idea that she would present her case by reading a script was all wrong. Here she was reading from a script and it just looked as if she was reading what had been written for her. It is not the way leaders of important countries do business. And yet the British were incredulous at what had happened and couldn't understand why they came away looking like the bad guys as far as the rest of the EU was concerned.

A flavour of that mood can be found in the assessment of British Cabinet Secretary Jeremy Heywood.

It's not been such a good day for the Prime Minister. She has been beaten up in Europe ... Donald Tusk has been unbelievably rude but the fundamental problem is that the EU thinks that, if we implement the new customs partnership, we won't be rigorous in applying the tariffs on our borders. And now we only have three weeks left to get all this sorted or risk a no-deal Brexit.

Heywood was seriously ill with cancer at the time and died tragically young just a few weeks later. He had worked right to the end to serve his country's best interests.

The British media presented the entire Salzburg summit as a humiliation for the Prime Minister. The tabloid press went wild. The *Sun* caricatured Tusk and Macron as gangsters, describing them in the front page headline as 'EU Dirty Rats', with the subheading, 'Euro Mobsters Ambush May'. Other British newspapers used strong but less emotive terms – 'fury', 'humiliation', 'disaster' – to describe the rejection of May's Chequers plan. The *Guardian* put it more calmly; May was fighting to save her Chequers Brexit plan and with it her authority as Prime Minister 'after she was ambushed' at the end of the Salzburg summit when EU leaders unexpectedly declared that her proposals would not work.

May's response was to come out fighting. In a statement on the doorstep of 10 Downing Street the following day she suggested that she had been treated with a lack of respect by the EU leaders. She acknowledged that while some progress had been made there were two big issues on which the UK and the EU were still far apart. One of those issues was the backstop, and she repeated the line she had taken at the summit.

Creating any form of customs border between Northern Ireland and the rest of the UK would not respect that Northern Ireland is an integral part of the United Kingdom, in line with the principle of consent as set out clearly in the Belfast/Good Friday Agreement. It is something I will never agree to – indeed in my judgement it is something no British Prime Minister would ever agree to.

Ironically, her nemesis, the arch-Brexiteer Boris Johnson, was to prove her wrong on that score.

May also took on Tusk directly saying he had not shown how the British proposals would undermine the single market. 'He didn't explain how or make any counter-proposals, so we are at an impasse. Throughout this process I have treated the EU with nothing but respect. The UK expects the same.'

Barnier professed himself perplexed at May's reaction and denied that she had been treated with a lack of respect. He felt that while Macron had been 'rather blunt', the French President's hostile comments were mainly directed at Boris Johnson and Nigel Farage. 'All of this reinforces my resolve to avoid any form of aggression, emotion or passion, to shove my fists in my pockets after any provocation from the British and to continue to stick to the facts, the figures and the legal basis if we want to succeed.'

Gavin Barwell felt that Conservative MPs and the Tory press had reacted positively to May's fighting response. 'Although it hadn't felt like it at the time Donald Tusk had done the Prime Minister a favour. She hadn't wanted a row, that wasn't her style, but it was how the Conservative Party liked to see its leaders negotiate with Europe. And we received a number of messages of support from national capitals appalled at how the Prime Minister had been treated.'

There was no great surprise on the Irish side about the general rejection of May's plan. Varadkar put his views on the record, suggesting that the outrage in the UK was the result of misleading media speculation in Britain for the previous few weeks that had led to false expectations about the outcome. 'There was a sense created in the UK press that there was division around the EU table, among the EU-27. There is not. The EU is totally united, not just united behind Ireland but also united behind the single market. Perhaps the sense was created that Prime Minister

May would come away with something more positive than occurred. I don't think anyone in the EU or Ireland is to blame for that.'

One of Varadkar's team put it more bluntly. 'She came in to the dinner in Salzburg, pissed them all off and walked away again. What part of that plan was supposed to persuade the EU leaders that they could do business with the British?'

The big question after Salzburg was whether the two sides would ever be able to find any basis on which to compromise.

10

A Done Deal?

'The colours on our flag are white, orange and green in equal measure.
Sometimes I feel that we haven't fully lived up to that.'
Leo Varadkar, after a meeting with leaders of the
Orange Order, 26 November 2018

* * *

The shape of a compromise emerged quickly after the Salzburg debacle when the British shifted ground and pushed for a UK-wide backstop rather than a Northern Ireland-only one. The Irish government was happy to go along with this change of plan and it met the overriding objective of keeping an open border, but the European Commission and many of the member states needed a lot of persuasion.

Theresa May received a morale boost after a confident performance at the Conservative Party conference in early October. In a successful effort to poke fun at her awkward attempt at dancing on a recent visit to Africa, she made her entrance sashaying onto the stage as Abba's 'Dancing Queen' played. It was a marked contrast to the coughing episode that had ruined her speech at the previous year's conference.

She called on Conservatives to unite behind her Brexit plan, warning that divisions within the party could lead to Britain remaining in the European Union, and she rounded on hard-line Brexiteers who rejected compromise. She also criticised the EU for offering what she called two unacceptable options. 'Either a deal that keeps us in the EU in all but name, keeps free movement, keeps vast annual payments and stops us signing trade deals with other countries. Or a deal that carves off Northern Ireland, a part of this country, effectively leaving it in the EU's customs union.'

The speech bought her some time, but there were ominous developments at the conference which were a harbinger of things to come. Boris Johnson got a rousing reception at a fringe event at which he urged May to 'chuck Chequers' while DUP leader Arlene Foster warned that her party's red-line opposition to a border in the Irish Sea was 'blood red'.

By this stage May's new strategy of attempting to break the impasse by proposing a UK-wide backstop was out in the open. While the Irish government was happy enough to go along with it as it would settle the border issue, Barnier and his team were distinctly unhappy. They felt it would allow the UK some of the benefits of the customs union and the single market without many of the obligations, the very cherry picking about which Tusk had made a fuss at Salzburg.

Varadkar visited Brussels on 4 October to meet Barnier and his team. In his diary Barnier described Varadkar as 'a courageous young man' for the way he had campaigned to change the Irish law on abortion. 'We have established a relationship of trust and friendship with his team, especially his diplomatic Sherpa John Callinan,' noted Barnier, but he warned the Taoiseach that the negotiations ahead would be risky and difficult and he should be prepared for failure. 'Of course it is he [Varadkar] who will set the tone on 17 October at the European Council meeting, by approving the agreement, if there is one.'

Despite Barnier's reservations the Commission indicated that it was prepared to move away from the Northern Ireland-only backstop. However, given the difficulty in getting agreement on the nature of the UK-wide backstop in the short time left until the October deadline, the Task Force proposed that the Northern Ireland-only one should remain as the backstop to the new UK-wide backstop.

When May travelled to Brussels on 17 October for another meeting of the European Council she met Varadkar, who told her he was comfortable with the proposed change to the backstop. The atmosphere was more restrained than that at Salzburg but Varadkar stoked up some tension with the British at the dinner by showing the other EU leaders a copy of the previous day's *Irish Times,* which carried a story about the bombing of a customs post at the Irish Border in 1972. Irish officials recall that their British counterparts were furious at the gesture, but Varadkar was unapologetic. He described it as 'a useful prop to demonstrate to all the European leaders the extent to which the concerns about the re-emergence of a hard border and possibility of a return to violence are very real'. Questioned by journalists the following day he said: 'I just wanted to make sure that there was no sense in the room that in any way anyone in the Irish government was exaggerating the real risk of a return to violence in Ireland.'

May took heart from a conversation she had with Merkel in which the Chancellor told her that the difficulties in finding a solution to the Irish Border issue should not be allowed to derail the EU–UK relationship. Merkel said the solution lay in the future relationship; if the UK wanted a close relationship 'the problem of the Irish Border becomes smaller'. The problem was that a sizeable number of May's MPs wanted a very distant relationship, not a close one. Merkel told May: 'I want your success and not your rivals',' but the Prime Minister would have to have been a political Houdini to succeed.

One thing that was clear after the summit was that the October 2018 deadline for the conclusion of the Withdrawal Agreement would not be met. Barnier described the meeting as 'an exercise in futility', but some things had become a little clearer. The British were now aiming for a UK-wide backstop and the EU leaders were inclined to agree, despite their reservations. Barnier told them that the Irish question was the central issue in the negotiations. He warned that the solution being proposed by the British for 'frictionless trade' risked giving UK firms a serious competitive advantage.

Varadkar was happy enough with the new version of the backstop but was concerned to ensure that it was not time-limited. 'It can be temporary by all means but it can't have an expiry date ... unless and until we have an alternative agreement that also assures us that we will have no border on the island of Ireland. This is not just an issue of principle but one of trust.' Some senior British ministers who backed May had precisely the opposite concern; they were prepared to live with a UK-wide backstop but only if there was a clear exit mechanism.

At the end of October the new Brexit Secretary, Dominic Raab, met Simon Coveney for dinner at the Irish embassy in London and tried to persuade him to agree to an exit mechanism from the backstop. Their testy exchange was described by an Irish source as 'a frank ninety-minute discussion'. Coveney rejected Raab's demand that the Irish should agree to an exit mechanism from the backstop and told him that Britain should not mistake Irish patience for a change in position. A British source said 'Raab had got precisely nowhere'.

A few days later the *Daily Telegraph* reported that at the dinner Raab had demanded the right of the UK to pull out of the backstop after just three months. Coveney went public with a tweet saying that a backstop that could be unilaterally ended by the UK would never be agreed to by the Republic or the EU. He elaborated on it to reporters: 'I had dinner with Dominic Raab in London last week ... I made it absolutely crystal clear to him that Ireland and, in my view, the EU could never support a time-limited backstop or a backstop that could be ended unilaterally by the UK alone after any review mechanisms in the future.'

May phoned Varadkar on 5 November to clarify matters. The Taoiseach told her that Ireland would consider a review mechanism for the backstop but this could not involve a unilateral decision to end it. A government statement said he had raised in the conversation the prior commitment that the backstop must apply 'unless and until' alternative arrangements were agreed.

Over the following ten days the EU and UK negotiators inched towards an agreement. On 13 November Olly Robbins and Sabine Weyand agreed on a draft Withdrawal Agreement and referred it back to their respective political leaders. May spoke to cabinet ministers individually and scheduled a full cabinet meeting for the next day to sign off on the 585-page document which contained 185 articles, three protocols and numerous annexes. The Remainers in the cabinet were reasonably happy, but ministers who had campaigned for Brexit were uneasy. Michael Gove told colleagues he needed a drink after reading the documents, but while he foresaw problems getting it through parliament, he would support it as the alternative was a no-deal.

In Brussels the mood was one of joy mingled with relief when Robbins got in touch on 14 November to say the British government had agreed the deal. Sabine Weyand even shed a few tears at the news and Barnier prepared to meet the press to unveil the deal. Raab was supposed to join him at the press conference but failed to turn up as he had decided to resign from the British government in protest at the agreement. Barnier adopted a low-key, sober tone with the media, conscious of the fragile political situation in London. When a British journalist quipped, 'So, champagne,' Barnier replied, 'Certainly not, we're going to drink water and continue with our work.'

In Dublin there was also huge relief that the deal had finally been agreed. Varadkar told the Dáil that the agreement would see the entire UK remaining in the customs union and would include additional measures for Northern Ireland to ensure there was no hard border. 'The backstop does have to be there, it does have to be legally operable, it can't have an expiry date, it can't be possible for one side to withdraw from it unilaterally. It is our intention that the backstop should never have to be invoked and if it is invoked it should be temporary,' he said. He also went out of his way to emphasise that the Irish government respected the territorial integrity of the UK and the principle of consent enshrined in the Good Friday Agreement.

However, DUP leader Arlene Foster denounced the Irish government as being the aggressor in the Brexit talks and said that on a first reading of the agreement she could not support it. The resignation of Raab and Esther McVey from the British cabinet indicated that May was going to have serious difficulties getting the deal through parliament.

At a press conference in Dublin Varadkar described the agreement as 'one of the better days in politics' but he recognised the political problems ahead. 'There is, of course, a bit of a way to go, there is the possibility of this being defeated in Westminster or even the European Parliament but I think we are in a stronger position than we were last December. We have turned a joint report, a political promise, into a legally binding treaty agreed by the UK government.'

As part of his continuing efforts to persuade unionists of the government's good intentions Varadkar invited Orange Order Grand Secretary Reverend Mervyn Gibson to visit Government Buildings in Dublin in late November. The two men posed for photographs and had a meeting which was also intended by European Affairs Minister Helen McEntee. The meeting was an opportunity to discuss support for Protestant schools in the border area as well as the community, sporting and cultural needs of Protestants living in these areas. Jim D'Arcy and Eamon Molloy, the assistant secretary in the Taoiseach's office with responsibility for North/South issues, had been involved in exploring these issues with the Protestant community.

'The colours on our flag are white, orange and green in equal measure. Sometimes I feel that we haven't fully lived up to that,' Varadkar said after the meeting. 'The Good Friday Agreement acknowledges that people in Northern Ireland have the right to be British, Irish or both, and accepted as such. We should acknowledge that there are many people in our state that feel themselves to be both British and Irish. It's something that we should accept too.'

On the Brexit front the European Council on 25 November formally approved the amended Withdrawal Agreement and the Political Declaration on the future relationship between the EU and the UK. 'The atmosphere is solemn,' recorded Barnier. 'Everyone has the feeling that we are living through a historic moment, the moment of a break-up desired by a member state and a divorce that we have tried to deal with as well as possible.' Macron recommended that the same method should be employed for the next stage of the negotiations and Merkel agreed, congratulating Barnier and his team on 'a masterpiece of diplomacy'.

The mood on the British side wasn't nearly as upbeat. Barwell maintained that May had managed to get the EU to agree to a new model between the single market/customs union and a free trade agreement but he accepted that the EU had refused to agree to the British ambition to have zero customs checks. 'As we were driven away from the Commission's headquarters the Prime Minister and I were both relieved that the deal was finally done and anxious about what was to come.'

Varadkar insisted after the summit that the only alternative to the agreement was a no-deal scenario. Echoing other EU leaders, the Taoiseach said that the withdrawal treaty was the only deal on the table. 'So you see that is the core difficulty with people who are arguing that there is a better deal on offer or a better deal can be negotiated. They don't agree among themselves what a better deal could be, they probably wouldn't have a majority in parliament for an alternative deal, and they certainly wouldn't have twenty-eight member states signed up to it.'

'There is no Plan B,' said Dutch Prime Minister Mark Rutte. 'If anyone thinks in the United Kingdom that by voting No something better would come out of it, they are wrong.' The difficulty was that a wide cross-section of MPs in the House of Commons did believe that there was a better alternative to the Withdrawal Agreement, ranging from the ERG who wanted a deal on the UK's terms or none at all, to those in all parties who wanted to remain in the EU.

One worrying straw in the wind was that just as the European Council was meeting in Brussels the DUP was holding its annual conference in Belfast, at which Arlene Foster and Nigel Dodds repeated their opposition to the deal. The star attraction at the DUP conference was not any of the leading party figures but former Foreign Secretary Boris Johnson who wowed the delegates with his usual mixture of buffoonery and a hard-line anti-EU message. 'Junk the backstop' was his theme as he regaled the audience with a speech about the UK's rightful place as one of the main trading nations of the world.

His speech was comical in more ways than one, given what was to happen over the following year. He told the DUP faithful that when he was Mayor of London 'we got those German-made bendy buses off the street'. Instead, he brought back the wonderful red London Routemaster bus, which is manufactured in Northern Ireland with the best of British parts. Wright Bus was a fine example of how Britain could trade with the world. With the right Brexit deal 'we can turbo-charge the areas in which this country already leads Europe, if not the world,' he declared.

On a more serious note, he said that if the UK wanted to agree free trade deals, cut tariffs or vary regulations, it would have to leave Northern Ireland behind as an 'economic semi-colony of the EU'. He said this would mean damaging the fabric of the UK, with regulatory checks and customs controls between Britain and Northern Ireland on top of additional regulatory checks down the Irish Sea in the divorce treaty. 'No British Conservative government could or should sign up to any such arrangement,' he said, to applause from the DUP members.

An interesting aspect of Johnson's appearance at the DUP conference was the role of Christopher Moran, the chair of Co-operation Ireland, who facilitated his trip to Belfast. Johnson kicked off his speech by saying, 'I would like to thank my friend Christopher Moran, for everything he has done for Northern Ireland, and for helping me to secure this invitation.' Later that day Johnson travelled back to London with Moran on the businessman's private aircraft. On the same flight were DUP leader Arlene Foster and Conor Burns, a Tory MP who was Mr Johnson's parliamentary aide when he was Foreign Secretary.

Back in London, the *Sunday Times* front page for 25 November was being finalised: the lead story described how more than a hundred prostitutes were operating out of an apartment block owned by Moran in one of the wealthiest parts of London. The newspaper stressed there was no suggestion that Moran had any involvement with the prostitution but the revelation prompted some negative publicity for aspiring Conservative leader Johnson.

Moran, a property tycoon and Tory donor, had been chair of Co-operation Ireland for fifteen years. Peter Sheridan, the chief executive of the organisation, which promotes peace and reconciliation on the island of Ireland, had facilitated a number of visits from EU politicians and officials on fact-finding missions to the Border region. Moran made no secret of his sympathies with the Tory Brexiteers and was to play a behind the scenes role as a fixer for Johnson on Irish issues after he became Prime Minister.

Johnson's role in encouraging the DUP to reject the Withdrawal Agreement was just one of the strands of the emerging opposition to the deal. The deep-seated hostility of the Brexiteers and the DUP was compounded by the cynical opposition of the Labour Party and the naive belief among a cross-section of pro-Europe MPs that rejecting the deal would lead to a second referendum. Barwell observed that socialist parties around the EU, and the Irish government, were horrified by Labour leader Jeremy Corbyn's attack on the backstop. May's team heard from Irish sources that Labour made no bones about the fact that it was adopting an anti-backstop stance purely for partisan advantage.

'I was frustrated that so many MPs were living in cloud cuckoo land about the choices available but the government had to take some responsibility for that,' wrote Barwell. 'If it had spelt out clearly what the choices were at the outset we might have had a more constructive debate.'

One example of an MP living in cloud cuckoo land was the once and future Minister Priti Patel who reawakened memories of the Irish Famine by proposing that the British government should use the threat of food shortages in Ireland in the event of a no-deal Brexit as leverage to get the backstop abolished. Ireland's EU Commissioner Phil Hogan responded by saying the comments showed how out of touch the MP was given that the UK was a massive food importer with a substantial amount of the food consumed in the country coming from the Republic. 'So if she wants to advocate a policy that brings about starvation of the British people this is a good way of going about it,' he said.

Patel's intervention was one example of many of how extreme political debate in the UK had become and it illustrated just how difficult May was going to find it to get parliamentary approval for the deal. The problems facing the Prime Minister were compounded by parliamentary procedure. She had to get the Commons to approve the deal in a so-called meaningful vote before bringing the Withdrawal Agreement Bill itself through the Commons and ensuring that the large and complex piece of legislation was not amended in any way that would undermine the agreement with the EU.

May and her ministers went on a tour of the UK to try to sell the deal to the public in the hope that they would put pressure on their MPs to back it. Northern Ireland was the one place where the tactic worked. The DUP was so embarrassed by the strong support for the deal from the business community that a DUP delegation came to see May to ask her to stop Northern Secretary Karen Bradley and her team promoting it.

Unfortunately for May, the response in the rest of the UK was not as supportive. While the public didn't appear to have any great problem with the deal, MPs in all parties found reasons to oppose it and it became clear to the Prime Minister that she was in for a serious drubbing in the Commons. So on 10 December, with just twenty-four hours to go she pulled the 'meaningful vote' and announced to derisive jeers in the Commons that she intended to seek further reassurances on the backstop from the EU.

In a phone conversation with Varadkar the previous evening she had pleaded for a softening of the Irish position to allow for some form of time limit to be applied to the backstop. May had already been told by the British Ambassador to Ireland, Robin Barnett, that if Varadkar agreed to a time limit or an exit mechanism, Fianna Fáil would pull the plug on the confidence and supply arrangement that underpinned the government in Dublin. According to Gavin Barwell, Varadkar told May in their phone conversation on 9 December that he could not compromise, even if he wanted to, because politics trumped economics in Ireland as well as the UK. 'There are things worse than recessions. I couldn't as Taoiseach acquiesce in a return to a hard border,' he is quoted as saying.

The following day May set off on a tour of European capitals to see if she could persuade other EU leaders to take a softer line on the backstop ahead of another European Council meeting due at the end of the week. Mark Rutte told her he was willing to come to the UK parliament to tell MPs it was the best deal on offer. His Sherpa, Michael Stibbe, told Olly Robbins that the EU leaders were only likely to offer something if they thought it would make a difference. Angela Merkel was less positive, telling May it would be tough to achieve anything that looked like a re-opening of the Withdrawal Agreement. Donald Tusk was also negative, but Jean-Claude Juncker was more positive, suggesting that something interpretative was possible as long as the Irish were onside.

To highlight her difficulties May had to cut short her tour and return to London to face a motion of no confidence in her leadership from opponents in the Conservative Party. Responding to the news, Barnier summed up the feeling of many foreign observers:

> It is madness to see the extent to which the future of this great country, and our relationship with it, has for three years now been dependent upon the bickering, backstabbing, serial betrayals and thwarted ambitions of a handful of Conservative MPs. Boris Johnson ... will , along with David Cameron and a few others, carry a real burden of responsibility in their country's history.

May opted to face the challenge head-on within 24 hours and won the contest by 200 votes to 117, but the price she paid was a promise to step down before the next general election. She also committed herself to finding a legally binding solution to the backstop that would allow the DUP to support the Brexit deal. 'I have heard what the House of Commons said about the Northern Ireland backstop and, when I go to the European Council tomorrow, I will be seeking legal and political assurances that will assuage the concerns that members of parliament have on that issue,' she told her party.

As May took a breather before heading off to Brussels the next day for the European Council meeting, Varadkar had a serious phone conversation with Juncker to clarify where matters stood. After the call the government issued a statement saying both had agreed that the Withdrawal Agreement 'is a balanced compromise and the best outcome available. While they agreed to work to provide reassurance to the UK, the agreement cannot be reopened or contradicted.'

When May arrived in Brussels for the European Council on 13 December she followed Juncker's advice and met Varadkar before the meeting to try to persuade him of the need for some sort of time limit to the backstop. During the course of an hour-long meeting the Taoiseach expressed a willingness to consider clarifications on the content of the Withdrawal Agreement but refused to consider a time limit on the backstop. He was insistent that the EU needed the guarantee of the backstop without a time limit because British politics was so uncertain. Varadkar also told May she was wasting her time trying to get the DUP onside; they would only be happy if the Irish government was unhappy.

John Callinan was even more frank in a conversation with Olly Robbins. He spelled out that the EU side was concerned that if there was a time limit to the backstop the UK government would try to use the Border issue as leverage in the future relationship negotiations.

When the Council meeting got under way the following day May was given an opportunity to put her concerns to the EU leaders. She told them that if there had been a vote in the Commons the text would have been rejected, adding that the whole debate was crystallising around the backstop. 'I am not asking for new commitments. The backstop remains but we must be able to say that it will never be used or only for a short period of time.' Questioned by other leaders, she repeated the point. 'We need to find a way out or an end date for the backstop. We need to show more than good will, and more than "our best endeavours", to find an alternative to the backstop.'

While she received a polite hearing for her presentation, which lasted almost an hour, several leaders made the point that the Irish Border was their border too, as it was the only land border between the UK and the EU. Later, after May left, Barnier reiterated the need to stick by the agreement already concluded and to be absolutely clear that there could be no time limit on the backstop. A number of leaders responded to his presentation by saying they would not accept any change to the backstop unless Varadkar agreed to it.

At his post-summit press conference the Taoiseach maintained that he and other EU leaders were willing to help by providing clarification about the content of the Withdrawal Agreement, but the backstop would have to remain. 'When it comes to the assurances that Prime Minister May is seeking the EU is very keen to offer explanations, clarifications, assurances, anything that may assist MPs to understand the agreement and, hopefully, to support it. But the backstop is not on the table,' he told journalists. As for a time limit to the backstop, Varadkar was firm. 'If the backstop has an expiry date, if there is a unilateral exit clause, then it's not a backstop ... and that would mean reopening the substance of the Withdrawal Agreement and the EU is unequivocal that's not happening.'

At a joint press conference Juncker and Tusk reiterated their support for the backstop but said they had given May assurances they would seek to agree a future trade deal with Britain by 31 December 2020, so that the backstop would never be triggered. It wasn't much of a concession, but May had no choice but to make the best of it and hope that the Christmas break might take some of the heat out of the political atmosphere in the UK.

11

Chaos in the Commons

'Can technology solve the Irish border problem? Short answer: not in the next few years.'

Sabine Weyand on Twitter, 3 February 2019

* * *

It was an anxious beginning to 2019 for Europe's political leaders as the 29 March deadline for Brexit loomed and the British parliament prepared to vote on the Withdrawal Agreement. It was a particularly nervous time for Taoiseach Leo Varadkar and Prime Minister Theresa May as they faced decisions that would impact on their respective countries for decades to come.

Varadkar had a long phone conversation with Angela Merkel on 3 January to review their strategy on the backstop and see if there was anything they could do to help May win parliamentary approval for the Withdrawal Agreement. 'We agreed that we would stand by the agreement we made with the United Kingdom at the end of last year. We are happy to offer reassurance and guarantees to the United Kingdom but not reassurances and guarantees that contradict or change what was agreed back in November. We also discussed no-deal planning,' Varadkar told journalists after the forty-minute call.

The Taoiseach was relieved that the Chancellor seemed determined to stick by the backstop, despite her desire to help May, but there was some concern on the Irish side about Merkel's focus on no-deal planning. While the Germans were willing to support the Irish on the backstop they were becoming increasingly anxious about how the Irish would protect the single market in the event of a no deal. This was a question the government in Dublin was strenuously avoiding.

The European Commission had been pressing for answers to this question over the previous six months but had got nowhere. What the Irish didn't want to admit was that there would have to be some system of customs checks at or near the Border in the event of a no-deal. The Barnier Task Force was not interested in pursuing the issue as it might undermine its negotiating strategy, but contingency preparations were being made by another division of the Commission.

'We were having quite a different set of conversations with them because every time we went to the meeting the tactic was to try and avoid giving any answers but to try to prize out of them what tolerances there would be in the event of a no-deal for solutions that frankly did not involve putting back the border. They were very, very, difficult conversations and a big part of the strategy was to keep playing for time and avoid giving definitive answers,' said Callinan. In Brussels Declan Kelleher had the job of fending off EU officials and had to come up with increasingly lame excuses to postpone scheduled meetings and evade discussions about Irish contingency planning for a no-deal.

With the EU and Germany now beginning to look seriously at the issue Varadkar began to feel uncomfortable. He had told Theresa May in December 2017 that he didn't want to be remembered as the Taoiseach who agreed to the reintroduction of a border between North and South, but in the event of a no-deal there would be huge pressure on him from the EU to do just that.

The dilemma facing Varadkar at this stage was that while he could count on Germany and other EU states to support him on the backstop, the corollary was that they would expect him to do what was necessary to protect the single market in the event of a no-deal and a customs border of some kind was the only way to do it. That was something the government in Dublin simply did not want to admit.

Minister for Trade Shane Ross let the cat out of the bag at a press conference in Dublin at which he shared the platform with Simon Coveney. Asked a question by a journalist about what would happen in the event of a no-deal Ross breezily conceded that border checks would be necessary. Coveney quickly intervened to say that there were no plans for border checks in any circumstances. To compound the embarrassment in a recording of a private conversation between the pair just as the press conference ended, Coveney was heard chiding Ross: 'Once you start talking about checks anywhere near the Border people will start delving into that, and all of a sudden we'll be the government that reintroduced a physical Border on the island of Ireland.' Ross's typically casual response was 'Yeah, but I didn't know what to say.'

While neither Varadkar nor Coveney was prepared to admit that a customs border of some kind would be required if Ireland was to remain part of the single market there were no illusions in Brussels about what would be required. Looking back a senior EU official put it bluntly. 'The Irish refused to come up with a contingency plan so we had to devise one that involved checks on goods coming across the border from Northern Ireland. If Ireland refused to implement it the only option would have been checks at French ports on all goods coming from the island of Ireland.'

Varadkar may have said that he did not want to be remembered as the Taoiseach who presided over the reintroduction of Border checks, but the alternative would have been to go down in history as the leader who took Ireland out of the single market. Luckily for him that dreadful choice did not arise, but it could still emerge at some point in the future if the UK government reneges on the Brexit deal.

As the Irish struggled to avoid commitments on the Border, the UK was heading inexorably towards a resounding defeat in parliament for the Withdrawal Agreement. The publication of an exchange of letters between May, Juncker and Tusk, which was designed to reassure MPs that the EU had no interest in trapping the UK in the backstop and would proceed to negotiations on the future relationship without delay, had no impact.

When the House of Commons held a 'meaningful vote' on the Withdrawal Agreement on 16 January 2019, May made a last-ditch plea to colleagues to support her, warning them not to break their promise to the British people to deliver Brexit.

This is the most significant vote that any of us will ever be part of in our political careers. After all the debate, all the disagreement, all the division, the time has now come for all of us in this House to make a decision. A decision that will define our country for decades to come. Together we can show the people we serve that their voices have been heard, that their trust was not misplaced.

When the vote was taken at the end of an eight-day debate she suffered a humiliating defeat, losing by 432 votes to 202. The Brexiteer and Remain wings of the Conservative Party joined with the Opposition and the DUP to trounce the government. It was the heaviest parliamentary defeat sustained by any British prime minister in the democratic era and it fatally undermined May's authority.

In Dublin Varadkar was adamant that he would not back down on the backstop.

We have said it from day one that Brexit cannot result in a hard border between Ireland and Northern Ireland. We have made that commitment to the people of Ireland, North and South. And the United Kingdom and the United Kingdom Government has made that commitment to the people of Ireland, North and South, so it needs to be honoured.

He again rejected the notion of a time-limited backstop. 'A guarantee with a time limit is not a guarantee. What we are trying to achieve here is a guarantee that there be no hard border between Ireland and Northern Ireland.' He pointed to the fact that in another vote in the Commons a proposal to accept the Withdrawal Agreement with a time-limited or deleted backstop was defeated, with only twenty-five MPs voting for it. The response of Arlene Foster was to call on May to go back to Brussels and compel the EU to make fundamental changes to the EU–UK Withdrawal Agreement. It was an illustration of just how detached from reality the DUP was, and continued to be, throughout the entire Brexit process.

After her overwhelming Commons defeat May had to deal immediately with an opposition motion of no confidence. She tabled a motion of confidence in her government the following day and survived by a margin of 325 votes to 306. The DUP, whose ten MPs supported May as required by their confidence and supply agreement, boasted afterwards that its backing was the difference between victory and defeat for the Tories.

Winning the vote of confidence gave the Prime Minister some breathing space. She invited the leaders of the other parties to meet her to discuss what could be done. Various sets of talks followed, some involving the Opposition and others Conservative MPs who were against her deal for diametrically opposed reasons. On 29 January there was another day of drama in the House of Commons as MPs voted on seven contradictory amendments to the Withdrawal Agreement.

One of them, proposed by Conservative MP Graham Brady, the chair of the influential 1922 backbench committee, proposed a reopening of the Withdrawal Agreement to find an alternative to the backstop. The party, with May's acquiescence, rallied behind the amendment and it was passed by 317 votes to 301. It gave some temporary comfort to the Prime Minister. She said:

> A fortnight ago, this House clearly rejected the proposed Withdrawal Agreement and Political Declaration with just 202 members voting in favour. Tonight a majority of honourable members have said they would support a deal with changes to the backstop. We will now take this mandate forward and seek to obtain legally binding changes to the Withdrawal Agreement that deal with concerns on the backstop while guaranteeing no return to a hard border between Northern Ireland and Ireland. My colleagues and I will talk to the EU about how we address the House's views.

The EU response was immediate. Donald Tusk released a statement saying, 'the backstop is part of the Withdrawal Agreement and the Withdrawal Agreement is not open for renegotiation.' Barnier was shocked at May's apparent change of direction. 'This position marks an important shift on the part of the British government since it amounts to a direct calling into question of the outcome of two years of negotiation, without any detailed indications as to what they want instead. This is not acceptable.' He went on to observe that a time-limited backstop or a unilateral withdrawal from it were simply not on.

May was not the only one having to face contradictions in her position. In Davos a week earlier Varadkar had told an international audience that a no-deal Brexit would be a major dilemma which would require Ireland, the UK and EU to sit down after a period of chaos and hammer out an agreement to honour commitments that there would be no hard border between the Republic and the North.

> Ireland has obligations to protect the single market – it's our market, our jobs, our standards. Both the UK and Ireland would have a responsibility to honour the Good Friday Agreement and the peace process. So, I think we'd end up in a situation where the EU, Ireland and the UK would have to come together in order to honour our commitments to the people of Ireland that there'd be no hard border and agree on full alignment on customs and regulations.

That was a reasonable statement of the Irish position but, in an interview with Bloomberg, Varadkar raised the prospect of a return of soldiers to the Irish Border in a worst-case Brexit scenario. He said a hard border 'would involve customs posts, it would involve people in uniform and it may involve the need, for example, for cameras, physical infrastructure, possibly a police presence or army presence to back it up. The problem with that in the context of Irish politics and history is those things become targets.'

The Opposition pounced on the ill-considered remarks. 'When the Taoiseach tells an audience in Davos that the Army may have to be sent to the Border, he is contradicting everything that we have been told by him and the Tánaiste about preparations. It is hard to see how this helps our case,' said Fianna Fáil leader Micheál Martin. Varadkar also got into hot water for mentioning in passing during a briefing with opposition leaders that one option that was getting some traction in Europe was that if an open border was maintained in Ireland after a no-deal, checks would be required on the continental mainland at ports like Calais and Rotterdam for all goods coming from Ireland. This was a nightmare scenario that would effectively exclude Ireland from the single market and Varadkar rushed to clarify the issue, saying that he would never agree to it. Nonetheless, it was a worrying glimpse of what could happen if there was a no-deal Brexit. Ireland would have to choose between implementing some form of border checks or being excluded from the single market.

In the UK Brexit Secretary Steve Barclay began highly publicised talks with Conservative MPs about technological alternatives to the backstop. They were immediately dismissed by Brussels officials as unrealistic, with Politico reporting that Sabine Weyand had described such suggestions as 'unicorns' and 'magical thinking'. On Twitter she was more diplomatic. 'Can technology solve the Irish border problem? Short answer: not in the next few years.' However, the more eye-catching descriptions of 'magical thinking' and 'unicorns' quickly entered the Brexit lexicon in Brussels.

The episode demonstrated that May was attempting the impossible in trying to persuade the EU to drop or modify the backstop. She decided that as well as travelling to Brussels in early February she needed to go to Northern Ireland to reassure people that she was committed to avoiding a hard border and to Dublin to see if she could persuade the government to move a little and accept some kind of time limit on the backstop. First she sent Barwell to Brussels to see if he could find any room for flexibility among influential backroom people there ahead of the Council meeting.

Accompanied by UK Ambassador Tim Barrow, Barwell met the Commission's Secretary-General, the forceful Martin Selmayr, who told the British that the patience of most people in Brussels had been exhausted. He added that it was 'disingenuous' of the UK to try to keep negotiating something after it had been agreed. Selmayr went on to say that a time limit to the backstop 'was not going to happen' but he did concede that it might be possible to agree something 'complementary to the Withdrawal Agreement.' It wasn't much but it gave Barwell some hope. The Secretary-General of the European Council, Jeppe Tranholm-Mikkelsen, had a similar message.

The British met Irish Commissioner Phil Hogan the next day and he was a little warmer. He explained that there was a nervousness about reopening the Withdrawal Agreement as 'at the moment we've all the hens in the pen', so the British should focus on the technical side of their argument.

When Varadkar arrived in Brussels on 6 February Donald Tusk again triggered a huge controversy. At a press briefing with the Taoiseach after the meeting he suddenly said: 'I've been wondering what that special place in hell looks like for those who promoted Brexit, without even a sketch of a plan about how to carry it out safely.' Varadkar whispered to Tusk: 'They'll give you a terrible time in the British press for that,' but Tusk merely smiled. 'Yes, I know.' On cue the British media went into a frenzy with Brexit-supporting newspapers like the *Daily Telegraph* going wild with indignation. The BBC was not far behind.

The pro-Remain *Guardian* took a calmer view. 'This was Donald Tusk unplugged. A politician tired of diplomacy that kept going nowhere. "What bit of backstop doesn't the UK get?" and happy for once to speak his mind ... He no longer cared that much what anyone thought. He had tried to be nice to the Brits but all you got in return was news bulletins with Theresa May in a Spitfire and people comparing the EU's aims with Hitler.'

When Varadkar met with Juncker and Barnier, he too got a reality check. 'I tell him of the sensitivity of the member states on the issue of the internal market which is directly linked to the issue of the border in Ireland,' noted Barnier. 'We must be clear among ourselves. Controls to protect the internal market must be implemented somewhere, whether around the island or within it, or on the mainland with the risk of excluding Ireland from the single market, which we do not want.' It was a message Varadkar did not want to hear.

Barnier recalled in his diary that two days before this senior Commission officials had been in Dublin to explore what might happen in the event of a no-deal. The message they got from the Irish was that in these circumstances they wanted a return to the Northern Ireland-only backstop with controls between Britain and Northern Ireland, which would remain in the single market and customs union. The Irish insisted this would ultimately be accepted by the government in London, despite May's adamant opposition to it.

May arrived in Brussels the following day to meet Juncker and other senior officials, including Barnier. 'For some days now I have been hearing that she does not know where to turn or which direction to go in. On all sides doors are being shut on her and the walls are closing in. And yet she seems unsinkable,' recorded Barnier.

When Juncker met May he told her the problem seemed to be the inclusion of the whole of the UK in a customs union. He said he was prepared to ask the twenty-seven member states to revert to a backstop for Northern Ireland only, if that would help her. That option was not acceptable to May, so the meeting ended in stalemate.

Speaking to the media afterwards she put a brave face on it. 'I am clear that I am going to deliver Brexit. I am going to deliver it on time. That is what I am going to do for the British public, I will be negotiating hard in the coming days to do just that,' she insisted. May also responded to Tusk, saying that she had raised with him 'the language that he used yesterday, which was not helpful and caused widespread dismay in the United Kingdom'. A joint statement from May and Juncker said their talks had been 'robust but constructive' and added that they would meet again before the end of the month to take stock.

The following day May came to Dublin for a meeting which had been carefully planned by Irish and British officials to see if the Taoiseach and the Prime Minister could establish some kind of rapport in a more relaxed atmosphere than normal. It was something that should have been done much earlier in the process, but both sides felt it might still do some good.

Earlier in the week, before travelling to Brussels, May had gone to Belfast to talk to politicians and leaders of industry. Her meeting with business people was far more friendly and productive than her engagement with the political parties. Speaking to journalists she said: 'We are absolutely committed to there being no hard border between Northern Ireland and Ireland.' She also said she wanted 'to work closely with the Taoiseach Leo Varadkar and the Irish government, as so many of our predecessors have before, to strengthen the bilateral relationship we have built'.

Barwell noted that the visit to Belfast had a profound impact on May and was key to her determination not to leave the EU without a deal. 'Nigel Dodds had told her he didn't believe there was anything about Brexit that threatened the Good Friday Agreement but this was in sharp contrast to what she would hear from the people of Northern Ireland over the next thirty-six hours.'

As May headed from Belfast to Brussels, Barwell, who had accompanied her to Northern Ireland, took a train to Dublin for a meeting with Brian Murphy. 'Brian and I had both been concerned that some of the Prime Minister and Taoiseach's meetings had been a bit scratchy. We had come up with the idea that the two of them, plus a small number of officials, should have dinner on Friday night [8 February] and the purpose of my meeting was to agree what they might cover.'

The two chiefs of staff had got to know and trust each other and they immediately got down to some straight talking. Murphy commented favourably on May's Belfast speech but told Barwell the government in Dublin had been upset by her decision to back the Brady amendment. Far from encouraging the Irish to compromise, it had hardened their resolve to have a watertight backstop as it was becoming clear that they might soon have to deal with a different British government that wanted a more distant relationship with the EU. Without a backstop, there would inevitably be a hard border.

Murphy was clear that there was no appetite on the Irish side for reopening the Withdrawal Agreement, but he asked what the British would propose. 'I ran through the options we had considered to check whether our assessment of their relative negotiability was accurate,' recalled Barwell. 'He was dismissive of alternative arrangements (not on this planet) and of an end date but seemed less implacably opposed to an exit mechanism in certain circumstances.' Barwell also explained the coalition that May was trying to build with some Labour MPs, which was why she was talking about workers' rights. He explained that those MPs would only move if they were sure there were enough Conservatives onside to get the deal through. That was why assurances were needed that the UK would not be trapped in the backstop. 'Our conversation was frank but warm and it went on well into the night.'

Two days later, having received another rebuff in Brussels, May arrived in Dublin to meet Varadkar for a private dinner at Farmleigh House, the former home of the Guinness family on the edge of the Phoenix Park that is now an official government residence. May was accompanied by a group of senior officials including Barwell, Olly Robbins and the British Ambassador to Ireland, Robin Barnett. The Taoiseach's party included Callinan, Murphy and the secretary general of his Department, Martin Fraser.

Newspaper reports described the meeting as 'warm' – in contrast to earlier meetings between the two leaders. They discussed Brexit and the continuing absence of a power-sharing administration in Northern Ireland. Before the meeting started Varadkar said it was not a day for negotiations but an opportunity to 'share perspectives'. There was no press conference afterwards and officials were tight-lipped about what had transpired.

John Callinan recalled that the Farmleigh dinner was different from most of the other meetings between the two leaders.

> The plan for that meeting, it was a Friday night, was not to do any business but to see could we create a different dynamic. Most of the previous meetings were done in the margins of the European Council in one or other delegation room. They are not exactly designed for comfort and intimacy, and you'd get about twenty minutes or so. That format did not encourage real interaction so we said we need to try and construct something. Olly and I did a fair bit of work to try and construct an engagement where they could really just try and get to know each other a little bit better. So we arranged this fairly intimate kind of dinner meeting up in Farmleigh but I thought she found it hard to relax.

Callinan was surprised to hear afterwards that May had felt it was one of the more enjoyable meetings she'd had in a long time, precisely because it was a relaxed and informal engagement and there wasn't any awkward business to be done. 'It couldn't have been an easy meeting in fairness to her given all of the difficult meetings she was having to deal with in London and Brussels.'

Brian Murphy also recalled that the mood at the Farmleigh meeting was good. 'There certainly was more chemistry that night than there was on any other occasion. But in hindsight did it make a big difference? No. Part of this I suppose is that May was involved in an eternal civil war within her own party.'

Varadkar himself was not convinced that the dinner at Farmleigh was as relaxed an occasion some of the officials on both sides thought. 'I kind of felt that dinner was pleasant, and we had a good conversation but I never felt we ever had the conversation that I was able to have with Boris.' Part of the problem was that, whether or not the dinner improved relations, it had come far too late in the day. After her massive Commons defeat, the Irish and most of the other EU governments had lost confidence in May's ability to get a deal through the Commons.

Another attempt to improve relations and possibly find some grounds for compromise involved a meeting in Dublin that weekend between the Irish and British Attorneys General, Séamus Woulfe and Geoffrey Cox. The two had spoken on the phone on a number of occasions over the previous months about the wording of the backstop. 'Let's pretend we are two old barristers in the robing room, trying to find a way to grease the wheel and agree a settlement,' remarked Cox in their first exchange.

Cox had been the star turn at the Conservative Party conference the previous October, at which he had delivered a rousing warm-up speech for May. This was his first visit to the Irish capital and he met Woulfe in the Attorney General's office on Merrion Street. Varadkar had some concerns that Cox might be attempting a manoeuvre to lure the Irish into accepting some form of time limit for the backstop and one of his senior officials, Helen Blake, attended the meeting, as did Robin Barnett. In the event the meeting was amicable but there was little give on either side.

After her visit to Dublin May gamely kept pressing the EU to agree to clarifications in the Political Declaration that would enable her to get enough MPs onside. Her aim was to bring over between 115 and 120 of the Tory MPs who had voted against her, as well as the DUP. She also though it was feasible to get up to fifty Labour MPs to back the deal, but they needed evidence that she could deliver her own side. In early March, with a week to go before the second Commons vote, she made a fiery speech appealing to ordinary people to put pressure on their MPs to back her deal. 'Brexit does not belong to MPs in parliament but to the whole country.'

In Brussels Robbins got the Task Force to agree to amend the Political Declaration to state that the EU would not attempt to trap the UK in the backstop indefinitely. In tandem the British planned to make a unilateral declaration to reinforce the point but wanted to ensure that it would not be contradicted by the Commission.

On the day before the second 'meaningful vote' May and Brexit Secretary Steve Barclay made a dash to Strasbourg to meet Juncker, who was in the French city for a plenary session of the European Parliament. 'The British are incapable of planning things in advance. London is frantic in its attempts to achieve a positive second meaningful vote tomorrow,' recorded Barnier, who was also there. May's strategy was to formalise the provisional nature of the backstop so that Geoffrey Cox would feel able to issue a favourable legal opinion stating that the UK could not be trapped in it against its will.

When they arrived in Juncker's office the British found that Varadkar had been on the phone an hour earlier objecting to a sentence in the proposed unilateral declaration. The wording he was concerned about was: 'if it proves not to be possible to negotiate an agreement, the UK records its understanding that nothing in the Withdrawal Agreement would prevent it instigating an end to its arrangements under the proviso of full compliance with its obligations to avoid a hard border on the island of Ireland.' Varadkar objected to the use of the word 'end' in the declaration and this was put to the Prime Minister. She in turn rejected the word 'suspension' as not being strong enough and eventually Juncker came up with 'disapplication', which was sufficiently ambiguous to be acceptable to both sides.

Varadkar's objection arose from panic in Dublin that May might be on the verge of getting Juncker to agree to water down the backstop provision. Varadkar and his team had been due to travel to the USA on 11 March for the annual St Patrick's Day jamboree in Washington, but he decided to delay his departure until the wording of the British unilateral declaration was settled. Meanwhile the rest of the travelling party, Séamus Woulfe, Martin Fraser and Brian Murphy, headed to Dublin Airport to catch their flight. They were in the VIP lounge waiting to depart when they received an urgent summons to return to Government Buildings.

As Fiach Kelly wrote in the *Irish Times*, there was a serious worry that the British might succeed in neutering the backstop. Woulfe, whose luggage had already been checked in for the US flight, was needed to give his legal opinion so he rushed back with the others for an emergency cabinet meeting that evening. After a briefing about the content of the draft declaration the cabinet adjourned to allow Varadkar lodge his objections with Juncker. Once the modified wording was agreed it was given to the Attorney General for his approval. He concluded that there was no fundamental legal change to the backstop.

To May's disappointment the British Attorney General came to the same conclusion. She had been hoping that the declaration would reassure enough waverers to get the Withdrawal Agreement approved by the Commons. There had been strong signals that a significant number of Conservative MPs would come on board and even indications that the DUP might vote for it.

May's hopes were shattered when Cox published his legal opinion on the morning of the vote. It stated that a legal risk remained that the UK would be left with 'no internationally lawful means of exiting the protocol's arrangement, save by agreement'. Even though Cox had spoken forcefully in favour of the agreement during the Commons debate, his legal opinion was just what the ERG had been hoping for and they were able to persuade a number of Tory MPs back into the No camp. While thirty-nine Conservative MPs, including David Davis, returned to the fold and voted for the agreement on 12 March it was not nearly enough and the second 'meaningful vote' was lost by 391 to 242.

The next day the Commons voted against exiting the EU without a deal, but that didn't mean a lot because unless there was a vote in favour of the Withdrawal Agreement the UK would have to leave with no-deal by 29 March. Dutch Prime Minister Mark Rutte summed up the position saying: 'Voting against no-deal is a bit like the *Titanic* voting for the iceberg to move.'

The following day there was another critical vote. This time it was on whether the UK should seek an extension to the 29 March deadline. The motion was carried by 413 to 202. On 15 March chief whip Julian Smith told May that the DUP was close to signing up to support the government in a third meaningful vote on the basis of a package of commitments that Britain would stay aligned with Northern Ireland if the backstop was ever triggered, and that Stormont would have a veto on new regulations being added to the backstop. The Irish government was told that the DUP was on board and for a brief period there were high hopes that May would finally get her deal through. However, the speaker of the Commons, John Bercow, scuppered the plan, refusing to allow a third vote on the basis that the House had voted on the proposal twice already.

May vented her frustration at this disappointment by going on television to tell voters she regretted having to seek an extension to Britain's membership of the EU. She laid the blame squarely on MPs.

Of this I am absolutely sure. You, the public, have had enough. You're tired of the infighting; you're tired of the political games and the arcane procedural rows, tired of MPs talking about nothing else but Brexit. You want this stage of the Brexit process to be over and done with. I agree. I am on your side. It is now time for MPs to decide. It is high time we made a decision. So far parliament has done everything possible to avoid making a choice. Motion after motion and amendment after amendment has been tabled without parliament ever deciding what it wants. All MPs have been willing to say is what they do not want.

It was a statement of fact, but she was widely criticised for attempting to mobilise public opinion to pressurise parliament. When May met Varadkar in the margins of an EU summit the next day she assured him that she had no intention of crashing out of the EU without a deal. She told him she was still confident of getting the Commons to back the Withdrawal Agreement. That European Council meeting agreed to extend the UK transition period from 29 March until 12 April to allow time for another vote. The European elections were scheduled for 22 May 2019 and there was a strong desire to conclude matters by then because if the UK had not left, it would have to participate in the poll.

By this stage May had come to the conclusion that her long-term future as Prime Minister had become untenable. On 27 March, at a meeting of the 1922 Committee, she announced that she would not lead the UK into the next stage of the Brexit negotiations but she was still determined to make another attempt to get the Withdrawal Agreement passed before she left office.

On 29 March May made her third attempt to get the agreement approved by parliament in a meaningful vote. While the gap had become closer, she failed by 344 votes to 286. This vote was on the With-drawal Agreement only, in an effort to get the Opposition on side for that step, leaving the detailed terms of Brexit to be negotiated later. The Opposition refused to bite and, in a monumental strategic error, left the UK hostage to the Brexiteer faction in the Conservative Party. The vote set the UK on a trajectory out of the customs union and the single market, despite the fact that there was a big majority in the Commons for staying in both.

Another special European Council meeting was called for 10 April, two days before the next deadline. Most of the leaders were thoroughly fed up by this stage. One declared bluntly at the beginning of the discussion: 'I've had enough of all these meetings on Brexit,' and went on to say that it would be very strange to see the UK holding European elections.

Barnier was in favour of a short extension to force the British to make a decision one way or the other, but a majority of leaders decided that the risk of a no-deal exit was too high. Merkel supported a long extension, arguing that if the British parliament accepted the Withdrawal Agreement in the meantime the date could be brought forward. Varadkar also argued strongly for a long extension in order to avoid the real possibility of a no-deal exit. In the end the Council agreed to extend the UK's membership until 31 October 2019.

Barwell, who travelled to Brussels with May, found the whole process dispiriting. 'I wish we had been able to bring every single MP with us to see the humiliating position they had put our country in. The Prime Minister was invited to address the European Council but then had to wait outside while the other heads of government deliberated over our country's fate.' Eventually the British delegation was summoned back to the Europa Building in the middle of the night and told an extension until the end of October had been agreed.

Emerging from that meeting shortly after 1 a.m., Varadkar declared: 'From Ireland's point of view, it means we won't have a no-deal Brexit on Friday. If no-deal happens at all, it won't happen until the end of October. But that creates a period of time for the United Kingdom to essentially come to a cross-party agreement and ratify the agreement.'

12

Merkel Comes to Dublin

'As you face the challenges posed by Brexit, know that Democrats and Republicans in this House stand with you.'

Nancy Pelosi, Speaker of the
US House of Representatives, in a speech to
a special sitting of the Dáil, 18 April 2019

* * *

As the Brexit process moved towards the end game, Varadkar and his officials became increasingly worried that German support for the Irish position might waver. It was clear to everybody at this stage that the backstop was the only reason Theresa May had been unable to get the deal through the UK parliament, so there was growing apprehension in Dublin that, faced with the prospect of a no-deal, Merkel might decide the price was too high.

'We were acutely conscious that Germany and Merkel in particular really mattered,' recalled Callinan. 'They had questioned the EU tactic of allowing the Northern Ireland issue to be dealt with upfront as part of the Withdrawal Agreement because you can't know some of the things you need to know until the trade deal is done. Merkel was fairly consistently of the view that this was the cart before the horse.'

The Chancellor's logic unnerved the Irish team because they knew only too well that she had a point. The Irish counter-argument, which was strongly shared by Barnier, was that if the Irish Border was left until last it would become a huge bargaining chip for the UK and give it enormous leverage to get the most favourable possible trade deal.

The reason Merkel's apparent doubts so worried the Irish was that everybody accepted that she was the key figure in the European Council, not simply because her country was the richest and most powerful in the Union but also because she had established herself as the dominant personality at the table. Keeping her onside was crucial and Irish officials regarded it as a significant achievement when she was persuaded to come to Ireland in April 2019 to judge the situation for herself.

Callinan summed up the mood in Dublin at that stage.

> We thought there was a risk that the Germans might say, 'Look. We did our best for you lads but let's just forget about the backstop now.' So we had to try and lock it in. And at that time we were starting to move into a phase where Brussels was saying to us, 'Well, what are you actually going to do if there's no deal?' That was another thread. So with Merkel we were trying to think of how to get beyond the normal standard stuff for these official visits.

Merkel's Sherpa, Uwe Corsepius, was a tough civil servant who had served in the Chancellor's office under Helmut Kohl and Gerhard Schröder before becoming European adviser to Merkel when she became Chancellor. In 2009 he went to Brussels as secretary-general of the European Council, but he came back to Berlin as head of EU policy in 2015 and remained in that position right through the Brexit process. He was described by Barnier as 'precise, direct, and competent' and was a crucial intermediary on Merkel's behalf with all the actors in the drama.

The other key official on the German side from an Irish perspective was the Ambassador to Ireland, Deike Potzel, who had been sent to Dublin in 2017 precisely because Brexit was so important. Unlike many previous German ambassadors who had come to Ireland for a relaxed final posting, Potzel still had a lot to achieve in her career. She quickly made an impression by cultivating a wide circle of contacts at all levels of Irish society and did not confine herself to official/diplomatic circles in Dublin.

A native of East Berlin, like Merkel, she had an instinctive grasp of the importance of the border issue for Ireland and understood that the restoration of a hard border would have not only a negative political and economic impact on the country but a psychological one as well. As an East Berliner she was on the same wavelength as the Chancellor and that rapport was important in ensuring that Irish concerns were understood at the highest level in Germany.

Callinan recalled:

So Merkel came to Dublin. And we worked closely with her Sherpa and the Ambassador in Dublin to set it up. So at one level we wanted to have the political symbolism of herself and the Taoiseach in Dublin having a meeting in solidarity, a bit like the Donald Tusk moment in 2017, but we wanted to go deeper than that.

With the agreement of her people we set up a meeting with 'real people' from border areas. We didn't try and arrange a meeting with representative types but had about a dozen individuals who had their own personal stories to tell. And there were people who had been the victims of horrible violence or people whose businesses had gone belly up or people who are trading successfully but were worried, and people who lived a cross border existence. She met these people for over an hour, and it was very, very powerful, really powerful and she engaged with them.

One of the people who made a strong impression on Merkel was Kathleen Gillespie from Derry. Her husband, Patsy, became known as the 'human bomb' when the IRA strapped him into a van and forced him to drive a bomb into a British Army checkpoint on the border between Derry and Donegal on 24 October 1990. He was killed, along with five soldiers, but his shouted warning saved the lives of others. Patsy was forty-three when he died and he and Kathleen had three children. Sinn Féin described him as a 'legitimate target' because he worked in the army canteen. In the years that followed his death Kathleen became a campaigner for reconciliation, including working with former IRA prisoners.

Gillespie and Merkel sat facing each other as the Derry woman told her harrowing story. She recounted the events of that dreadful day and the impact it had had on her and her children. It was actually one of her children's birthday. The articulate and dignified way Kathleen recounted the event had a profound impact on Merkel and everybody else in the room. There were other people from the border areas there, along with the Chancellor and the Taoiseach, but not the normal retinue of officials, which made the impact of the story all the more powerful.

Potzel recalled the emotional power of that meeting. 'Angela Merkel is very good at putting herself in other people's shoes and that meeting made a huge impression on her,' she said. The Ambassador was adamant that there was never any prospect of Germany changing tack and abandoning the backstop but she felt the meeting between the Chancellor and the people from the border region was an important moment in the process. 'Having lived behind a wall that kept people apart, the Chancellor was very conscious of the need to avoid a return to a hard border in Ireland.'

Having made a huge effort to ensure that Merkel and Germany stayed onside, Irish attention turned to the United States, which has played an important role in Irish affairs since the Famine. In recent times Ronald Reagan made a key intervention with British Prime Minister Margaret Thatcher to pave the way for the Anglo-Irish Agreement of 1985. In the 1990s President Bill Clinton took a direct role in the peace process and sent Senator George Mitchell to Ireland to chair the talks that led to the Good Friday Agreement.

From an Irish perspective a positive American influence looked more problematic in 2019. Donald Trump had been president for more than two years and had made no secret of his support for the hard-line Brexiteers and his contempt for the EU. He openly derided Theresa May, cultivated Nigel Farage and was lavish in his praise of Boris Johnson. However, there were other key players in the USA who took a different view, most notably the Speaker of the House of Representatives, Nancy Pelosi, who would have a huge influence on whether the holy grail of the Brexiteers, a free trade agreement between the UK and the USA, would get the approval of Congress.

In April 2019 Pelosi visited Ireland, the UK and Germany with a group that included members of Congress, among them Richie Neal, the chair of the powerful House Ways and Means Committee, and Brendan Boyle, a leading Democrat, both of whom had strong family ties to Ireland. Pelosi also had Irish ties, but very different ones from her Irish-American Congressional colleagues. Unlike them she had no Irish ancestors, but she did have a more immediate connection, her Irish grandchildren Liam, Sean and Ryan Kenneally. She had long taken an interest in the country and was well known to leading Irish politicians.

The US delegation visited London first and there was some apprehension in Dublin that they might be swayed by the British line on Brexit. While in London they had talks about the Brexit process with Deputy Prime Minister David Lidington and Chancellor of the Exchequer Philip Hammond but they did not get to meet Theresa May as they had hoped and expected. They had a fractious exchange with Jacob Rees-Mogg and leading members of the ERG and got to see the Labour leader Jeremy Corbyn. Their visit was virtually ignored by the British media.

It was covered by the *Washington Post*, whose London correspondent Willam Booth reported that when Pelosi was asked what was being discussed she replied 'Brexit, Brexit, Brexit'. Booth went on to note that in the past US–UK bilateral talks would have been dominated by issues like counterterrorism, intelligence sharing, NATO, Russia and China, and the special relationship between the two countries. 'Today, Brexit dominates. And on one particular point, Pelosi is emphatic: Don't mess with the Irish peace accord.'

The report went on to say that Pelosi had warned Prime Minister Theresa May's government, Conservative pro-Brexit hard-liners and the Labour leader Jeremy Corbyn that if their approach to Brexit in any way weakened the Good Friday Agreement, the US Congress would block any trade deals Britain might seek with the United States.

While Pelosi and her delegation did not publicly vent their frustration at what they regarded as a dismissive attitude adopted towards them in the UK they were scathing in private when they arrived in Dublin. 'They felt they had been treated like shit,' said one Irish source. 'By the time they got to Dublin, they were fuming at the Brits. They were absolutely fuming. Now it may have been that Pelosi was wearing her colours on her sleeve, and the British took a dim view of that, but the Tories made a complete bags of it and Corbyn was no better.'

By contrast the delegation was greeted with open arms in Dublin and the red carpet was rolled out as far as it could go. Pelosi and her delegation were received by President Higgins and they had productive meetings with Varadkar and Coveney to discuss Brexit. She was invited to address a special sitting of the Dáil, as part of the one hundredth anniversary celebrations of its foundation, and a state dinner in her honour was held in Dublin Castle.

It was the classic Irish approach to making foreign dignitaries feel welcome and loved and the Americans lapped it up, particularly as it was such a marked contrast to the way they were greeted in London. Of course they were already predisposed towards giving comfort to the Irish view of Brexit, but the episode turned warm sentiment into hard political support.

Speaking after the first official engagement of the Irish visit, a meeting with Coveney, Pelosi was adamant that a future US–UK trade agreement was 'just not on the cards' if Brexit damaged the Good Friday Agreement in any way. She told a gathering at Iveagh House that Brexiteers should not take 'any kind of consolation or comfort' from the notion that a trade deal with the USA was likely.

Addressing a special session of the Dáil the following day she repeated the message. 'If the Brexit deal undermines the accord [Good Friday Agreement] there will be no chance of a US–UK agreement' on trade. 'As you face the challenges posed by Brexit, know that Democrats and Republicans in this House stand with you,' she said to sustained applause from TDs and senators. Former Taoiseach Enda Kenny, who had established strong relations with a range of US political leaders, including Joe Biden and Pelosi, was in the chamber to reinforce the message, while one of Ireland's best known celebrities, Bono, was in the distinguished visitor's gallery along with his wife, Ali.

That night, at the state dinner in honour of the American visitors in Dublin Castle, Varadkar told the guests, who included DUP leader Arlene Foster, that 'no matter what happens with Brexit we will do everything we can to prevent the return of a hard border between Ireland and Northern Ireland.'

The following day the delegation went to the Border, visiting Donegal and Derry, before going on to meet Northern politicians at Stormont. During their visit the journalist Lyra McKee was shot dead by dissident republicans in Derry, reinforcing the point about the constant danger of a return to violence. The upshot of the visit was that the Americans went home even more strongly supportive of the Irish position than when they arrived.

Part of the reason the Americans were given such an off-hand reception in the UK was that Theresa May, in the final stages of her premiership, was making one last effort to see if she could assemble a coalition to get the Withdrawal Agreement through parliament. She established a negotiating team to have detailed discussions with the Labour Party over how their concerns, particularly with regard to workers' rights, could be assuaged. After eight meetings over a number of weeks it became clear that Labour would not do a deal, even though many of its MPs were in favour of one. Surprisingly, Corbyn was relatively open to a deal but Keir Starmer, who was in theory strongly pro-EU, raised obstacles at every turn. Michael Gove described Starmer as 'harder to please than anybody [he had] ever met'.

Barwell was angry at what he regarded as Labour's pig-headedness in killing off the last chance of a soft Brexit.

> The collapse of the talks meant the end of Theresa's premiership and her successor was bound to be a hard Brexiteer. I presume they thought they could stop whoever came next from leaving without a deal and then win the subsequent general election. If they did, they were right on the first point but the latter was a colossal misjudgement. If they had done a deal it would have been much harder for Boris [Johnson] to portray them as blocking Brexit. Jeremy Corbyn wanted to do it but Keir Starmer stopped it – it seems fitting that he's now dealing with the consequences.

As the talks with Labour were in progress May came under renewed pressure to resign. Former party leader Iain Duncan Smith called on her to go shortly after the Conservatives suffered an expected drubbing in local elections on 2 May. The chair of the backbench 1922 Committee, Graham Brady, made a similar call a few days later. Down but not yet out, May made one final effort to persuade MPs to back a compromise plan around which a majority could gather. On 21 May she made a speech outlining her intention of introducing, in June, a new version of the Withdrawal Agreement which would allow the Commons to make amendments in favour of one form or other of a customs union, or even a second referendum. 'I say with conviction to every MP of every party: I have compromised. Now I ask you to compromise too,' she said. The offer made no impression on the Opposition and it angered many Conservative backbenchers. May decided that there was no point trying to go back to parliament one more time. Instead, on 24 May she announced that she intended to step down as party leader on 7 June.

Announcing the decision on the steps of Downing Street she said: 'I have done everything I can to convince MPs to back the deal. Sadly I have not been able to do so. I tried three times ... It will be for my successor to find a way forward that honours the result of the referendum. To succeed, he or she will have to find a consensus in parliament where I have not. Such a consensus can only be reached if those on all sides are willing to compromise.'

Getting to the final part of her statement, in which she said it had been the honour of her life to serve as Prime Minister of the country she loved, May almost broke down but she pulled herself together and carried on till the end. When she went back into Downing Street she apologised to Barwell for getting emotional, but he was cross with her for apologising, as he had urged her for two years to show a bit more emotion in public. He told her that no one watching the footage on the television news that night was going to think less of her for being upset about having to stand down from a job she had worked her whole life to get. 'You wait and see. The papers will use those pictures differently because I'm a woman,' she told Barwell, and she was right.

Watching the television footage in Brussels, Barnier too was impressed by her show of emotion. 'She cannot suppress a sob and frankly who can blame her, except the writers of a few unworthy tabloid headlines?' He went on to record in his diary, 'I admire the courage of this woman of politics who did not vote to leave the European Union. She nonetheless made it her mission to implement Brexit in order to respect that demo-cratic decision, despite the many obstacles placed in her path, not least by the Brexiteers who have done their best to shirk their responsibility for the past three years.'

Varadkar paid a similar tribute. 'I got to know Theresa May very well over the last two years. She is principled, honourable and deeply passionate about doing her best for her country, and her party. Politicians throughout the EU have admired her tenacity, her courage and her determination during what has been a difficult and challenging time.'

The question, though, is whether Varadkar and Barnier could have done more to help May and keep the UK in a closer relationship with the EU. Varadkar, looking back, said:

> I do often wonder about that. It is one of the things that I think about. Could we have done more to help May win votes and get it through? The main thing that May wanted from us was an exit mechanism from the backstop, to end after five or ten years. I often wonder if we'd offered her an exit mechanism. We would never have been able to accept a ten-year expiry date. But could we have offered her a similar exit mechanism that we offered Boris? I don't think she would have accepted it but I do wonder if that offer had been made. She would have had to accept it and carry it and it would have to have been both.

Varadkar has also pondered whether May might have been able to handle her party differently.

> It is impossible to put yourself in somebody else's shoes. I just wonder if she'd stood up to her critics and opponents at home might she have got the deal through. Ultimately Boris was willing to kick people out of the party, including people [like] Nicholas Soames, honoured people. He was ready and willing to put up it to his opponents in a way she wasn't. I kind of wonder if she'd made less of an effort to get her critics on board and taken them on. But that would have been harder for her as she was suspected of not being a true Brexiteer.

> Whereas I think it was easier for Boris to make a deal for that reason. It's bit like the Ariel Sharon thing. Sharon could make a deal and get it through where an Israeli Labour politician couldn't. That's politics, I suppose.

One thing Varadkar is definite about is his revulsion at the way May was treated by the Conservative Party. 'Her party treated her appallingly. In any political party there are rivalries, and there are people who have ambitions for higher office, and all the rest of it, but this was on a different level.'

Following May's announcement of her intention to resign, the jostling for position in the succession race began. First, though, the party had to face into contesting the European elections on 23 May in the worst of all possible scenarios. European elections were never taken that seriously in the UK but this time around the contest was surreal, given that the UK was leaving the EU and elected candidates would be leaving the European Parliament within months. It was a contest nobody wanted, apart from Nigel Farage. Having walked away from his original creation, UKIP, after the 2016 referendum he had now launched a new political organisation, the Brexit Party, and gleefully took to the hustings for another shot at getting elected to a parliament he despised.

The outcome was a disaster for the Conservative Party, which was relegated to fifth place with just 9 per cent of the vote and four seats. The big winner was Farage's Brexit Party, which won 31 per cent, hoovering up support from voters who wanted the UK to leave the EU. The Labour Party didn't fare much better than the Conservatives, dropping to 13 per cent, while the Liberal Democrats came in second place with 20 per cent. The scale of the collapse in the Tory vote sent shockwaves through the party.

A subsequent study of the voting patterns found that Brexit Party voters were generally older, less-educated men who were not particularly badly off, and who had abandoned the Conservatives and UKIP. The focus of these voters had shifted from opposing immigration to achieving Brexit. While European elections have never been a guide to subsequent general elections the message this time was unmistakable. Unless they managed to find a way of winning voters back the Conservatives would face a drubbing at the next general election, whenever it took place.

Observing from Brussels, Barnier noted, 'For the next Conservative Prime Minister, whoever that may be, this should serve as a clear incentive to avoid the marginalisation of their party by settling the Brexit issue as soon as possible. The latest turn of events may end up increasing the possibility of a no-deal.'

In Ireland the result of the European elections was reasonably good for Fine Gael, which increased its vote to 30 per cent, a rise of seven points, while gaining an extra seat to give it five out of the thirteen available. It was not a spectacular performance but it showed solid backing for the Brexit strategy Varadkar had been pursuing.

In the UK the race for the leadership began immediately after May named a date for her resignation. In all, ten candidates put their names forward to the parliamentary party, which had the job of narrowing down the field to two. The top two would then be put to a vote of the party's 160,000 or so members. Johnson started off as the clear favourite and the first cabinet minister to endorse him was Liz Truss. After five rounds of voting by the parliamentary party, Johnson and Foreign Secretary Jeremy Hunt emerged as the two candidates whose names would go to the membership.

On 5 July Barwell met Johnson's chief strategic adviser Edward Lister and Hunt's adviser Ed Jones, one of whom, he assumed, depending on the outcome of the leadership contest, would take over his job. 'I wanted to give them the handover I'd never had and prepare them for what life would be like in the job,' wrote Barwell, behaving to the last like the conscientious public official he was. In the end the result was as had been widely predicted. The party membership, who voted by postal ballot, elected Johnson by a margin of two to one. The result was announced on 23 July, almost two months after May's decision to resign.

Johnson won the leadership with an unambiguous pledge to leave the EU by 31 October 2019, deal or no-deal, and that caused deep trepidation in Ireland. A no-deal Brexit would mean a hard border on the island with all the negative consequences that entailed, or the departure of the country from the single market. It would also have the potential to cause a massive disruption of trade with the UK. The challenge facing Leo Varadkar in the summer of 2019 was whether he would hold his nerve and stick with the backstop, given that it had the potential to do such serious damage to the country, if Johnson called his bluff.

13

Boris in Downing Street

'I have one message that I want to land with you today, Leo, that is I want to find a deal, I want to get a deal.'
Boris Johnson after his first meeting as Prime
Minister with Leo Varadkar, 9 September 2019

* * *

Boris Johnson had a boyhood fantasy of becoming King of the World and he achieved the adult version of that ambition by being elected Prime Minister of the United Kingdom on 23 July. He immediately declared his intention of leaving the EU on 31 October, whether or not there was a deal. He insisted that the 'anti-democratic' backstop would have to go, maintaining there would be no checks at the Irish Border. Johnson sacked most of the senior ministers in the outgoing government in a purge that was dubbed by one ally as 'not so much a reshuffle as a summer's day massacre'. He appointed a raft of Brexiteers to the cabinet, including Dominic Raab, who became Foreign Secretary, Priti Patel, Liz Truss and Michael Gove. He kept Steve Barclay as his Brexit Secretary and appointed former chief whip and Remainer Julian Smith as Northern Ireland Secretary.

Varadkar tweeted his congratulations, saying he looked forward to an early engagement with the new Prime Minister on Brexit, Northern Ireland and bilateral relations. However, in a radio interview he was adamant that an entirely new Brexit deal was not going to happen, adding that he would like to hear Johnson put some flesh on the bones about what he was proposing. 'I look forward to having the opportunity to sit down with him one to one and also for our teams to meet together and really see if he can put a little bit of detail behind some of those slogans and statements because we haven't got that yet.'

Varadkar anticipated things to come by raising the prospect of the backstop applying only to Northern Ireland, as had originally been intended in December 2017, rather than keeping the entire UK in the EU customs union and elements of the single market. At that stage Johnson was having none of it: 'I do not accept the argument that says that these issues can be solved only by all or part of the UK remaining in the customs union or in the single market.'

A few days later the two men spoke by phone. Their only previous meeting had been at a St Patrick's Day event in Trafalgar Square in March 2012, when Johnson was Mayor of London and Varadkar Minister for Transport in Dublin. The official account from both sides described their first engagement as leaders being warm and friendly. According to a statement issued by the Irish side Varadkar told Johnson that the backstop was needed because of decisions taken by the UK, but he went on to offer a glimmer of hope. 'Alternative arrangements could replace the backstop in the future, as envisaged in the Withdrawal Agreement and the Political Declaration on the future relationship, but thus far satisfactory options have yet to be identified and demonstrated.'

A statement from Downing Street said the Prime Minister had made clear that his government would approach any negotiations 'with determination and energy and in a spirit of friendship, and that [Johnson's] clear preference is to leave the EU with a deal, but it must be one that abolishes the backstop'. As well as talking about Brexit they dealt with the situation in Northern Ireland, where the Assembly and Executive were still in suspension, and they had an exchange of views about the challenges of being a new Prime Minister and particularly the difficult task of choosing a cabinet.

This surprisingly matey discussion about prime ministerial responsibilities signalled the beginnings of a very different kind of relationship between Taoiseach and Prime Minister than had been the case during the May years. 'The chemistry between them worked and that was terribly important,' said Johnson's chief strategist Edward Lister.

Looking back on his exchanges with Johnson from the vantage point of November 2021, Varadkar remarked:

I always figured he was the kind of person that you would be able to do a deal with because he had shown himself to be relatively flexible. Before the referendum it was unclear as to whether he would be for it or against it. He did in the end vote for the 'Theresa May deal' though it wasn't really her deal but the EU's deal, but anyway the name stuck. Remember he voted for that in the end.

So I always got the impression that he was keen to have an election mandate. I was also keen to have an election mandate. And I kind of thought that as two politicians who wanted an agreement, and were potentially both heading into elections within six months, that it would be possible to cut a deal with him, despite the sabre-rattling and diplomatic posturing that was going on.

One message that Varadkar took from that first phone call was John-son's overriding priority to get rid of the backstop. 'I remember one thing he did say in the first phone call was that he had to perform a backstopectomy. I am not sure if the term was for my benefit as a doctor, or simply because he is very good at words, but he kept saying he had to have a backstopectomy.'

After this telephone exchange with Varadkar, Johnson travelled to Northern Ireland to meet all the parties at Stormont. His first engage-ment was a private dinner with the DUP leaders Arlene Foster, Nigel Dodds and Jeffrey Donaldson at the five-star Culloden Hotel in east Belfast. He spent the following morning at Stormont House, holding bilateral meetings with all the parties in an effort to encourage them to do what was needed to get the devolved Assembly and Executive up and running again. All the other parties were critical of the Prime Minister's decision to hold a private dinner with the DUP but as events turned out it did not signify as much as they thought.

An astute assessment at that stage of Johnson's likely course of action was made by Jonathan Powell, former adviser to Tony Blair and the

UK's chief negotiator of the Good Friday Agreement. He forecast that Johnson would ultimately abandon the DUP and pursue a free trade arrangement with the EU. 'That means Northern Ireland would have to go back to the original backstop. There would definitely have to be special measures for Northern Ireland in that case and there would definitely be a border down the Irish Sea.'

Barnier also took Johnson's initial sloganeering with a grain of salt. 'Behind the slogans I detect a strategy that comes as no surprise. "Deliver Brexit; unite the country; defeat Jeremy Corbyn." This is clearly the route he has chosen and that should allow him to reach an agreement with us for an effective and orderly exit on 31 October.'

In tandem with his sweeping cabinet changes, Johnson brought in an entirely new team at senior official level. Dominic Cummings, the main architect of the Vote Leave campaign, took over the running of Downing Street. From an Irish point of view the key new arrival was Edward Lister, who was installed as chief strategic adviser to the Prime Minister. Lister had been Johnson's deputy mayor and chief of staff during most of his period as Mayor of London and he was as emollient as Cummings was abrasive. He took charge of the contacts with the Irish government and quickly established a rapport with Brian Murphy, which was to prove critical in the months ahead.

Out went Olly Robbins as the Prime Minister's EU Sherpa and in came the pugnacious David Frost, a former career diplomat who had left the Foreign Service in 2013 to become chief executive of the Scotch Whisky Association. He was a Leave supporter during the 2016 referendum campaign and struck up an alliance with Johnson, who appointed him as a special adviser during his period as Foreign Secretary.

Johnson followed up his initial sloganeering with a four-page letter to European Council President Donald Tusk on 19 August simply demanding that the backstop be abolished, without making any alternative proposals about how a border in Ireland could be avoided. The EU side were taken aback at both the tone and content of the letter. Tusk tweeted, 'those against the backstop and not proposing realistic alternatives in fact support the reinstatement of a border. Even if they do not admit it.'

Two days later Johnson flew to Berlin to meet Merkel. He repeated his mantra that the Irish backstop would have to go if there was to be a Brexit deal. 'We do need the backstop removed. If we can do that I am absolutely certain we can move forward together. Once we get rid of it, there is chance to make real progress.' Merkel responded by giving Johnson a thirty-day deadline to come up with a solution and he appeared to accept the challenge. 'I must say I am very glad listening to you tonight, Angela, to hear that at least the conversations that matter can now properly begin. You have set a very blistering timetable of thirty days, if I understood you correctly, I am more than happy with that.' The *Guardian* commented that the Prime Minister's acceptance that the onus was on him to find a solution was significant because up to then the UK government had been arguing that it was up to the EU to move first, by abandoning its stance on the backstop.

The exchange with Merkel was polite and constructive but that atmosphere did not carry over into Johnson's early interaction with the EU. On 27 August he had a testy phone conversation with Juncker, again stetting out his demand that the backstop must be scrapped. 'This backstop is not democratic. It's not consistent with the direction we want to go in. And Theresa May wasted too much time negotiating with you on a text where too many options remain open that we don't want, like the customs union and links with the single market.' On a more positive note the Prime Minister suggested that when it came to Ireland he was prepared to accept a single framework for agriculture and animal control.

A little over a week later, on 9 September, Johnson flew to Dublin for his first face-to-face meeting with Varadkar. The two men held a joint press conference before getting down to business in Government Buildings. At the press conference Varadkar welcomed Johnson, but his message about the consequences of a no-deal was blunt: 'It will cause severe disruption for British and Irish people alike. We will have to get back to the negotiating table quickly. When we do, the first and only items on the agenda will be citizens' rights, the financial settlement and the Irish Border.' The Taoiseach then outlined a more optimistic scenario. 'If there is a deal, and that is also possible, we will enter talks on a future relationship agreement between the EU and UK.'

Johnson was decidedly more upbeat. 'I have one message that I want to land with you today, Leo, that is I want to find a deal, I want to get a deal. Like you I've looked carefully at no-deal, I've assessed its consequences both for our country and yours. And yes, of course, we could do it, the UK could certainly get through it but be in no doubt that outcome would be a failure of statecraft for which we would all be responsible.' To reinforce the point he added, 'So for the sake of business, for farmers, and millions of ordinary people who are counting on us to use our imagination and creativity to get this done, I want you to know I would overwhelmingly prefer to find an agreement.'

Most of the media reporting of the press conference focused on the obstacles in the way of a deal and Johnson's optimism was widely regarded as bluster. There was also considerable comment on Varadkar's poise and fluency in contrast to Johnson's typically dishevelled appearance and his somewhat bumbling delivery. Watching the television coverage from Brussels, Barnier noted: 'When placed alongside the Taoiseach, who speaks so lucidly and with great poise, Boris Johnson seems a little maladroit in his remarks.' This view was even reflected in some of the British press coverage.

The subsequent meeting between Varadkar and Johnson, both of them accompanied by officials, went a lot better than the press conference might have indicated. Varadkar was quickly convinced that Johnson wanted to do a deal, even if they didn't come close at that meeting to finding enough common ground. The Prime Minister's acceptance of an all-Ireland solution for agriculture and food products was one positive, but, more important, the chemistry between the two men was good and Varadkar sensed that they could do business.

John Callinan recalled that while Johnson had set out a hard line, Varadkar had come to the conclusion that a way to engage simply had to be found. Just saying 'no' could be dangerous. 'It was all very strange. First of all you had to adjust to the personality of Boris and second you had to try and gauge what sort of game it is behind the bluff and bluster. There was a new team to get to know as all the key officials we'd been used to dealing with were gone.'

'When he [Johnson] stepped off the roundabout in Dublin he looked dizzy, like a dishevelled Dougal, aimlessly waffling around in circles,' wrote Miriam Lord in the *Irish Times*. 'The Prime Minister didn't look or sound good alongside the measured Varadkar, who answered questions clearly and didn't rely on waffle.'

Yet behind the bluster the Irish side sensed that something big was in the offing. One of the few journalists to understand that something important had happened at that first face-to-face meeting between the two leaders was Tom McTague of *The Atlantic*:

On the way back to London that day, on board a small Royal Air Force plane with his closest advisers, Johnson had been in a buoyant mood, full of bravado. 'We're going to get a deal,' he declared to his aides, pacing up and down the aisle, throwing his arms out wide and pushing out his chest, according to one first-hand account. At this point Johnson had been Prime Minister barely a few weeks, but the mood had changed inside 10 Downing Street. A new team had moved in, with new tactics and ideas.

While nothing of substance had been achieved in Dublin, Johnson, like Varadkar, felt that the atmosphere had changed and that an opening might just be possible. According to his aides Johnson had simply aimed to convince Varadkar that he wanted a deal, and they felt the message had been heard. 'I was told the Irish leader and his team got the clear impression that despite Johnson's gung-ho promises and "do or die" commitments to leave the EU on 31 October, he was actually someone whom they could work with,' was McTague's accurate assessment. 'They were personality meetings,' said one British official. Johnson 'did a bit of freewheeling, but he convinced Varadkar he wanted to do a deal.' Another concluded that he had convinced Varadkar that he wanted to do business.

One of the people in the political world to grasp what was happening was Ireland's EU Commissioner, Phil Hogan. 'The penny is finally dropping' with the UK, he predicted in an interview with Paddy Smyth of the *Irish Times* on the day he was nominated to the key European Trade portfolio. He referred to the fact that Johnson had spoken just days before of an all-Ireland food zone, saying this pointed to an acceptance of some level of divergence between Northern Ireland and the rest of the UK. 'If we can build on that we certainly might get closer to one another in terms of a possible outcome,' said Hogan, who forecast that the idea of an Ireland-only backstop was likely to come back on the agenda.

The work of British and Irish officials in the search for a compromise formula during September 2019, was carried out under the radar of the media and most of the political world. One of the reasons for this was that Johnson kept his ambition for a deal hidden in his public pronouncements and in most of his political engagements. The day after he met Varadkar in Dublin he had detailed discussions with the DUP leaders in Downing Street. In a statement afterwards Arlene Foster said she had been encouraged by the tone and language used in Dublin.

> History teaches us that any deal relating to Northern Ireland which cannot command cross-community support is doomed to failure. That is why the Northern Ireland backstop is flawed. Not one single unionist MLA in the Northern Ireland Assembly supports it. The Prime Minister rejected a Northern Ireland-only backstop in a letter to Donald Tusk on 19 August. It is undemocratic and unconstitutional and would place a tariff border between Northern Ireland and the rest of the United Kingdom. That would be unacceptable.

Foster went on to say that Johnson had confirmed his rejection of the Northern Ireland-only backstop, while a spokesman for the Prime Minister was quoted as ruling out such a solution. 'We are not seeking a Northern Ireland-only backstop,' he said.

As he wrestled with the conundrum of the Irish Border, Johnson was also in the throes of a massive political crisis at home. Having replaced May with the pledge to rescue the UK from political stalemate with a no-deal Brexit on 31 October if a deal proved impossible, the first two months of his tenure resulted in more political chaos in London. There were knife-edge votes in parliament, embarrassing defeats for his government and mutiny in the Conservative ranks.

On 28 August Johnson dropped a political bombshell by declaring that he had asked the Queen to prorogue parliament from 10 September to 14 October. The clear intention was to ensure that parliament would not be able to block a no-deal Brexit. A political storm ensued, with some of his opponents suggesting that the move amounted to a prime ministerial coup. There were protests in towns and cities throughout the UK and three separate court actions were launched to challenge his action.

When parliament resumed on 3 September Johnson announced his intention of calling a general election under the Fixed-term Parliaments Act. This prompted a rebellion in the Commons, with some Conservative MPs joining the Opposition to vote to take control of the order of business to prevent a no-deal exit if Parliament failed to endorse a deal by 19 October. The following day a piece of legislation that became known as the Benn Act, which ruled out a no-deal Brexit, was passed by a majority of twenty-eight. The Bill, dubbed 'the Surrender Act' by Brexiteers, required the Prime Minister to seek an extension of Article 50 if there was not a deal by 31 October.

A total of twenty-one Conservative MPs had crossed the floor of the Commons to vote for an opposition motion; and one MP left the party to join the Liberal Democrats. Among the rebels were some of the leading figures in the Conservative Party, including former chancellors of the exchequer Kenneth Clarke and Phillip Hammond; Nicholas Soames, grandson of Winston Churchill; and former cabinet minister David Gauke, who had been a leading opponent of Johnson. The group, dubbed 'The Gawkward Squad', immediately had the whip removed for defying party orders. The move meant that Johnson's initial wafer-thin majority of one had been turned into a deficit of forty-three. To add insult to injury, on 5 September the Prime Minister's brother Jo Johnson resigned as a minister and announced he would step down as an MP, describing his dilemma as being 'torn between family and national interest'. Two days later, senior minister and personal friend of Johnson Amber Rudd resigned from the cabinet, describing the withdrawal of the whip from the rebel MPs as an 'assault on decency and democracy'.

Johnson, who said that he would 'be dead in a ditch' before requesting an extension of Article 50, then proposed a general election on 15 October, but his motion was unsuccessful as it failed to command the support of two-thirds of the House. Having suffered six parliamentary defeats in six days, Johnson advised Queen Elizabeth to prorogue parliament from 12 September to 14 October in a transparent manoeuvre to avoid any more Commons defeats in the run-up to the deadline for Brexit. The decision was challenged in three separate court actions. On 11 September, three Scottish judges ruled the prorogation of the UK Parliament to be unlawful. On 12 September the High Court in Belfast rejected claims that his Brexit plans would have a negative impact on

Northern Ireland's peace process. The most important decision of all came on 24 September when the Supreme Court in London ruled unanimously that Johnson's advice to the Queen to prorogue parliament 'had the effect of frustrating or perverting the constitutional role of parliament in holding the government to account' and that the prorogation was therefore unlawful.

As turmoil raged in the UK during September Varadkar's team began a cautious exploration with their British counterparts about what form of compromise might be possible. Since early 2017 the Irish side had been very careful not to be seen to engage in bilateral discussions with the British that might be regarded as an attempt to stray outside the common EU position as articulated by Barnier and the Task Force. Now, however, they began a tentative diplomatic dance to see how far the British might go. 'We lifted the skirt a little bit on the idea of some sort of a consent mechanism. That was the key piece at the time that was new, that hadn't been on the table with Theresa May,' said one Irish official.

McTague observed that the Irish side, having come to the conclusion that Johnson was willing to compromise in the search for a deal, took a risk and began talking to the British on the substance of Brexit. He also wrote that officials in 10 Downing Street believed that Johnson's commitment to preparing for a no-deal exit, and apparent willingness to go down this route if he could not reach an agreement, played an important role in encouraging the Irish and the EU to the negotiating table. 'In September, the Irish began, bit by bit, to dilute the purity of their position.'

As part of this process a back channel was set up between 10 Downing Street and Varadkar's office in Dublin. On the British side the key figures were Lister and two cabinet officials, Brendan Threlfall and John Bew. Threlfall had headed the section in the UK Brexit Department dealing with Northern Ireland and had moved to the Northern Ireland Office for a time to continue the work. At this stage he was back in the cabinet office, leading the work on drafting alternatives to the backstop. The historian John Bew was a more recent addition to the process having been appointed to the cabinet office by Johnson after his accession to Downing Street. Bew, a respected historian in his own right, was the son of one of the foremost Irish historians, Paul Bew, who had been an adviser to David Trimble and had been elevated to the House of Lords.

Threlfall and Bew did the detailed drafting on the British side and worked closely with Fraser, Callinan and Murphy on the Irish side to establish how an alternative to the backstop could be found. The British were encouraged by their assessment that the Irish were prepared to take the risk of annoying the EU in pursuit of a deal, although Varadkar and his officials insisted that they kept Barnier and his team in the loop, just as Johnson did with the DUP.

It was crucially important for the Irish side not to keep the EU in the dark, particularly as some of the officials in Dublin believed they were being played by Johnson. They feared that any concessions made in private would be used against them in leaks to the British media by Dominic Cummings or other hard-line Brexiteers in Downing Street. While the fear of being double crossed lingered, Varadkar was reasonably sure that Johnson's desire to do a deal was real.

That confidence survived despite Johnson's publicity tricks during September. In an interview with the *Daily Mail* he claimed that huge progress had been made in the talks and he compared his negotiating tactics to those of the cartoon character the Incredible Hulk. 'The madder the Hulk gets the stronger the Hulk gets. Hulk always escaped no matter how tightly bound he seemed to be and that is the case for this country.' Barnier drily commented in his diary that the comparison had its limits as no one had tied down the UK and nothing was stopping it from leaving the EU except the difficulty they were having agreeing among themselves.

On 16 September Johnson flew to Luxembourg for a working lunch with Juncker and Barnier at which the Commission President reminded him that the abolition of the Irish backstop was simply not possible, but he added that 'we are prepared to replace it with another solution provided it is operational and fulfils the same objectives of peace in Ireland, the absence of a hard border and obviously the protection of the single market.'

Barnier observed a mêlée outside the restaurant before lunch, with more than a hundred reporters and photographers jostling for position around the Prime Minister. 'Mr Johnson appears as he wants to be: tough, moving like a bulldozer, clearly trying to force his way through.

But there is something genuine and mischievous in his eyes and in the expression on his face. All in all, a rather likeable character.'

That likeability had also helped to persuade Varadkar that a deal was possible and the developing relationship between the two leaders was cemented when they met in New York on 24 September while attending the general assembly of the United Nations. The meeting took place on the same day as the UK Supreme Court delivered its bombshell decision that the prorogation of parliament was illegal. The main focus of the British media was on the fact that Johnson would have to telephone the Queen to apologise for giving her the unsound advice to prorogue parliament. Before he made that cringing phone call he met Varadkar for their second face-to-face meeting. 'The meeting in New York was against the backdrop of the court finding against him closing down parliament,' recalled Brian Murphy. 'And they were clearly flustered. We knew from his staff that he was going to have to phone the Queen shortly thereafter to basically apologise. It was just a demonstration of all the crazy politics that was going on.'

John Callinan recalled that in spite of the craziness some real progress was made at that UN meeting.

> We had a follow-up meeting with Boris in New York, when we were all at the UN, and that was where some of the ideas that eventually made it into the final deal came into play. At this point the discussions were going on very quietly at official level but the meeting between Leo and Boris was fairly serious. The one in Dublin was a sort of introduction with some high-level stuff but the one in New York was a detailed enough conversation about the protocol. There was a little bit of talking past each other but the key thing for us was to try and get behind the bluff and bluster and see what Boris was willing to live with. So we established at that point that some kind of a consent mechanism that we could go along with might be possible and that would unlock the whole thing.

Brian Murphy has a similar recollection of the importance of that New York meeting. He recalled that by this stage a number of channels of communication had been opened, apart from the direct talks between the leaders.

There were the conversations that John [Callinan] was having with his opposite number, and there would have been a channel between myself and political staff in Downing Street. So that meant there were ways of having contact. And then obviously Simon Coveney was having separate series of meetings at Minister of Foreign Affairs level. But after New York with Barnier talking about the clock running down it was clear that the thing was coming to an end.

Journalist Tom McTague, who was clearly well briefed on the meeting, concluded that it was in New York that that Varadkar glimpsed a different side to his British counterpart than the widely accepted caricature that Johnson himself created of a bumbling, chaotic, amusing, but ultimately unserious character. At the UN, Johnson was tired and distracted by events at home and was unable to hide his vulnerability.

According to three people familiar with the events, Johnson's demeanour that day had the effect of drawing Varadkar out. Both leaders went off-script, going back to the basics of Brexit and offering ideas, Johnson gesticulating with his arms in a physical expression of frustration that they had not found a compromise. The meeting – a moment in which one national leader who understood the vicissitudes of political life saw the struggles of a counterpart – revealed a genuine desire on both sides to find a compromise. Varadkar, according to one senior official, concluded that despite Johnson's political difficulties at home, a deal was still possible. 'The currency between leaders', the official said, 'is something they both understand.'

The personal relationship was a key element in persuading each of the leaders that they could do a deal with the other but they were also pushed towards compromise by the realisation that the looming no-deal Brexit would be a disaster for both countries. Johnson and his team had been disabused of the notion, a feature of the British approach since 2016, that when it came to the end game the big powers, particularly Germany, would override Barnier and the Commission, abandon Ireland and do a deal with the UK that suited its own interests.

Merkel's clear desire for an amicable settlement had led the British to misread the German position at various points in the Brexit process in the vain hope that she would at the last minute attempt to override Barnier and the Commission. It was no accident that Johnson's first foreign trip as Prime Minister had been to visit Merkel in Berlin. While she encouraged him to come up with a solution to the backstop conundrum she was quite clear that Germany would not abandon it unilaterally. By the end of September the penny had finally dropped with everybody in Downing Street that the Germans were not going to bend. While Merkel was particularly conscious of the strategic importance of the UK as a security ally of the EU, her absolute priority was the protection of the single market.

Varadkar too was pushed towards compromise by the appalling vista of a no-deal outcome, which would be disastrous for the Irish Border and also for trade between the UK and Ireland. He was also influenced by a nagging suspicion that if it came to a cliff edge in October, Merkel, despite all her assurances, might still abandon Ireland in order to keep the UK close to the EU. 'It was in the back of my mind that that might happen. I remember the prime minister of another small country saying to me once, in Davos, that I should bear in mind that as far as the big countries are concerned there's a game that we don't see. His warning to me was just to be aware of this possibility and I was very aware but it never happened. It never arose.'

The other concern Varadkar had at the back of his mind was whether pressure would be applied to change the Irish corporation tax regime.

And again that never happened. So the principle of solidarity held. What I always knew was that Merkel did want a deal. More so than Barnier and the Commission, she was open to *sui generis* solutions that we could have a special arrangement with Britain. It didn't have to be a choice of a Canada-style deal or the single market. So I think she was always more open to an agreement with Britain. She was definitely never in the camp of people who felt the British should be punished, or that we needed to demonstrate that Brexit was a bad thing or other people might leave. I think she had a much more pragmatic approach. For the Germans it's different because Britain is such a big security partner. It is not just about the economics of it.

It was certainly the case that Merkel was always aware of the wider geopolitical context. We're less aware of it. For us, it's Britain, Europe and America and the rest of world doesn't impinge greatly. For her it's Russia and Turkey and China and keeping Britain as an ally was really important.

Varadkar also came to the conclusion that the structure of the German federal state has served to make the government in Berlin far more aware than other powerful countries of the concerns of smaller EU states.

I think what is admirable about Germany is the way their federal state works. So the whole job of being a German Chancellor is meeting with the minister presidents of each of the federal states and taking their views into account. So Saarland is important. So is Bavaria, so is Niedersachsen and Schleswig-Holstein. Whereas, I think the French President and British Prime Minister think differently. So that helps when you're a smaller country like Ireland. The German system is more understanding of our concerns.

The Germans were well aware of Irish worries that something might happen at the last moment to change the picture. Deike Potzel was adamant in 2021 that Irish fears on this score were always groundless and there was never the remotest prospect that Merkel would go behind the backs of Ireland or the Barnier Task Force to do a deal with the UK. 'We knew the Irish had this suspicion but it was never justified.' She pointed out that German car manufacturers who were alleged by the British media to be pressuring the government to cut a deal with the UK had in fact done the exact opposite. 'For the car makers as for everybody else the preservation of the single market was far more important than doing a deal with the British but it took a long time for that to sink in.'

However groundless the Irish fears about the prospect of Germany abandoning the backstop, the reality was that a no-deal outcome would have presented the Irish government with the cruel dilemma of having to introduce some form of border controls on the island or facing expulsion from the single market. While the government in Dublin had dodged efforts by the EU and the Germans to pin them down on what exactly they intended to do in that doomsday scenario it was looming ever larger as a real possibility as the October deadline grew closer by the day.

What it all amounted to was that there was enormous pressure on both Varadkar and Johnson to find a way of avoiding a no-deal outcome.

Having first established a personal rapport, they deployed advisers and officials to work out how disaster could be averted. While most of the public commentary was resigned to a no-deal Brexit, and the mood in Brussels was downbeat, decisive moves were already in train to ensure that the worst would not happen.

14

The Frontstop

'The negotiations will probably end this week. Varadkar doesn't want to negotiate.'

Senior Downing Street source, quoted in the
Spectator, 6 October 2019

* * *

The developing relationship between Varadkar and Johnson set the talks on a new trajectory, but finding a formula to break the two-year-long impasse over the backstop challenged the ingenuity of Irish and British officials. The Prime Minister was committed to getting rid of the backstop; the Taoiseach was equally committed to ensuring that there would be no hard border. There was no easy way to square that circle.

Officials got down to serious work immediately after the Dublin meeting of the two leaders in early September. Following a series of phone calls and an exchange of documents a team from Downing Street came to Dublin on 16 September to meet the senior figures in the Taoiseach's office. The British team was led by Edward Lister, Johnson's chief strategic adviser and personal emissary. Journalist Tom McTague described Lister, who was then aged seventy, as 'an unassuming figure, besuited, gray-haired, respectable, like the head of a medium-size business'. One of Johnson's most trusted advisers from his time as London mayor, Lister was a stark contrast to the other central figures in Johnson's administration, Dominic Cummings, the brilliant and obsessive disrupter who had masterminded the Leave campaign, and the Prime Minister's combative and dour EU Sherpa, David Frost.

Lister's role was to build a relationship of trust and see if the other officials on the British team could work with their Irish counterparts to agree a new strategy. The key British officials were Threlfall and Bew. Having worked on the Irish aspect of Brexit for more than two years, Threlfall was familiar with the minute details of the backstop and the possible alternatives to it. Bew, with an established reputation as a historian, had a deep insight into the unionist thinking and the contacts to establish what might be acceptable to the DUP.

The Irish side was led by the country's top civil servant, Martin Fraser, the secretary general of the Taoiseach's Department; and John Callinan, Varadkar's Sherpa. Lister's counterpart, Brian Murphy, was also in attendance, along with other officials involved in the process. Both sets of officials knew they had just one last shot at trying to unpick the Gordian knot if a no-deal Brexit was to be avoided.

'So you had this situation where Boris had made it clear that something has to give if we're to get this done,' recalled Callinan. 'He was playing very hard ball saying he wasn't afraid to go with no-deal. I don't believe he would have gone with no-deal but who knows. Nobody could say that for sure. Leo was thinking, well, we're going to have to find some way to engage here. Just saying no is a dangerous game.'

Lister recalled that the UK side was also struggling to find a way through. 'It was a very difficult time. It was very bitter in British politics at that stage with two sets of extremists in Parliament, one set who just wanted out of the EU and didn't care whether or not there was a deal and the other group who wanted us to remain in the EU and ignore the vote of the people to leave. We had to find a middle path.' Lister accepted that the Irish side was entitled to do everything possible to avoid a hard border. 'We thought the Irish had reasonable concerns and we knew that a compromise formula had to be found to reassure the government in Dublin that it would not happen. We also knew that a no-deal would be hugely damaging for Ireland so it was in the interests of both countries to find agreement. The same was not true of Brussels; they didn't seem to care whether or not there was a deal.'

Another person on the British side who played an important role in smoothing the way towards a deal was the new Northern Secretary, Julian Smith, who made an immediate impact when he was appointed by Johnson to replace the hapless Karen Bradley. An experienced and able politician, who had served as chief whip in the May government, he was determined to do everything he could to restore the power-sharing institutions at Stormont, which had been in abeyance for almost three years. He saw immediately that implementing the provisions of the Good Friday Agreement would be impossible if a no-deal Brexit resulted in the restoration of a hard border on the island. 'My focus was on Stormont and getting the Executive up and running again and I pushed back on the idea of a no-deal. I made the case that there should not be a border between North and South and spoke at the Commons select committee making that point. I worked against a no-deal outcome,' said Smith.

Appearing at the House of Commons Northern Ireland select committee in October, Smith stated bluntly that while his first aim since taking over as Northern Secretary in July had been the effort to get the Stormont Assembly up and running again, 'the second priority was doing everything we can to avoid no-deal'. He went on to say: 'I think no-deal is a very, very bad idea for Northern Ireland.' It was a coura-geous statement that provoked Johnson's ire and ultimately cost him his job.

While Smith did not have a direct role in the Brexit talks, his inter-ventions helped to create an atmosphere in which a deal could take place. 'I did a lot of work with Jim [D'Arcy] to improve relations. I tried to show positive aspects of a good British–Irish relationship and to de-dramatise some of the rhetoric. Ruling out a border on the island was important as the Tory right tried to keep the prospect open,' said Smith.

Phil Hogan also played an active role at this critical time in attempting to avert a no-deal outcome by bringing clarity into the political discus-sion about thinking in Brussels. He travelled to Hillsborough Castle in Northern Ireland for a discreet meeting with Julian Smith at which a positive exchange of views took place. The meeting was arranged by Jim D'Arcy, who had been working tirelessly developing links with all strands of opinion in Northern Ireland and had quickly struck up a good relationship with the new Northern Secretary.

His meeting with Hogan at Hillsborough was an aspect of Smith's approach that stood in stark contrast to the bellicose public posturing of Johnson. After his first formal meeting with Simon Coveney to discuss the restoration of the Northern institutions, Smith suggested that they should adjourn to a pub for a pint. It was part of his strategy to establish trust between the two governments so as to facilitate the return of the power-sharing institutions at Stormont and inject a positive mood into the negotiations.

Johnson's core objective, as he had made clear to Varadkar at their first meeting, was that the UK-wide backstop had to go. Finding something to replace it to meet the Irish objectives was now the issue. As well as 'binning the backstop' Johnson was determined that the future relationship between the UK and the EU would be as distant as possible. That meant there was no prospect of the border problem being solved by a close trading relationship in the future, as many had hoped might be the outcome of Theresa May's strategy. During the month of September it became clear to both sides that the only alternative to having the backstop as a last resort was an upfront, immediate solution to the border issue. A 'frontstop', as Varadkar termed it.

The complex task facing Johnson's officials was to find a formula that would be acceptable to the Irish and the DUP. The DUP's most powerful backroom figure, general secretary Timothy Johnson, made numerous visits to Downing Street in September and October 2019 to discuss the options and try to influence British officials to devise a solution his party could live with.

The Conservative Party conference at the beginning of October was a key test for Johnson's leadership. He desperately wanted to get the endorsement of the membership and planned to deliver a rousing speech about his Brexit strategy to ensure their support. However, he didn't want his tough talking to derail the prospects of a deal with Varadkar. With the European Council due to meet in two weeks and the deadline of 31 October coming up fast, time was running out, especially as he had pledged not to seek another extension.

Lister and his team were sent back to Dublin again on 1 October to emphasise the Prime Minister's ambition to do a deal. The following day, Johnson was due to deliver his keynote speech to the Tory faithful and to publish his much-anticipated revised Brexit plan in the form of a letter to Juncker. Lister visited Dublin with the ambition of keeping the window open for a deal, as an overly negative Irish reaction could kill it off before it had a chance to breathe.

While Threlfall and Bew engaged in discussions about how a 'front-stop' solution might work, Lister had a long chat with Brian Murphy to brief him on the content of Johnson's speech. The core of Johnson's proposal was that Northern Ireland would remain in the EU single market, initially for four years, but would stay outside the EU customs union. That would inevitably entail some form of customs checks between North and South. The other key element of the plan was that Stormont would have a vote on whether or not to remain in the single market after the four years were up.

The officials in the Taoiseach's office had deep concerns about both proposals. Any form of customs checks on the island were simply unacceptable. On the question of giving Stormont a role in the process, Varadkar and his team had come around to the accepting the need for a consent mechanism, but only as long as it did not amount to giving the DUP a veto. The Irish team wondered if Johnson was taking advantage of their willingness to move and attempting to exploit it for his own purposes, but Lister convinced them that the Prime Minister was serious and just needed some room to manoeuvre. He urged the Irish side to be as restrained as possible in their reaction to Johnson's speech and leave room for further compromise.

Lister made a good impression on the Irish officials, who had come to respect his sincerity, and they agreed to urge Varadkar to take a cautious line the following day. Lister then flew to Manchester, the venue of the Conservative Party conference, and by 9.30 that evening was sitting down for dinner with colleagues in the corner of Mr Cooper's Restaurant and Bar in the Midland Hotel. He explained that he had delivered the message and all they could do was wait and see what the Irish response would be.

The next day Johnson duly made his conference speech, to great acclaim from his supporters, and published his Brexit plan in the form of a letter to Juncker. He again demanded the abolition of the backstop and as an alternative proposed that Northern Ireland should leave the EU customs union but remain aligned with the EU's single market rules on standards. The plan would have effectively kept the North in the European single market but outside the customs union, leading to checks on the island of Ireland, with the entire arrangement subject to approval from Stormont every four years. Although they fell short of meeting the requirements of Dublin and Brussels the proposals did represent significant movement.

To the relief of the British, Varadkar responded in the way that Lister had suggested. Questioned by journalists the morning after the conference speech the Taoiseach was careful not to be too dismissive of the proposals, but he was emphatic that he would not accept a deal that included checks on goods moving between the two parts of the island. That evening Varadkar and Johnson had an amicable thirty-minute phone conversation. They still differed on how Northern Ireland could remain in the single market but still be outside the customs zone. Nonetheless, the Taoiseach promised to take a careful look at the Prime Minister's plan and consult the EU institutions about it. Johnson also spoke to Juncker that evening to emphasise that he was serious about being open to a deal.

The response of the DUP, which had been kept in the loop through the consultations with Timothy Johnson, was also restrained. Arlene Foster said that her party would support the Prime Minister's proposals, which she described as 'a serious and sensible way forward' that would enable the UK to leave the EU by 31 October.

The media was slow to grasp what was happening. The message from the London *Daily Telegraph*, which supported Johnson, was not encouraging. Under a front page banner headline 'Pressure on Dublin to back deal' the lead story proclaimed, 'It means Leo Varadkar, the Taoiseach, is now the main obstacle in the way of Britain leaving the EU with a deal on 31 October.' The Irish media was also generally pessimistic, although it portrayed Johnson as the obstacle to progress. European Council President Donald Tusk was also downbeat, declaring that the EU stands 'fully behind Ireland' and adding in a tweet that the EU remained 'open but still unconvinced' by the UK plans.

Barnier noted that there were positive elements in the Johnson proposal, particularly the alignment of Northern Ireland with EU rules on goods, supported by a system of controls for goods entering the North from Britain or from third countries. However, he concluded that while the stated objective was to avoid a hard border it was not spelled out how this would be achieved. 'Finally, all the proposed solutions are conditional on a positive and unilateral decision being made by the Northern Ireland institutions, both before they come into force and then every four years. This is simply unacceptable. We will not discuss a solution with such a Sword of Damocles hanging over it.'

A few days later Johnson initiated a crucial phone call with Chancellor Merkel. In a breach of normal diplomatic protocols, Downing Street briefed the British media on its version of the call, claiming that the Chancellor had 'made clear a deal is overwhelmingly unlikely and she thinks the EU has a veto on [the UK] leaving the customs union'. The Germans declined to make any comment on the leak. Merkel's spokesman said he would not comment on 'private, confidential' talks between government leaders.

Senior German sources said privately the conversation between the two leaders was not as described in the UK media. While the Germans were doubtful about the UK customs proposals for Northern Ireland and their consequences for the integrity of the EU single market, the officials were adamant that the Chancellor said in her conversation with Johnson that she would continue looking for a solution to the Brexit deadlock until time was up.

Whatever the truth about what was said, the Downing Street leak reflected the continuing British frustration that Merkel was not for turning in her support for the backstop. Johnson followed up his call to the Chancellor with one to the Taoiseach. They spoke for forty-five minutes and the atmosphere was good. A government spokesman in Dublin said that both sides had 'reiterated their desire to reach a Brexit deal' and hoped to meet in person later in the week. Varadkar himself said he and Johnson would work until the very last moment to secure a deal, but not at any cost. 'I think it's going to be very difficult to secure an agreement by next week. If there's no-deal the countries worst affected will be Ireland and Britain.'

At this stage, amid leaks and counter-leaks, mostly emanating from London, even the principals found it difficult to know what was going on. The night before Johnson spoke to Merkel and Varadkar, the *Spectator* published a response from a Downing Street source to one of its senior and respected journalists, James Forsyth, who had asked for an update on the negotiations. The contact, who everybody concluded from the tone was Dominic Cummings, had this to say:

> The negotiations will probably end this week. Varadkar doesn't want to negotiate. Varadkar was keen on talking before the Benn Act when he thought the choice would be a new deal or no-deal. Since the Benn Act passed he has gone very cold and in the last week the official channels and the back channels have gone very cold ... If this deal dies in the next few days it won't be revived. To marginalise the Brexit Party we will have to fight the election on the basis of 'no more delays. Get Brexit done immediately.'

The Cummings leak helped to fuel the widespread pessimism about the chances of a deal being done just at a time when the opposite was the case, with British and Irish officials working furiously to find an alternative to the backstop. Creating confusion may have been the point of the leak or possibly the Downing Street team were keeping all their balls in the air to give Johnson different options as the deadline grew every closer.

On the evening of 9 October the Irish media was surprised to be told that Varadkar and Johnson would meet the following day. 'This will be a private meeting to allow both leaders and their teams to have detailed discussions about the process for securing agreement for a Brexit deal,' a government statement announced. No venue for the meeting was announced, but word got around that it would be in the Liverpool area and Irish media scrambled to book early morning flights to that city.

The venue for the meeting was in the Wirral, not far from Liverpool, at a country house hotel called Thornton Manor, a popular location for weddings. Callinan recalled that there was no particular reason to meet in the Wirral but the venue emerged because of reservations on the Irish side about going to Downing Street in case it created the wrong look. As Johnson had been to Dublin just a few weeks earlier the two sets of officials discussed potentially neutral venues. Northern Ireland was mentioned, as was Chequers, but ultimately it was agreed that the Liverpool area would fit the bill as a neutral venue. 'So anyway we settled on Liverpool and jokingly on the basis of "sure it's more Irish than English." And then there was a bit of a scramble to find a suitable place once we had agreed on somewhere near Liverpool. They came back with a suggestion of this lovely stately home Thornton Manor.'

Brian Murphy remembers that the location of the meeting also indicated the wish of both sides that it should not be a usual run-of-the-mill leaders' summit.

We took the view that it should be a different type of event. That meant not going into Downing Street, not having all the press conferences before and afterwards. We would do it in a different way. We suggested somewhere up towards Liverpool and they came up with the Wirral. And, that worked because while the media was camped outside they were not inside. There were no press conferences done afterwards. We did a briefing at the airport, but we didn't have the two prime ministers, answering questions and potential differences, nuances emerging.

Varadkar recalled being a little bemused at the fuss being created by his officials over the location of the meeting.

I was never particularly pushed but there was a view from my officials that as Boris had been to Dublin and I'd been to London it should be a neutral venue. I wasn't particularly bothered but I accepted the advice and so eventually they proposed the Wirral. So I flew over there into John Lennon airport, the first time I'd been in Liverpool, and then drove up the road to the Wirral.

Officials on both sides assumed the two leaders would meet privately for about twenty minutes before being joined by their teams for the substantive talks. Instead the Taoiseach and Prime Minister went for a walk in the grounds for about twenty minutes and then shut themselves away in a room for an hour and a half, when they really got down to business.

We did a walk around the garden largely exchanging small talk as a kind of icebreaker type thing. And then we were in the room on our own for a good while. That was the longest time we were together, just the two of us over tea and biscuits. And that's when I had a chance to put to him the concept that if the UK backstop is a non-runner then the alternative option is a Northern Ireland-only solution. I think I called it a frontstop because, unlike the backstop which would only apply at a later point if there was no trade agreement, this would apply immediately.

Varadkar remembered Johnson's jokey reference in their first phone call that he had to perform a 'backstopectomy' and he emphasised that the 'frontstop' alternative would achieve that objective. The focus of both was whether they could agree on the basic principle of how the Northern Ireland-only solution would work and what form of consent mechanism would be used to underpin it.

> Both of us were of the view that the technical details, around customs checks and so on, were not to be worked out by us, because neither of us would have had an expert understanding of how those things work. So the real issue that we discussed was how there would be democratic consent because that was their [the British] issue. I think that the idea of a sort of referendum in the north had been floated at some point but we very much didn't pursue that because we just thought it would be too dangerous.

Varadkar, though, did accept the idea that some form of consent within Northern Ireland was necessary.

> I was in favour of a democratic consent mechanism. There had been talk of a time limit, which I was never willing to accept unless it was a very long time, like, maybe fifty years, but ten years was definitely not on. So we needed some other mechanism by which the protocol backstop/frontstop could end. I said we can accept the need for a consent mechanism but it would have to be a cross-community vote to disapply it. The arrangement would apply until it was disapplied. And the discussion then went on to how the consent mechanism would be approved. Would you need a majority of both communities or would it just be a straight vote in the Assembly?

Obviously his preference was the opposite of mine. He favoured an Assembly vote to apply it, with the decision being based on a cross-community vote. To me that represented a lack of permanency and it would be too easy to disapply it.

The officials on both sides were taken aback by how long the two men spent closeted together and on the Irish side there was some trepidation about what might emerge. Varadkar, though, had no hesitation about seizing the historic opportunity the meeting offered to frame a solution to a seemingly intractable problem that had bedevilled European politics for two years and threatened the long-term welfare of both Ireland and the UK.

Varadkar said:

The officials came in and we briefed them on what we had agreed in principle and it was for them to write it up ... Of course I would have discussed my ideas in advance with my officials so that I had a clear idea of what I was going to put to him. So it wouldn't have been a huge surprise to them but there were some people whose view would have been 'you have to hold out for the backstop and make them go to the brink.' But I just thought that was too risky. If there was any prospect of an agreement we should take it. Something I would have always said to Boris in various conversations was 'I'm not wedded to the backstop. It's the objective that matters.' I would have said that publicly too. The bottom line was to avoid a hard border between north and south and that was done.

The Irish team for the debrief was led by the top civil servants in the Taoiseach's office, Martin Fraser and John Callinan; and Varadkar's chief of staff Brian Murphy was also present. All were pleasantly surprised and relieved at the scale of the progress that had been made. After both sets of officials had been debriefed they discussed how the agreement in principle would work in practice. The explored the detail of what had actually been agreed and what would require further clarification at a technical level.

At the start the Irish side had noted that Dominic Cummings was with the UK team, as was Edward Lister. While they worried that Cummings might attempt to throw a spanner in the works he did nothing of the kind and his presence ended up being a reassurance that whatever was agreed by the two leaders would stay agreed. Johnson's EU Sherpa David Frost was also there along with the British Ambassador to Ireland Robin Barnett and officials from the Cabinet Office and the Northern Ireland Office. Brendan Threlfall and John Bew, who had come to Dublin in September, were in close attendance and their presence was another signal that Johnson was serious about doing a deal and was not simply preparing the ground for the blame game after a breakdown.

The officials worked out an agreed joint statement. The key sentence was that the two leaders could now see a pathway to an agreement. It was the message that both sides wanted out of the meeting because there was still great uncertainty about whether any deal would survive the inevitable pressures that would arise in the following weeks. While there was relief and even some quiet jubilation on the Irish side at the level of progress that had been made, a deliberate decision was taken not to overhype the outcome for fear of undermining it.

Varadkar recalled:

So a common line was agreed that we had a joint pathway. And I didn't know how it was going to go down. I may have done a clip for the television news at the airport. And it was Nick Miller [Irish government press secretary] who said to me that it had been well received and that it was being seen as a breakthrough. I had a concern that it might have been seen as me backing down. We were now giving up the 'bulletproof backstop'. We were giving it up for something that did the same job, but I was a bit concerned that it might be seen as us backing down rather than being a breakthrough so I was kind of relieved. You never really know in politics what the public reaction is going to be. I was also very careful not to oversell it because I would have had a concern that it could yet fall apart either at the EU/UK level or that Boris might not be able to get it through parliament.

The two leaders put out a short joint statement:

The Taoiseach and Prime Minister have had a detailed and constructive discussion. Both continue to believe a deal is in everybody's interest. They agreed that they could see a pathway to a possible deal. Their discussions concentrated on the challenges of customs and consent. They also discussed the potential to strengthen bilateral relations, including on Northern Ireland. They agreed to reflect further on their discussions and that officials would continue to engage intensively on them. Following their discussions, the Taoiseach will consult with the EU Task Force and the UK Brexit Secretary will meet Michel Barnier tomorrow morning.

Varadkar made his own statement to the cameras and it was upbeat but careful:

I think sometimes at this point in negotiations and discussions, the less said the better. But what I can say is that I had a very good meeting today with the Prime Minister and our teams together – very positive and very promising. I am now absolutely convinced that both Ireland and Britain want there to be an agreement. That's in the interests of Ireland, the United Kingdom and the European Union as a whole. And I do see a pathway towards an agreement in the coming weeks.

Varadkar deliberately sought to play down any notion that he had secured a win. 'I don't think this should be seen in the context of who's making concessions or who the winners and losers are. I don't think that's the game any of us want to play. What this is about is securing an agreement that works for the people of Ireland and also the people of Britain and Europe.'

The Taoiseach's cautious tone could not disguise the fact that something truly significant had happened in the Wirral. 'Suddenly, in the space of a few hours, everything changed,' wrote *Irish Times* political editor Pat Leahy. He noted that few observers had any expectations that the two men would report any progress. Several British media outlets had predicted that the talks between the EU and the UK would collapse before the weekend and some even suggested that Johnson would not attend the summit of EU leaders.

'But, as we know now, that's not what happened. The two men spent about three hours together – some of it with their senior officials, some of it with just each other and some sort of very significant breakthrough took place,' wrote Leahy.

The first task facing Irish officials on the way back from the Wirral was to make urgent contact with the Task Force in Brussels to report what had happened. The positive outcome came as a surprise to EU officials, who were not expecting a serious breakthrough. It was only a week before the critical European Council meeting which would determine whether it was going to be deal or no-deal and a lot of work remained to be done. Varadkar explained:

> I think the EU side was definitely pleased that an outcome had been reached that was acceptable to the Irish because the European Union and Germany in particular wanted there to be a deal. They were never going to roll us over but I think they were relieved that we were able to come to an arrangement that was satisfactory to us. Obviously we had to make sure that that was okay with the Task Force, which it was. The most important principle from their point of view was that nothing should be done that would undermine the integrity of the single market; nothing that would allow Britain to use Northern Ireland to get a better deal for Britain. And that was one of the things that was very clear all along. Whereas some people in London thought that we were using Northern Ireland to keep Britain closer to the EU, the view in Brussels was the opposite of that. It was that Britain would try to use Northern Ireland to get a better deal for Britain.

Barnier's response to the emerging deal was supportive but guarded, as his diary entry for following day indicates. 'Boris Johnson and Leo Varadkar met again yesterday in Liverpool in a more positive atmosphere. According to the Irish government, with whom we had set up this meeting and who reported back to us immediately afterwards, Mr Johnson is now ready to accept the absence of customs controls on the island, even if it means strengthening customs controls between Britain and Northern Ireland. This is essential if we are to make progress.' Barnier went on to say that Varadkar had agreed to work 'on a mechanism that would strengthen democratic support for our solution.' That mechanism would ultimately become part of the Northern Ireland Protocol.

UK Brexit Secretary Steve Barclay flew to Brussels for breakfast with Barnier and confirmed the two-step solution agreed by the Taoiseach and the Prime Minister. 'I welcome them but have to put them into context,' noted Barnier. 'The need for movement comes primarily because the UK government has reneged on major commitments made by Theresa May. Removing the backstop represents a huge step backwards. The new proposals are therefore far from sufficient.'

Barnier spelled out to Barclay that getting a deal would require the British to accept some fundamental points. The first was that the EU would not accept any mechanism that made the entry into force of the Protocol conditional on the agreement of the DUP, which would inevitably question its existence every four years. 'As Leo Varadkar said to Boris Johnson yesterday we are still prepared to work on a mechanism that would strengthen democratic institutions.' The second point was that the EU would not agree to any proposal that created a customs border on the island. 'We cannot accept any ambiguity on that point. What is at stake is the all-island economy which is very important for Leo Varadkar but also to the integrity of the single market.' The final two points related to the timing of the Withdrawal Agreement and the creation of robust level playing field guarantees as a precondition for a broad and ambitious free trade agreement.

Barnier told Barclay that he would have to brief the ambassadors of the twenty-seven member states in three hours and they would want to know if the UK government was serious about an agreement. 'So there are two options: either you tell me that you are ready to accept these four points as a working basis and my team and I can prepare to enter into intensive negotiations this weekend, or you do not and I will have to tell the ambassadors that nothing is expected between now and next week's European Council, where Brexit may not even be on the agenda.'

Barclay said yes to the four points as the basis on which to work on an agreement. Just after noon on 11 October Barnier informed the ambassadors of the EU-27 about the agreement and they authorised him to open intensive discussions with the UK.

It was still far from done and dusted as the detailed negotiations between the EU and the UK got under way. Irish officials recall a tense few days between the Wirral meeting and the European Council the following Thursday, with multiple further rounds of contact in the triangle between London, Dublin and Brussels. 'It was a busy and tetchy process with the Brits, of course, coming back to try and peel off a little bit more each time. And there were some things that we were happy to give; others that we weren't. So that went on for a few days. Even on the morning of the meeting it wasn't clear if we were going to get a deal. In fact I think we were on the flight to Brussels and we didn't know until we landed whether we were getting the green light from London,' recalled Callinan.

15

Endgame

'The key change in comparison with the earlier version of the deal is Prime Minister Johnson's acceptance to have customs checks at the points of entry into Northern Ireland.'

Donald Tusk, 17 October 2019

* * *

It was by no means certain that the outline deal struck by Varadkar and Johnson at the Wirral would lead to an agreement between the EU and the UK. For a start the complex details remained to be hammered out and the outcome would then have to be ratified by the European Council and British parliament. Given the record of chaos in the House of Commons since the beginning of the year anything was possible.

Then there was the attitude of the DUP, which had been critical up to that point. The party was wrong-footed by Johnson's willingness to accept the unthinkable – a border in the Irish Sea. To cover his volte face Johnson's team put a lot of effort into trying to persuade the DUP to go along with the deal on the basis of the consent mechanism that gave Stormont a long-term role in determining whether the agreement would remain in place. However, Foster reiterated her party's opposition to any provision that treated Northern Ireland differently from the rest of the UK. 'Anything that traps Northern Ireland in the European

Union, whether single market or customs union, as the rest of the United Kingdom leaves, will not have our support,' she proclaimed.

In Brussels Barnier and his Task Force got down to business with their UK counterparts over the weekend after the Wirral summit. They had just days to reach agreement before the European Council meeting the following Thursday. Barnier concluded that it would not be possible to reach agreement on legally binding texts in time unless the British delegation received new political impetus.

He noted that David Frost, who headed the UK team, had not back-tracked in principle on the concession made by Johnson at Thornton Manor, and confirmed by Barclay, so there was no longer any question of there being a customs border between Northern Ireland and the rest of the island. 'In our view all the customs procedures and controls that we need in order to protect the single market must therefore be put in place around the island,' he wrote.

The two teams then started haggling about how Northern Ireland could remain inside the EU single market while being a part of the UK customs area. The problem with this was that the North would be part of two customs areas yet there would not be any border on the island. It meant that the EU customs code could potentially be unravelled in Ireland with serious consequences for the single market. 'There is simply no precedent for such an arrangement. But we remain willing to keep working to find legal and practical solutions to the problems raised by the British provided they accept our concept of a full customs regime upon entrance to the island,' noted Barnier.

The other big issue was the consent procedure. Barnier told the ambassadors of the EU-27 that the British had given up on the idea of granting the DUP a unilateral veto on the process. 'We are aware that the Taoiseach and Prime Minister Johnson have discussed other ideas apart from this for ensuring that the consent of both communities can be obtained at regular intervals.' He also observed that some questions remained unanswered, particularly whether it would be a yes vote – to continue with the proposed system, or a no – to discontinue it.

Initially the talks in Brussels were inconclusive, with Frost trying to unpick some things already agreed. However, after days and nights of negotiation the two sides resolved most of the outstanding issues. As the talks were going on in Brussels, the British engaged with the Irish and the DUP to pin down the detail of the consent mechanism. Threlfall and Bew returned to Dublin to pore over the options with their Irish counterparts. They finally worked out the detail of how, four years after the agreement came into force, the Stormont Assembly would decide by a simple majority whether it should continue to be applied. If there was cross-community support for its continuation it would apply for eight years. If it was just a simple majority there would be another vote every four years. If there was a simple majority against it in the Assembly, the Protocol, as it came to be known, would cease to apply after a cooling-off period of two years during which time the necessary measures to replace it would have to be agreed.

As the detail of the agreement was being slowly hammered out in Brussels and Dublin it seemed to the outside world as if this was yet another stage in a tortuous process that had no end. There was still considerable worry in Dublin political circles at what might happen. Labour Party leader Brendan Howlin said experience showed that people needed to be very wary of Johnson. 'That's why I thought it was a significant risk for the Taoiseach to go in a room alone with him and come to an agreement,' noted Howlin, who said he did not know if there was a clear pathway to an agreement as the opposition parties had not been briefed on the talks. 'We are a little over two weeks away from a catastrophic outcome which would be a hard Brexit,' he said.

Fianna Fáil leader Micheál Martin took a more positive view, welcoming the progress made at the Wirral and expressing the hope that it would finally lead to an agreement. 'The agreement at the Wirral was different to what was originally there in the backstop but that didn't matter. It avoided a hard border and also gave a potential which I had been arguing for from day one that Northern Ireland could have access to both the UK and EU markets,' said Martin.

The public reaction to Varadkar's efforts to strike a deal with Johnson were overwhelmingly positive. An Ipsos MRBI opinion poll in the *Irish Times* showed a dramatic rise of 15 points in Varadkar's satisfaction rating, with a huge majority backing the government's Brexit strategy. The concerns being expressed by the DUP at the prospect of a border in the Irish Sea certainly served to boost support for the deal south of the Border.

In Brussels the two sides hammered out the detail of the deal agreed in principle by Varadkar and Johnson. On the day before the EU summit, just when Barnier thought it was in the bag, David Frost and Tim Barrow came back to him accompanied by group of tax experts to argue for a rewrite of the VAT chapter of the Protocol. 'On a pretext of being able to assure the UK that control of tax services remains in British hands, what they actually want is to give Northern Ireland a major tax advantage within the single market itself. Not a chance.' After this rebuff it was all finally pinned down and Barnier briefed the Brexit steering group, including Guy Verhofstadt and other European Parliament leaders, before going back to his office for a well-earned pizza with his negotiating team.

As this was going on in Brussels Johnson struggled to get the DUP and some of his own hardliners on board. He had a phone conversation with Varadkar urging him to agree some flexibility on the Stormont consent mechanism in the Protocol, but the Taoiseach held firm, insisting that any decision would have to be by a simple majority and would not require cross-community support. The Prime Minister was deliberately vague when he addressed a meeting of the 1922 Committee, comparing the state of the negotiations to the final stage of climbing Mount Everest. 'We're on the Hillary Step going strong for the summit, but it is shrouded in cloud,' he said.

The following day, Thursday 17 October, the European Council was scheduled to sign off on the deal. At nine o'clock that morning Boris Johnson rang Juncker attempting to obtain further concessions on VAT. He was given a firm 'no' and shortly afterwards began a cabinet meeting in Downing Street to get formal approval. 'All these years we have done so much waiting for the British!' sighed Barnier who, without waiting for the green light, began preparations for the various steps that would have to be taken during the day.

Johnson called Juncker again later in the morning to confirm that the cabinet backed the plan; then he spoke to Barnier about the steps he intended to take to ratify the deal. There would be a 'meaningful vote' in the Commons two days later, with the Withdrawal Bill going to parliament the following Monday and Tuesday. Johnson's strategy was to get it done as quickly as possible to exert maximum pressure on MPs. Juncker committed to help him.

Barnier briefed the Commission at 11.30 a.m. and then went to meet the media in the Commission press room where, to his great surprise, the journalists gave him a round of applause. Later in the day Johnson kicked off the European Council meeting in an emotional fashion, telling the other heads of government that one of his daughters was born in Brussels and speaking about 'the two sides of the British heart'. More to the point, he told them that the agreement would have to win the vote in the House of Commons and he promised that when that was done the UK and the EU would be able to rebuild their relationship. 'I am here for the first time and, I hope, the last,' he concluded.

When Johnson left the room to allow the twenty-seven to give their verdict on the deal, Tusk gave the floor to Barnier. He told the EU leaders that the trigger for the agreement was the meeting in Liverpool a few days earlier between Varadkar and Johnson, since it was there that the Prime Minister had moved on two fundamental points: first accepting that de facto customs procedures would have to be implemented around the island of Ireland; and second by withdrawing the right of the DUP to veto the deal.

After a round table discussion during which Barnier dealt with a range of queries from the EU leaders, Tusk checked that all twenty-seven were in agreement. In his diary Barnier noted Tusk's contribution to the unity among the heads of government. 'Over the years I have developed a deep respect for this courageous Polish politician.'

The EU leaders then went off to brief their respective media delegations, but there was one notable change to the usual format. Instead of going to the Irish delegation room, a beaming Varadkar joined the leaders of the EU institutions, Jean-Claude Juncker and Donald Tusk, to announce the approval of the full legal text by EU leaders.

Tusk turned to Varadkar to acknowledge the special place of Ireland in the talks: 'Why has a deal that was impossible yesterday become possible today?' he asked. 'First, the new version of the deal has been positively assessed by Ireland. I've said from the beginning that we would always stand behind Ireland, and not force a deal unfavourable to Dublin.' True to his word, Tusk, along with Barnier, had ensured that the UK's road to Brexit had to go through Dublin.

At that press conference Tusk explained why a deal had finally been possible. 'The key change in comparison with the earlier version of the deal is Prime Minister Johnson's acceptance to have customs checks at the points of entry into Northern Ireland. This compromise will allow us to avoid border checks between Ireland and Northern Ireland, and will ensure the integrity of the single market.'

Varadkar also paid tribute to the solidarity the other EU leaders had shown with Ireland. 'As the leader of a small nation I have felt enormous solidarity from my European partners, and I think what's been demonstrated in the past few years is a union of peoples and one in which small states are protected.' He went on to express his regret that the UK was leaving the EU. 'I have mixed feelings today, I regret the UK is leaving but respect the decision to do so, like an old friend going on a journey without us, and we really hope it works out for them. There will always be a place at the table for them if they ever want to come back.' Merkel expressed similar sentiments. 'We have shown that the EU-27 have stuck together. I am feeling quite optimistic.'

The remarkable thing was that after all the drama in Brussels, London and Dublin, the final Withdrawal Agreement reflected only slight changes, mainly involving amendments to the six paragraphs dealing with Ireland, to the 600-page Withdrawal Agreement negotiated by Theresa May. It meant that apart from the Irish clauses the agreement, which had been rejected three times by the UK parliament, remained intact, and would go back again to the House of Commons for ratification.

The new text was entitled the 'Ireland/Northern Ireland Protocol' and under its terms it was agreed that Northern Ireland would continue to follow EU rules on product standards (part of the EU's single market rules) to prevent checks along the Irish Border. Checks would instead take place on goods entering Northern Ireland from England, Scotland or Wales. Inspections would take place at Northern Ireland ports, and customs documents would have to be completed.

While the new deal was remarkably similar to the one negotiated by Theresa May, Johnson had succeeded in two key political objectives. First, he got the EU to reopen the Withdrawal Agreement, something that Barnier had insisted was never going to be possible. Second, the backstop as it applied to the entire UK was removed; instead, he had agreed to a border down the Irish Sea. While this was something that Ireland and the EU had argued for from the beginning, his climb-down allowed him to claim that he had got rid of the hated backstop. The fact that the solution entailed abandoning the DUP didn't appear to bother the ERG group of Brexiteers in the Conservative Party.

A rueful Gavin Barwell noted in 2021 that Johnson's threat of leaving without a deal did not extract any meaningful concessions from the EU. 'Despite all the talk from his chief negotiator David Frost about how the May government had blinked at key moments, the truth is that the deal Boris negotiated was 95 per cent Theresa's deal with the 5 per cent that was new involving concessions by the UK. Boris went back to what the EU had wanted all along: special arrangements for Northern Ireland that created a partial border within our own country.'

The big question after the agreement in Brussels was whether Johnson could do what May had failed to do and get his deal through parliament. In characteristic style he professed total confidence that he could get the deal passed even though the DUP declared that its ten MPs would vote against the government in the meaningful vote scheduled for 48 hours later. 'These proposals are not, in our view, beneficial to the economic wellbeing of Northern Ireland and the integrity of the Union,' said a statement from the party.

Varadkar tried to reassure unionists that the constitutional position of Northern Ireland would not be affected by the agreement. 'The queen will still be the queen, the pound will still be the pound, people will still post letters in Royal Mail red letter boxes,' he said before leaving Brussels. He pointed out that the North would remain part of the United Kingdom because of the Good Friday Agreement. 'That is protected until such a time, should that time ever arise, when the majority of the people in Northern Ireland vote otherwise.' He also pointed out that there were already differences between the North and the rest of the UK which didn't affect its constitutional position. 'It's been the case for a hundred years now that Northern Ireland has its own legal system, has a different education system, has lots of different laws, lots of different rules from the rest of the UK. And that's a reflection of devolution and autonomy and doesn't change the constitutional position of Northern Ireland.'

DUP deputy leader Nigel Dodds was not impressed by the reassurance.

If Leo Varadkar thinks unionism is just about red post boxes then he is either very ill-informed or else just wishes to be offensive. Of course we will still use sterling and Her Majesty the Queen will be our head of state, but a new trade barrier will have been erected between Northern Ireland and the rest of the United Kingdom without the consent of anyone who lives here.

What was particularly galling for the DUP was that its allies in the ERG, with whom it had conspired to vote down Theresa May's deal, now deserted them and rallied behind Johnson, even though he had agreed to a border in the Irish Sea, something that May had refused to do. The sheer foolishness of the DUP's involvement in ensuring that the May deal, which respected the integrity of the UK, was rejected was now apparent to all. The humiliation of having their gullibility and political incompetence exposed to the world was hard to bear.

Looking back, Varadkar admits that he had some sympathy for the position in which the DUP found itself. 'I did feel bad for the DUP. Now, I didn't feel sympathy for them in the sense that they had created this mess themselves but I did feel sorry for them. Someone in the Orange Order said to me once that there was a long history of unionists being betrayed by British prime ministers and he wouldn't be surprised if it happened again. And it just felt like that was happening and I felt bad for them. They walked into it but I definitely knew it wasn't a good thing.'

Similar sentiments were voiced at the time of the deal by Jonathan Powell, who wrote that Varadkar and his team deserved huge credit 'for their patience, calmness and, above all, imaginative approach in the face of *Raider of the Lost Ark*-style negotiation tactics by the British side.' He went on:

The problem is, however, that Brexit was always going to trample on someone's rights in Northern Ireland, and it has ended up being the DUP. It might be tempting to just say the DUP had it coming, given their misplaced trust in the two-timing Johnson, but that would be a mistake for the long-term peace of the island.

Instead it is important to understand why the DUP object to this deal and to acknowledge that they have a point. The hard border in the

Irish Sea is a real problem for them. It will grow wider over time as the UK diverges in terms of regulation and as we introduce new tariffs. More and more items will have to be on the list drawn up by the new joint committee. And that widening border will threaten their British identity.

Two former British prime ministers, John Major and Tony Blair, who steered the process that led to the Good Friday Agreement, also warned that Johnson's Brexit deal could upset the delicate balance in Northern Ireland. In a joint video with Blair for the People's Vote campaign that advocated a second Brexit referendum, Major said a border in the Irish Sea would fuel unionist fears.

It was not clear initially if the DUP's rejection of the deal would be enough to scupper it in the House of Commons. Some on the Irish government side felt that the agreement could well go down to defeat in a parliament that had demonstrated again and again that it knew what it didn't want but could not make up its mind what it would accept.

When the Commons met on Saturday 19 October, Johnson's plans for a vote on the agreement were thrown into disarray when a majority of MPs backed an amendment that would oblige the government to implement the provisions of the Benn Act and seek an extension of the transition until 31 January 2000, in order to avoid a no-deal. Johnson was forced to go back on his pledge and wrote to Tusk seeking an extension. He didn't sign the letter – to make the point that it was parliament's wish rather than his own. He sent a second, signed, letter saying he would still push for ratification the following week and hoped to have the whole procedure completed by the end of the month so that the extension would not be necessary.

On Tuesday 22 October the road to Brexit was finally cleared when the Commons voted by 329 votes to 299 to support the Withdrawal Agreement Bill. While MPs refused to vote for an accelerated legislative process to get withdrawal done by 31 October, there was no longer anything in the way of an orderly withdrawal on 31 January 2020. The DUP voted against the government in both divisions but the party's ability to influence the course of Brexit was now at an end.

Leo Varadkar was the first EU leader to react to the vote. 'It's welcome that the House of Commons voted by a clear majority in favour of legislation needed to enact the Withdrawal Agreement. We will now await further developments from London and Brussels about next steps, including [a] timetable for the legislation and the need for an extension,' he said. There was immediate speculation in Dublin about the impact of the vote on the likelihood of a November general election in the UK. 'And if they're having an election, we're having an election,' said one Irish government source.

One of the more bizarre speeches in the Commons debate came from hard-line Tory Brexiteer and member of the ERG Owen Paterson. He quoted with approval the speech delivered by Michael Collins to the Dáil after he had signed the Anglo Irish Treaty of 1921. Collins famously said the Treaty gave Ireland not the freedom it wanted but the freedom to achieve freedom and in time he was proved right. Paterson, who had served as Northern Secretary under David Cameron, had clearly boned up on Irish history during his time in office but the irony of quoting one of the founders of the Irish State in support of Brexit was clearly lost on him.

Johnson's hope of getting the Withdrawal Bill through parliament by the end of October were not realised and he was forced to accept the extension of EU membership until 31 January 2020. He then made a determined attempt to get the general election he had been angling for since he took over as Prime Minister. He made another attempt to get the two-thirds majority required by the Fixed-Term Parliaments Act and when that failed announced he would come back with a short Bill which would require just a simple majority to set aside the provisions of the Act.

He was facilitated in his ambition to have a general election by the naivety of the Opposition. The Liberal Democrats and Scottish National Party (SNP) proposed a motion calling for an early election and Johnson managed to win a decisive victory in the Commons setting aside the Fixed-Term Parliament Act and calling a general election for 12 December.

He set off on the campaign with a slogan that had emerged from a focus group in Bury in the north of England: 'Get Brexit Done'. The message was simple but powerful and it resonated with voters in all parts of England who had become utterly weary with the endless political manoeuvring over Brexit and the interminable negotiations with the EU.

Outside Northern Ireland there was little interest or understanding of the Protocol but it did become an issue towards the end of the election campaign. Early in the campaign Johnson told Northern Ireland exporters that under the terms of the Protocol they would not need to fill in customs declarations when they sent goods across the Irish Sea to the rest of the UK. He added that if firms were asked to, they should call him and 'I will direct them to throw that form in the bin ... There will be no forms, no checks, no barriers of any kind.' This contradicted comments made by his Brexit Secretary, Steve Barclay, who told the House of Commons 'exit summary declarations will be required in terms of NI to GB'.

Simon Coveney, on a visit to Brussels, said he was not going to get into a debate with Prime Minister Johnson in the middle of an election campaign, but he insisted, 'The deal is the deal, it's there in black and white. People can read it for themselves and I think it's self-explanatory.'

Towards the end of the campaign Labour leader Jeremy Corbyn revealed the contents of a leaked British Treasury assessment of the impact the Protocol would have on trade between Northern Ireland and the rest of the UK if there were no free trade agreement at the end of the transition period. The paper suggested that Northern Ireland would be cut off from whole swathes of the UK internal market, would face shortages and prices rises in shops and would effectively be severed from the UK's economic union.

The gloomy report suggested that the impact on the Northern Ireland economy could be devastating, with 98 per cent of Northern Ireland export businesses 'likely to struggle to bear this cost' of customs declarations and documentary and physical checks on goods moving within the UK. It said there would be checks on trade going from Great Britain to Northern Ireland, including tariffs, food safety and security checks, and regulatory checks to ensure that goods coming into Northern Ireland were compliant with EU regulation.

None of this had any impact on the electorate outside Northern Ireland. Johnson campaigned in the jokey, bumbling style that so many English voters found endearing. His strategy, masterminded by Cummings, was to make gains in the so-called 'red wall' constituencies in northern England that had voted Labour for generations but that had also voted for Brexit. The slogan 'Get Brexit Done' had resonance all over England, but it was particularly potent in the 'red wall' constituencies. Johnson was helped greatly by the decision of Nigel Farage to pull Brexit party candidates from constituencies where the Conservatives were defending seats and contest only Opposition-held seats.

Johnson's strategy paid off in spectacular style. The Conservatives gained 48 seats, ending up with 365, while Labour dropped 60 to finish with 202, its worst result since the 1930s. The Liberal Democrats lost one – its leader Jo Swinson – while the SNP recovered ground it had lost in 2017, almost obliterating the other parties in Scotland. In Northern Ireland the DUP lost two seats to end up with eight while Sinn Féin held seven, the SDLP won two and the Alliance Party one. For the first time a majority of Westminster seats in the North went to non-unionist parties. It was a fitting outcome for the disastrous political miscalculations made by the DUP.

The result was a triumph for Johnson and his Brexit strategy. He had increased the party's share of the vote by 12 per cent and had a majority of eighty in the Commons. There were no longer any obstacles to leaving on 31 January 2020, or to proceeding to the next stage of the Brexit process, which was to negotiate the future relationship with the EU.

While Johnson capitalised on the breakthrough in the Wirral to put himself in an unassailable position in the UK, Varadkar failed to seize the moment to do the same in Ireland, even though he was initially bolstered by a wave of public support. An *Irish Times* opinion poll showed a jump of fifteen points in Varadkar's satisfaction rating after the deal, while Fine Gael was steady on 29 per cent of the vote, remaining the biggest party in the country. He was in a strong position to call a general election. A majority of Fine Gael ministers urged him to go to the country, but his closest advisers urged caution.

Having agonised over it for a few days, Varadkar opted for caution. He reportedly told his cabinet that he was Taoiseach first and Fine Gael leader second, 'that while an election now may be the best time for the party it might not be for the country'. On 30 October he told journalists that with the Brexit process still ongoing the UK general election had the capacity to change the picture at Westminster once again. 'I don't think it is the right thing for the country given the ongoing uncertainty around Brexit,' he said.

Varadkar quickly found himself in the worst of both worlds. The Opposition kept a relentless focus on the failures of the government, particularly in housing and health. Minister for Housing Eoghan Murphy barely survived a motion of no confidence in early December and Minister for Health Simon Harris was lined up as the next target for the Opposition in the New Year. As there was no guarantee the minister would survive a vote of confidence Varadkar had little choice but to seek a dissolution of the Dáil on 14 January. An election would be held on 8 February. He had lost all the impetus gained from the successful outcome of the Brexit process, and the election outcome was far worse than anybody in Fine Gael anticipated. The party dropped fifteen seats to end up with thirty-five in the 160-member Dáil, three behind Fianna Fáil and, sensationally, two behind Sinn Féin, which had suddenly become the biggest party in terms of the popular vote. It was nothing short of a disaster for Varadkar.

With the benefit of hindsight he regrets not having gone in November, but he does not accept that it would inevitably have been a better result. 'I always thought we'd get more than thirty-five seats. Some days I thought it might only be forty-something but we did much poorer in the election than that. So, if I could go back again I probably would have risked it in November. But I'm not so naive as to think the same dynamics might not have played out.'

As to why he got the opposite of the Brexit bounce won by Johnson, Varadkar is philosophical. 'The public reaction to the Brexit deal was great, but I was never naive about it. Look, Churchill won the war but lost the election. Elections are always about what are you offering me now. You shouldn't expect a reward for what you've done; the public will ask what are you offering us now? We hoped that our good record on the economy and on Brexit and international affairs would stand to us but it didn't.'

16

Buyer's Remorse

'I made a terrible mistake. We never realised that the Protocol was going to be so onerous'

Boris Johnson to Micheál Martin at Chequers,
14 May 2021

* * *

In the first half of 2020 Brexit receded from the headlines. The main reason was the emergence of Covid-19 as a global pandemic that threatened to kill an unquantifiable number of people and wreak havoc with the health systems of the developed world. Another reason for the relative calm was that nothing changed immediately as a result of the UK's departure on 31 January because of the transition period, which was due to continue until at least the end of 2020. The talks between the EU and the UK on a Trade and Cooperation Agreement got off to a slow start and were not helped by the Covid restrictions, which meant that the chief actors could not meet in person for long periods.

In Ireland the political stalemate that followed the inconclusive general election occupied the minds of leading politicians as they struggled with how to deal with the seismic changes that had shaken the system to its foundations. Most of them had concluded that the threat of a hard Border had gone for good following the agreement at the Wirral, and its endorsement by the European Council. In any case, the trade talks and the future relationship were matters for the EU and the UK to negotiate.

Faced with the twin threats of Covid and political instability Varadkar, somewhat ironically considering his poor election result, benefited from a massive surge in public support. He delivered a state of the nation address on St Patrick's Day that struck a chord with the public and generated strong public support for lockdown measures. 'We did enter one of those moments that don't happen a lot in politics,' said Varadkar later. 'That kind of wartime feeling where everybody was behind the government, behind the country and wanted us to succeed. That's rare. We experienced the same to a certain extent on Brexit where people felt Ireland was under threat and they wanted the government to succeed.'

In the immediate aftermath of the election Sinn Féin demanded to be in government and organised public rallies to support its claim, but when Fianna Fáil leader Micheál Martin ruled out coalition, reality dawned. It became clear that Sinn Féin and the small hard left groupings simply didn't have the numbers in the Dáil to form a government. The only viable option was a coalition of Fine Gael, Fianna Fáil and the Greens. Months of wary negotiations were to follow.

Meanwhile, in Northern Ireland the power-sharing institutions at Stormont were restored in early January after a gap of three years. The breakthrough was mainly due to the hard work and skilled diplomacy of Northern Secretary Julian Smith as well as the commitment of Simon Coveney. While the achievement was widely welcomed, Coveney's role did nothing to help Fine Gael in the general election, while Smith was casually dropped from the government by Johnson in a cabinet reshuffle in February.

Smith's sacking provoked a rare cross-party consensus in Northern Ireland, with Arlene Foster and Michelle O'Neill both expressing disappointment at the decision, as did Leo Varadkar. One leading British journalist, Peter Foster, said on Twitter it was a testament to Smith that both Foster and Varadkar had paid tribute to him. 'Despite his commitments to a young family Smith clearly gave everything to the Northern Ireland job at a time when the British government clearly didn't give a monkey's whatever about the province ... Smith was chopped because ultimately he refused to get with the crazier bits of the programme ...

And so revenge is taken. NI is worse off. Suspect in the long run we're all worse off.'

Another British political commentator, Stephen Bush, wrote in the *New Statesman* that Smith's dismissal was regarded as inexplicable across Westminster because 'he succeeded where his predecessors failed in negotiating a return to power-sharing in Northern Ireland.' Bush predicted that the decision would have major implications for Northern Ireland and for the next phase of the Brexit talks.

'Firstly, I wouldn't be shocked if it means that the return of power-sharing at Stormont proves to be brief. The second is that it will make the negotiations on the exact shape of the Northern Ireland Protocol – which will run concurrently with the next stage of the Brexit talks – more fraught. The headlines on this reshuffle will be about the appointments and big beasts. But make no mistake, the sacking of Smith is of far greater importance than anything else Boris Johnson will do today.' The truth of this was to become evident over the following two year.

The disappointment in Dublin at the departure of Smith was matched by relief that Barnier was asked by the Commission to stay on and handle the talks on an EU–UK Trade and Cooperation Agreement between the EU and UK. He was keenly aware that concluding the negotiations by the end of 2020 would be a race against time. There were three basic areas for negotiation. The first was establishing an economic partnership that would avoid tariffs or quotas for trade involving a 'level playing field' agreement and a deal on fisheries. The second was security co-operation, on which no big hurdles were anticipated. The third and potentially most contentious area was establishing a robust institutional framework to ensure both parties implemented the deal.

At the first formal meeting between Barnier and the UK's lead negotiator David Frost on 17 February Frost dropped a bombshell. He airily announced that Boris Johnson's government did not feel bound by the Political Declaration it had signed just four months earlier. 'We can accept some elements but not all. There is a philosophical gap between us about the so-called level playing field.' The implications for the operation of the Northern Ireland Protocol were ominous.

Over the following months, during the often tetchy talks between Barnier and Frost on the future relationship there were regular hints from the British side that they were unhappy with the Protocol. Barnier was having none of it and insisted that the agreement would have to be honoured. At the end of March he confided his determination to his diary.

In Ireland and Northern Ireland the British must put in place customs, regulatory and phytosanitary procedures for all products arriving from a third country or from Great Britain at Northern Ireland ports and airports. None of this can be left to chance. It requires personnel to carry out the controls and IT infrastructure. It is not a question of renegotiating the Withdrawal Agreement but of making it operational in practice on 31 December.

In May the British government issued what it called a command paper detailing how the Protocol would work in practice. Officials at Stormont started to prepare the ground for the various new checks that would be required on top of the animal health checks that already applied to trade between Britain and Northern Ireland.

Meanwhile the political system in Dublin was focused on forming the new government. After months of negotiations Fine Gael, Fianna Fáil and the Green Party agreed a programme for government with the Taoiseach's office rotating between the two biggest parties. It was agreed that Micheál Martin would be Taoiseach for the first two and a half years and that Leo Varadkar would take over for the second half of the government's life.

Assuming the Taoiseach's office was a remarkable political achievement for Martin. He had taken over the Fianna Fáil leadership in the dark days of the financial crisis and saw his party's Dáil representation plunge from eighty to twenty in the 2011 general election. It was widely speculated that he would be the first leader of the party never to become Taoiseach, but he clawed his way back from the brink of political disaster, doubling the party's seats in 2016 and entering the 2020 election as a realistic contender for government. The poor election outcome was a bitter disappointment for him but he resisted pressure to pursue a coalition deal with Sinn Féin and ended up as Taoiseach at the end of June 2020, after nine years as party leader.

Martin, a quietly spoken Corkman with vast ministerial experience ranging from Health and Education to Foreign Affairs, appeared initially to struggle with the responsibilities of Taoiseach. He was presented with a number of political challenges during his early months in office. He had to sack Minister for Agriculture Barry Cowen for allegedly attempting to evade a Garda checkpoint for a motoring offence years earlier. He appointed Mayo TD Dara Calleary in his place, but in August there was a political convulsion when the media reported that members of the Oireachtas Golf Society had breached Covid rules at a dinner in Clifden in County Galway.

Calleary, who had addressed the gathering, was forced to resign, but the big news was that Ireland's powerful and influential EU Commissioner Phil Hogan was also in the firing line. Following days of controversy Martin and Varadkar called on Hogan to step down and ultimately Commission President Ursula von der Leyen, who had succeeded Juncker in autumn 2019, told him his position was untenable. Hogan, who was widely regarded as one of Ireland's best ever EU Commissioners, of the calibre of Peter Sutherland or Ray MacSharry, felt he had no option but to resign. He was replaced by the experienced MEP Mairead McGuinness, but the loss of such a powerful figure with an established reputation at the heart of the Commission was a serious blow to Ireland's clout in Brussels.

In February 2022 Judge Mary Fahy in the Galway District Court ruled that there had been no breach of the law or of the Covid regulations at the golf society dinner. 'I'm satisfied the organisers did everything to comply, not in a court of public opinion, but in the court of law in my opinion. Unfortunately, very good people lost very good jobs,' she said in her ruling. By then of course the damage had long been done.

Not long after Hogan's departure, Ireland and the EU got a shock when the *Financial Times* reported that the British government was planning to set aside key elements of the Protocol. Under the headline 'UK plans to undermine Withdrawal Treaty puts Brexit talks at risk', the newspaper reported that the government's Internal Market Bill proposed to override parts of the Protocol. The report also said that Johnson was happy to accept a no-deal outcome if the talks had not concluded by his deadline of 15 October. Barnier was as shocked by the report as the government in Dublin.

A spokesman for the Commission insisted that the full implementation of the Withdrawal Agreement, and in particular the Ireland/

Northern Ireland Protocol, was essential. 'These are legal obligations under international law, this is a matter of trust, this is a prerequisite, a precondition for the negotiations on the future partnership. I think that's clear and I don't think we need to say any more,' he added. Northern Secretary Brandon Lewis confirmed in the House of Commons that a decision had been taken to override the Protocol. 'This does break international law in a very specific and limited way,' he said.

Barnier recorded that he was even more shocked when his team received a copy of the Internal Market Bill. 'This plan is even more serious than the leaks suggested. If passed, it would upset the delicate balance struck just a year ago with Boris Johnson himself to ensure there is no physical border on the island of Ireland, to protect all dimensions of the Good Friday Agreement and to preserve the EU's internal market.' He expressed his hurt at what the British were proposing to do. 'At this moment I feel that the threat is a betrayal of their word. It seems they will stop at nothing.'

Micheál Martin had a telephone conversation with Johnson in which he set out 'in forthright terms his concerns about the British move to unilaterally walk away from aspects of the Withdrawal Agreement signed last year'. A government statement said Martin had outlined his concerns to the Prime Minister about the 'breach of an international treaty, the absence of bilateral engagement and the serious implications for Northern Ireland'. In an interview with CNN the Taoiseach said the British move represented a new departure from the norms and conduct of diplomacy. 'I was annoyed and angry at the fact there was no heads-up. The degree to which it drags Northern Ireland back into the centre stage is very, very regrettable.'

After consultation with Barnier, Ursula von der Leyen sent Johnson a stiff message. 'Very concerned about announcements from the British government on its intentions to breach the Withdrawal Agreement. This would break international law and undermine trust. *Pacta sunt servanda* [agreements must be kept] – the foundation of future prosperous relations.'

European Commission Vice-President Maroš Šefčovič, who headed the EU team on the joint committee supervising the implementation of the agreement, travelled to London for talks with his UK opposite number, Michael Gove. Šefčovič insisted that 'peace on the island of

Ireland should never be used as a bargaining tool' and he called for the removal of the contentious clauses from the Bill.

The British sent out different messages in the following weeks. Frost temporarily adopted a more conciliatory tone, but Johnson claimed that normal EU procedures for food imports amounted to a food blockade in the Irish Sea that would destroy the economic and territorial integrity of the UK. Two former British prime ministers, John Major and Tony Blair, entered the fray to call the UK move 'irresponsible, wrong in principle and dangerous in practice'; three others, Gordon Brown, David Cameron and Theresa May, also declared they were against the Internal Market Bill.

The Irish used their influence in Washington to mobilise American opposition to the Bill. Coveney contacted Barnier to assure him that the British were meeting with strong resistance on Capitol Hill. Richie Neal, chair of the powerful Ways and Means Committee (which deals with trade issues), who was also president of the Friends of Ireland group in Congress, phoned Barnier for a briefing. Then Joe Biden, the Democratic Party presidential candidate, waded into the debate with a strong tweet: 'We can't allow the Good Friday Agreement that brought peace to Northern Ireland to become a casualty of Brexit. Any trade deal between the US and the UK must be contingent on respect for the Agreement and preventing the return of a hard border. Period.'

The US response was a clear warning to Johnson, but the tetchiness continued through the autumn. Frost told Barnier that it was not Brexit that was creating the problem in Ireland: 'It's more complicated than that. Northern Ireland is part of our country. These issues go back centuries.' Barnier replied that he knew a great deal about Irish history: 'I care very much for the country and its people.'

The Internal Market Bill remained on the table but the criticism continued from inside and outside the UK with Theresa May and French President Emmanuel Macron issuing messages of condemnation. Nonetheless the talks between Barnier and Frost dragged on past Johnson's own deadline of 15 October. Barnier came to the conclusion that Johnson wanted to wait for the result of the US presidential election in the hope that his ally Donald Trump would be re-elected.

The other side of the coin was that the election of Biden would weaken Johnson's hand. When Biden's victory in the US election was confirmed the President-elect wasted no time in nailing his colours to the mast. In response to a television reporter who called out: 'Mr President. A question from the BBC', Biden replied with a smile, 'The BBC! I'm Irish.'

Barnier watched the exchange with satisfaction:

The UK and the US will always have a special relationship, which is something other Europeans need to understand. But I doubt that Joe Biden will have a special relationship with Boris Johnson. What is certain is that this election means that the government in London has lost the leverage it wanted to generate in our negotiations by holding Ireland hostage. It is now certain that the famous Internal Market Bill will have to be dumped at some point.

That is exactly what happened in early December when Šefčovič and Gove agreed on a solution which ensured that controls and trade with Northern Ireland would be carried out in accordance with European law. The British government then announced that the Internal Market Bill would be withdrawn. 'A lot of wasted time and controversy only to end up simply honouring their own signature and applying what had already been decided upon and ratified,' commented Barnier.

In Dublin Martin kept a close eye on developments as British threats about non-implementation of the Protocol and a consequent no-deal Brexit emerged regularly in the closing months of 2020. 'We were obviously concerned about a no-deal and also about the fisheries issue but broadly we wanted something as close to a free trade deal as possible,' recalled Martin. 'I think the problem with the British position always was that the politics got in the way of sensible arrangements. The ERG's influence over the government was strong and so you have a very difficult negotiation which went right up to Christmas Eve.'

As the negotiations with the EU progressed Johnson's premiership lurched from one scandal to another. On 14 November, following a power struggle in Downing Street, his chief adviser, Dominic Cummings, who had masterminded the Leave campaign and the successful election strategy in 2019, resigned.

By that stage the focus had shifted to fishing, with the UK and the EU at loggerheads about the level of access boats from maritime countries, including Ireland, would have to UK waters in the future. Another bout of brinkmanship and bad-tempered negotiations finally ended with a deal on Christmas Eve.

'I remember it well because then we had the Alpha variant two days later so it was a horrendous Christmas,' recalled Martin. 'Even on Christmas Eve we were worried about a no-deal Brexit. We were concerned about the fisheries at the time, it was getting more heated and of course, a no-deal would have been calamitous for fisheries and everything else. Now I never quite thought Boris would go for a no-deal, do a kamikaze on it, but it was a serious worry.'

Because of Covid, Barnier's news conference had to be held virtually. He kicked off with a new twist on the phrase he had used throughout the negotiations – 'The clock is no longer ticking' – and he added that there were three objectives he had kept in mind all the way through the long process: the preservation of peace and stability on the island of Ireland; protecting the single market; and building a new partnership with the UK.

Barnier's job was done but the Protocol soon came back to haunt his successor, Maroš Šefčovič, the experienced Slovak Commissioner who was appointed to represent the EU in the partnership council established under the terms of the Trade and Cooperation Agreement. Throughout 2021 Šefčovič and his team had to deal with a concerted campaign by Johnson and his Brexit negotiator David Frost to undermine the Protocol.

'So eventually you get the deal,' said Martin. 'Boris signs up to it but then from then on they begin to drag their feet on the Protocol. And then we get to a position where the British government does not appear to realise that the stability of Northern Ireland needs to be a priority.'

The EU did not help itself with a serious misstep on 29 January 2021, when Commission President Ursula von der Leyen threatened to invoke Article 16 of the Protocol. This is a safeguard clause that allows either party to take unilateral 'strictly necessary' measures if the application of the Protocol creates serious economic, societal or environmental difficulties. Von der Leyen's threat to invoke Article 16 was made during a row between the EU and the UK over Covid vaccine supplies. There were fears in Brussels that the trade arrangements under the Protocol could be used as a back door to get around restrictions and send more supplies of the vaccine to the UK.

There was shock and outrage in Dublin, Belfast and London at von der Leyen's move. As Martin explained:

So they invoked Article 16 which, of course, was a mistake. John Callinan came in to me around six in the evening to tell me what had happened. I rang the President of the Commission immediately and in fairness to her she responded immediately. She said let me consult with my legal people and within an hour they had reversed the decision. Unionism conveniently ignores the speed at which the Commission put its hands up and said, 'Look, that was a mistake and we are not going to do it again.'

Varadkar is less forgiving:

I think the EU triggering Article 16 was a disaster, quite frankly. It was a really busy day and I was on the phone to Simon Coveney about something else that evening when it happened. I was driving through the Phoenix Park and my response was disbelief. I am not often speechless in life but I was this time. I could just not believe that this had happened and I think that was that was really damaging. Particularly as it was around vaccines of all things.

A senior Irish official also reflected on the 'absolute disaster' of the move. 'If anybody had forecast the Commission would do something like this you wouldn't have believed it. Of all the things that could go wrong this was not in our calculations. And of course the British have absolutely milked it. They're not wrong to say it did serious damage but they used it shamelessly.'

The same official observed that von der Leyen and her team operated in a similar fashion to Theresa May. 'It is a very tight, centralised team making decisions and not consulting and engaging.' He also pondered whether it would have happened if Phil Hogan was still Ireland's Commissioner. 'The question is would Phil even have known, but I think the answer is yes. Because of his sheer persona, his presence and ownership of the portfolio I think that he would have had to have been told.'

Another factor in the equation was that the Irish government was opposed to export controls in principle. As a former Minister for Health, Martin was aware of the damage controls could have done to the supply of vaccines because of the complex supply chains that are involved. 'From a supply chain perspective it was madness to do export controls and we resisted that at European Union level and we were proactive to say that this is not the way to go about this. And, you know, in fairness to the Commission, they agreed in the end.'

Northern Ireland First Minister and DUP leader Arlene Foster described the EU move as an 'incredible act of hostility' and demanded that Johnson respond in kind. 'At the first opportunity the EU has placed a hard border between Northern Ireland and the Republic of Ireland over the supply chain of the Coronavirus vaccine,' she added.

After the strong representations of the Taoiseach, and conversations between Johnson and the Commission president, the immediate issue was quickly resolved. The EU quickly reversed its position and UK cabinet minister Michael Gove said the EU had recognised it had made a mistake. However, the mistake gave the green light to those in the British government who preferred confrontation to conciliation over the terms of the Protocol.

In the early months of its operation in 2021 the Protocol did become an issue that affected not just politics in Northern Ireland but the lives of ordinary people. Some goods were missing from supermarket shelves and for a time some medicines were unavailable. This was partly due to the failure of British businesses to appreciate the level of paperwork that would be required by the fact that Northern Ireland was remaining in the EU single market, and partly due to a rigid interpretation of the rules by EU officials.

Varadkar conceded that the initial impact of the Protocol was more disruptive on trade between Britain and Northern Ireland than the Irish government had anticipated when the Protocol was devised. 'There was definitely a reality on the ground of some of these checks and controls having a greater impact on Britain to Northern Ireland trade than we had anticipated.'

Lord Lister made the same assessment. He said that neither the British nor the Irish negotiators had anticipated the rigidity of the EU approach to the operation of the Protocol when they agreed to it in October 2019. He blamed the difficulty on officials in Brussels for adopting a far too legalistic interpretation of the rules.

The teething troubles led to political tension in Northern Ireland as the DUP and other unionists became more vocal in their demands that the Protocol be scrapped. Micheál Martin called on the UK and the EU to dial down the rhetoric, saying there were 'elements the British government could sort out, but likewise on the European side I would say some member states need to cool it as well'. Negotiations between Šefčovič and Gove on the detail of the measure took some of the heat out of the row. The two men met in London and agreed to work on solutions to the problems and to extend the grace periods for business to comply with the new rules. More significantly, they both reiterated their full commitment to the Protocol.

However, the constructive mood did not survive the appointment of Frost to the cabinet on 1 March as minister with responsibility for Brexit and co-chair of the EU–UK Partnership Council. Frost immediately adopted a more combative approach and on 3 March Northern Secretary Brandon Lewis announced a unilateral six-month extension of the grace period for implementing checks, which was due to expire on 31 March.

The EU responded by instigating legal action against the UK for unilaterally breaching the agreement. One senior Commission official accused the UK of a second violation of international law over the Protocol. While Frost was blamed in Brussels for the UK's more aggressive line, Johnson's decision to appoint him to the role was a clear message in itself.

'Negotiating with Michael Gove was challenging as he came to talks fully prepared and made his points intelligently and forcibly,' said one senior EU official. 'The difference between him and Frost was that while Gove made strenuous efforts to mitigate the impact of the Protocol he accepted that it was an international obligation; Frost thought he could just abandon it even though he had been part of the team that agreed it in the first place. He was just impossible to deal with.'

Throughout 2021 Frost went out of his way to provoke one confrontation after another with the EU. The impact was to stoke tension in Northern Ireland, where loyalists were becoming increasingly restive about the symbolism as well as the substance of the Protocol. That spilled over into street violence in Belfast's Sandy Row in April when around three hundred people were involved in rioting, fifteen police officers were injured and a number of arrests were made. In the summer the Loyalist Communities Council, which represents a number of paramilitary groups that were active during the Troubles, cited the Protocol as justification for withdrawing support for the Good Friday Agreement, under which many of its members had been released early from prison.

On 28 April Arlene Foster resigned as DUP leader and First Minister following a concerted internal campaign to oust her. The majority of DUP Assembly members and a number of MPs signed a letter calling for her resignation as her authority had been fatally undermined by the British government's agreement to the Protocol. The more hard-line Edwin Poots was elected as her successor, but his tenure only lasted twenty-one days before he too resigned following an internal rebellion over his agreement to an Irish Language Act demanded by Sinn Féin. He in turn was succeeded by long-serving MP Jeffrey Donaldson and the DUP's internal turmoil gradually abated.

Later in May Martin and Johnson met at Chequers, the Prime Minister's country residence, to discuss the Protocol and other issues relating to Northern Ireland. They had an amicable conversation over lunch before getting down to serious discussions. Both sides issued statements afterwards saying they would continue to work together to find solutions to the Protocol and legacy issues in Northern Ireland.

'We had a long meeting at Chequers and it was a good meeting,' recalled Martin. 'Except he says: "Look, I made a terrible mistake. We never realised that the Protocol was going to be so onerous and that it would create such difficulties in the way of trade between Britain and Northern Ireland."' Martin restated the Irish and EU position and both of them agreed to ask the technocrats to make a big push to try to iron out the difficulties.

'Deep down he did reveal something. He is himself a unionist with a small u. He does believe in the union. Boris is Conservative Party leader and he is a unionist and he's proud of the union. I don't know if there is a lingering kind of guilt there that the Protocol landed unionism in it and feels he's agreed to something that he never anticipated would have the impact it did,' added Martin.

It's a bit hard to take some of that at times because he did agree it and basically it could be worked. Our passionate view is that if the political will is there this can be resolved. We are in no doubt about that. And the European Union through Šefčovič has been extremely patient and very anxious to reach an agreement, and our view has shown good faith.

Personally Boris is charming and we get on fine. He'll ring and he'll text. He's a force of nature. I think that he very often gets the wider picture and he tells me he is fond of Ireland. He has often told me how his daughter went to Trinity and enjoyed her time in Dublin.

Martin believes that Scotland is a complicating factor in the equation. 'Scotland is a looming issue and therefore, from a UK government's perspective, they want to ensure that nothing happens that promotes Scottish independence. To an extent the North is becoming a victim of that sort of political development. That's our assessment of it.'

Martin and Varadkar believe that the aggressive line adopted by Johnson and Frost during the first half of 2021 pushed the DUP and the UUP into taking a stronger line against the Protocol than they might otherwise have done. 'It was a really unfortunate set of events. Certainly before this year [2021] the ECJ was never an issue. It was not raised with me by unionist politicians and certainly not by the business community. So I think I think there is an element of buyer's remorse here and that the Prime Minister regrets signing up to this,' remarked Leo Varadkar

Varadkar is adamant that the Protocol has worked as intended.

It has prevented a border between North and South. It's strengthened the all-island economy, which was part of the original Declaration that we had agreed with Prime Minister May. It has preserved the integrity of the European single market. What it hasn't done is what I'd hoped it would do, which is to give Northern Ireland the best of both worlds. And I have to say that the level of checks and controls between Britain to Northern Ireland was greater than I thought they would be and needed to be. That is one of the areas where we have to take some responsibility for the problems that subsequently arose.

17

The Protocol Under Attack

'For a country like the United Kingdom to renege on an international treaty is something that does represent a new low point.'
Micheál Martin, 13 June 2022

* * *

Boris Johnson had been looking forward to the G7 meeting of the world's leading democracies in Cornwall in June 2021 as an opportunity to take his place at the centre of the world political stage but, to his consternation, the row over the Protocol overshadowed the event. US national security adviser Jake Sullivan warned before the event even started that President Biden had deep concerns that the issue could endanger peace in Northern Ireland, and when they met the President warned the Prime Minister not to renege on the deal. French President Emmanuel Macron got in on the act, demanding that Johnson honour the Protocol. The focus of the media on the Protocol rather than Johnson's efforts to project the image of global Britain was a humiliating outcome.

Later in the month the British asked the EU for an extension, to the end of September, to the grace period on chilled meats being sent from Britain to Northern Ireland. In advance of the move the Irish government made it clear it favoured the extension and Micheál Martin urged both Commission President Ursula von der Leyen and European Council President Charles Michel to allow it. The Taoiseach emphasised the need for both sides to dial down the rhetoric and he pointed to the positive aspects of the Protocol for trade which were getting drowned out amid rising tension.

In July both sides backed away from an immediate confrontation. The British called for a standstill period in which the EU would not ramp up its legal action and in return it promised to refrain from unilateral moves. The EU responded by pausing its legal action. 'In order to provide the necessary space to reflect on these issues and find durable solutions to the implementation of the Protocol, we have decided, at this stage, not to move to the next stage of the infringement procedure, started in March,' said a Commission statement.

In September Johnson travelled to the United States in an effort to build a positive relationship with the US President. He was given a warm welcome in the White House, but Biden repeated his concerns about the impact of the dispute over the Protocol on the Good Friday Agreement.

Meanwhile the EU, at the urging of the Irish government, made a determined attempt to find ways to mitigate the impact of the Protocol. Šefčovič went to Northern Ireland to meet a wide cross-section of people who had been affected by the arrangement as well as the political parties there. There were behind-the-scenes contacts between the government in Dublin and the unionist parties in an effort to prepare the way for the acceptance of a compromise.

In early October Šefčovič came forward with a much more significant set of modifications to the Protocol than the British had anticipated. The changes would have the effect of removing 80 per cent of the checks on goods from Britain destined for Northern Irish supermarket shelves and slashing customs formalities. They would have allowed unfrozen meat products into the single market, a move that in the eyes of some in Brussels opened a gap in the rules protecting EU agriculture and creating an opportunity for cross-border smuggling. It was a more wide-ranging offer than anybody had been expecting and some EU member states and senior officials in the Commission were worried that it was a step too far.

There were serious hopes in Dublin that this would be enough to defuse the problem and provide the unionists with an opportunity to claim a victory in getting the Protocol amended. Such hopes were dashed immediately when Frost, instead of welcoming the package as the basis for serious negotiations, demanded that the European Court of Justice (ECJ) should have no role in overseeing the operation of the Protocol. It was a demand he knew could not be met and it appeared to indicate that the British were intent on collapsing the talks and triggering Article 16 to suspend the operation of the Protocol.

'That put the unionists in a corner because they could not come out and accept something that had been rejected by their own government,' said Martin. 'That annoyed me more than anything because it displayed a lack of political will in Britain to getting this issue resolved.'

When Martin travelled to the COP 26 summit on climate change in Glasgow at the beginning of November rumours were rife that the UK was about to trigger Article 16. 'I was getting it from all quarters, getting texts from European prime ministers saying that they had met Boris and he told them he was going to invoke it,' said Martin. 'I got a text from Von der Leyen asking for an urgent meeting at COP. Charles Michel also wanted to meet me at COP. So I met them and also met a number of EU leaders, including Macron. They were all very strong in saying back to the UK, "You do this and it's a breach of an agreement and it's all-out confrontation." There were serious concerns about a very significant trade dispute between the European Union and the UK.'

Encouraged by the support, the Irish government responded forcibly to make sure Johnson and Frost understood that the triggering of Article 16 would have serious consequences for the UK. 'In my view it would be irresponsible, it would be unwise, and it would be reckless to invoke Article 16 as a response to the proposals from the European Commission,' Micheál Martin told the Dáil on 4 November. 'And I think if such an act was to be taken by the British government it would have far-reaching implications for the relationship between the United Kingdom and the European Union.'

A few days later Simon Coveney spelled out the warning, saying the EU would suspend its free trade and co-operation agreement with the UK if Article 16 was triggered. 'I think it is important that people like me and others who've been involved in this process make it very clear to the British Government the consequences of what they're considering doing in the context of the triggering of Article 16,' he said in a radio interview. 'I think I have a responsibility to perhaps set aside the diplomatic language that I'm expected to use as a foreign minister and be a bit more direct in relation to the consequences of that, as the Taoiseach has done this week.'

At that stage the government in Dublin braced itself for the worst. Interviewed for this book at the time, Leo Varadkar suggested that the row was not about what was best for Northern Ireland because the majority of Assembly members, as well as the business community, were broadly supportive of a protocol, albeit with modifications.

What's happening I think is not out of concern or interest in Northern Ireland or concern for the Good Friday Agreement. It's more about British nationalism. The worry I have is that Prime Minister Johnson has got to where he is by using English nationalism and Brexit. I think a confrontation with the EU, a confrontation with France in particular, and putting the Irish in their place a bit tends to play well with his base.

As it turned out, Johnson pulled back at that stage in the face of the determined EU response and worries expressed by senior cabinet figures like Michael Gove about the damaging impact a trade war with the EU would have on the struggling British economy. It seemed Johnson and Frost had expected that invoking Article 16 would set in train a year of technical talks and had not expected EU to call the entire trade agreement into question. There was a perceptible lowering of tension and soon there were even reports citing anonymous British sources that the government was prepared to modify its demand that the European Court of Justice should have no role in interpreting the Protocol. The EU then made a conciliatory move to waive the controls on medicines moving from Britain to Northern Ireland and it seemed that a compromise was finally coming into view.

'We got into a more even keel at that stage. It confirmed what I had suspected all along, that politics is more important that the substance of getting a deal,' said Martin. 'But to be fair Boris would consistently say he doesn't want to jeopardize Northern Ireland and he wants to get a deal, but feels that the arrangement isn't fair to the unionists.'

Johnson was also increasingly preoccupied by the internal threats to his own position, following a succession of scandals and controversies that had dogged him since the outbreak of Covid. The slide began in earnest with an attempt by the government to protect former Northern Secretary and Brexiteer Owen Paterson from sanctions after he had been found guilty by a parliamentary committee of unethical lobbying. The upshot was that Paterson resigned his seat but only after the government had undermined its own credibility by attempting to change the rules to save him.

The Paterson affair was embarrassing for Johnson and it was followed by a succession of leaks about a series of rule-breaking parties in Downing Street during the Covid lockdown. The leaks, which caused outrage in the UK, were orchestrated by Cummings, who had set out to undermine Johnson after his departure from Downing Street a year earlier.

On the Protocol front there was a rapid thaw in the mood after the threats in early November. All was sweetness and light when Martin met UK cabinet minister Michael Gove at a meeting of the British–Irish Council in Cardiff in late November. At a press conference later Gove said the EU Commission was taking a constructive approach and he was confident a deal could be done. Martin gave a similarly upbeat assessment. 'We thought there was a potential landing zone for Christmas,' he said later.

Then just before Christmas, Frost stunned everybody by resigning from the cabinet in protest at what he termed the government's 'current direction of travel'. His main gripe was that the UK had not embraced the alleged benefits of Brexit. Johnson immediately appointed his Foreign Secretary Liz Truss to take charge of the Protocol negotiations. Over the following months she had a number of meetings with Šefčovič and while the mood was more congenial than had been the case during Frost's tenure, big gaps still remained in the early months of 2022.

'I regarded Frost's resignation with some regret because sometimes the devil you know is better than the devil you don't know in the sense that he was fully abreast of the issues,' said Martin. 'Then Liz Truss came in and she certainly changed the mood music. She is nicer and more approachable but inevitably the impetus was lost. Before Christmas 2021 there was that real sense that we could bring this to a conclusion but it didn't happen,' said the Taoiseach.

Instead the British government began to ratchet up the tension as renewed pressure on Johnson's leadership began to develop in the early months of 2022, with former ally Steve Baker calling on him to go. Johnson tried to seize the initiative by comparing the Ukrainians fighting the Russian invasion to people in Britain voting for Brexit. The analogy angered politicians both in the UK and Europe. Donald Tusk, the former president of the European Council, called the comments offensive while Gavin Barwell, now a member of the House of Lords, said that voting in a referendum was not 'in any way comparable with risking your life in a war.'

In April the *Financial Times* reported that the government in London was preparing legislation to give Ministers sweeping powers to override the Protocol with Johnson and Truss signing off on the plan. Under the proposed legislation UK ministers would have unilateral powers to switch off key parts of the Protocol in UK law, including border checks on goods travelling to Northern Ireland from Britain. There was anger, but little surprise, in Brussels at the renewed sabre-rattling. One EU diplomat warned that any UK legislation that broke international law at a time when Western powers were seeking to present a unified front to Russia's invasion of Ukraine would be 'utterly irresponsible'.

During a visit to India Johnson confirmed that preparations for a confrontation were in train. He told a news conference in New Delhi that the Protocol 'really does not command the confidence of a large, large component of the population in Northern Ireland. We have to address that, we have to fix that.'

The reaction across the EU was unambiguous. German Chancellor Scholz ruled out any renegotiation of the Brexit deal relating to Northern Ireland. At a press conference in early May with Belgian Prime Minister Alexander De Croo, Scholz said that no one should 'unilaterally override, break or in any other way circumvent our deal.' De Croo was even more direct: 'Don't touch this, this is something we agreed on.' Šefčovič intervened to reinforce the point, saying the Protocol was part of an international agreement. 'Its renegotiation is not an option. The European Union is united in this position.'

The threats emanating from London followed the outcome of the Northern Ireland Assembly elections on 5 May where, as expected, the DUP lost its status as the biggest party, but not by nearly as much as opinion polls had predicted. Before the election was called Jeffrey Donaldson had announced that he would not serve in a new Executive if Sinn Féin became the biggest party and took the First Minister's position. However, during the election campaign he focused on attacking the Protocol and demanding that it be abolished.

When the votes were counted Sinn Féin ended up winning 27 seats, the same number of seats as in the previous Assembly election in 2019. The DUP dropped three to finish on 25, and the Alliance Party made significant gains ending up with 17 seats. Despite the DUP opposition there was a clear majority in the Assembly in favour of the Protocol. That did not deter Donaldson from proclaiming that his party would not enter the Executive as long as the Protocol remained in existence. The DUP's refusal to engage meant that the Assembly was unable to function and elect an Executive. This development fed into the British government's drive to override the Protocol, with Johnson and Truss citing the DUP position as evidence that there would have to be fundamental changes in its operation.

They also made a determined effort to pivot the argument on the Good Friday Agreement, insisting that the Protocol had undermined one of its basic principles as it did not have the support of the unionist community. While it was accepted in Dublin that Johnson was certainly influenced in part by a desire to get the DUP back into the power-sharing Executive, few in government had any doubt that his increasingly precarious hold on office was a major factor in his decision to ratchet up tension with the EU in May 2022.

In a long telephone conversation with Johnson on 10 May, Martin tried to dissuade the Prime Minister from taking unilateral action. He pointed out, to little avail, that the EU had engaged constructively in the Protocol discussions, had addressed the issue of medicines and had put forward a substantial package of flexibilities and mitigations for customs arrangements. It was a tetchy conversation with both men standing their ground and Johnson arguing that the EU had not done nearly enough to assuage unionist fears.

After the telephone call Martin wrote to Johnson setting out his views, copying the communication to von der Leyen and Šefčovič. He received a firm but courteous reply from Johnson, who said he was writing to the

Taoiseach in a spirit of friendship but, significantly, added that he was not copying his response to either von der Leyen or Šefčovič.

All the signals from London throughout May indicated that Johnson was determined to take unilateral action. Liz Truss announced on 17 May that it was the government's intention to introduce legislation in the near future to make changes in the Protocol, but she claimed that this was consistent with the UK's obligations under international law. This claim represented a dramatic shift from the acknowledgement a year earlier by Northern Secretary Bandon Lewis that overriding the Protocol would in fact be a breach of international law. Truss also claimed that the impending UK action would not undermine the Good Friday Agreement – on the contrary, it was necessary to protect it.

The London *Times* reported that the UK Attorney General Suella Braverman had advised the government that scrapping the Protocol would be legal because the EU's implementation of it was 'disproportionate and unreasonable'. She also claimed that the EU was undermining the Good Friday Agreement by creating a trade barrier in the Irish Sea and fuelling civil unrest.

Martin made a number of public appeals to Johnson not to abandon the Protocol, but he was increasingly critical of the British position:

> I think unionism has made a case to us and we have discussed it over time with the European Union. The European Union has met the unionist community and it has met with businesses and with industry in Northern Ireland and came forward with proposals. But the European Union really has never got a landing zone from the British government in relation to the Protocol. It's very unclear what will suffice for the British government. We have some sense of what would work with unionism, but we don't have that sense with the British government.

As in 2019, an American congressional delegation led by Nancy Pelosi and Richie Neal embarked on a fact-finding visit to Brussels, London and Ireland. Neal suggested that the dispute over the Protocol appeared to be a 'manufactured issue'. This drew a furious response from the DUP.

At this stage Johnson's leadership was coming under severe pressure from his own MPs who were increasingly perturbed by a steady drip of disclosures about the spate of parties in Downing Street during the Covid lockdown. An investigation by the London Metropolitan Police resulted in 83 people, including Johnson and Chancellor of the Exchequer Rishi Sunak, being fined for attending gatherings. The outcome was not as bad as Johnson's supporters feared as he was only fined £50 for one of the number of gatherings he had attended.

With the police investigation out of the way, a long-awaited report by senior cabinet office official Sue Gray into the lockdown parties, which had been delayed by the police investigation, finally appeared. Gray, a Londoner who had one stage had taken a career break to run a pub in Newry in Northern Ireland with her husband, had been tasked with looking into a number of alleged parties in Downing Street. Her remit was to report on the nature and purpose of the gatherings, who attended them and if any Covid rules were broken. In her report she gave details of sixteen events between May 2020 and April 2021. She was emphatic that 'what took place at many of these gatherings and the way in which they developed was not in line with Covid guidance at the time.'

Gray said the public had a right to expect 'the very highest standards of behaviour in such places, and clearly what happened fell well short of this'. Her report included a lot of damning evidence about the relaxed, boozy culture that prevailed in Johnson's Downing Street. It revealed that at a leaving do on 17 June 2020, pizza and prosecco were consumed and a karaoke machine used. During this event – which went on until 3 a.m. – one person was sick and there was a minor altercation between two others.

Speaking in the House of Commons after the publication of the report, the Prime Minister denied he had ever knowingly misled MPs about parties in Downing Street. He said he did not seek to absolve himself of responsibility, but insisted that progress had been made since the publication of Sue Gray's initial report earlier that year – including easier ways for staff to complain about behaviour. The leader of the opposition, Keir Starmer, called the report 'a monument to the hubris and arrogance of a government that believed there was one rule for them and another rule for everyone else'. He claimed it laid bare the rot of the government and how people in Number 10 'treated the sacrifice of the British people with utter contempt'.

The real worry for Johnson was not Starmer's criticism but the fact that a substantial number of his own MPs were appalled at the behaviour disclosed in the report. There was widespread public outrage at the fact that at a time when the vast majority of people were obeying the harsh lockdown regime, which included being unable to visit dying relatives and limiting the numbers allowed at funerals, Johnson and his staff felt free to engage in regular partying in Downing Street.

The depth of public anger was revealed by the response of a large crowd who gathered at St Paul's Cathedral in London to mark Queen Elizabeth's platinum jubilee. As Johnson and his wife, Carrie, climbed the steps of the cathedral he was met with a chorus of boos and jeers. The fact that a crowd of mainstream voters reacted so negatively came as a jolt to Johnson and it spooked a lot of Conservative MPs.

By that stage there was fevered speculation in the media that the number of MPs submitting letters of no confidence in the leader to the chair of the 1922 backbench committee, Graham Brady, had been steadily rising. Under party rules the threshold for triggering a vote of confidence was 54 letters and, given the number of MPs who had publicly declared their intention of submitting letters, it was clear by the jubilee weekend that the tipping point was close.

Early on the morning of Monday 6 June, with the Queen's jubilee celebrations out of the way, Brady announced that he had received the requisite number of letters to trigger a vote of confidence in the Prime Minister. With Johnson's agreement, the vote was scheduled for that evening, leaving little time for campaigning. The expectation was that Johnson would win, but the big question was by how much. Some of the rebels believed that they had moved too soon, ahead of two crucial by-elections scheduled for the end of the month, while the Johnson camp was confident of limiting the opposition to around a hundred votes or fewer.

Jeremy Hunt, whom Johnson had defeated in the leadership election in 2019, came out publicly against the Prime Minister, but no member of the cabinet joined the revolt. Leading figures like Rishi Sunak and Liz Truss, who had clear leadership ambitions, publicly backed Johnson. A worrying signal for him, though, was that opposition did not come from any particular faction but ranged from Brexiteers like Steve Baker and David Davis to openly pro-EU figures like Tobias Ellwood.

There was no great surprise that Johnson survived the vote of confidence, but the size of the rebellion was greater than anybody had expected. The Prime Minister won by 211 votes to 148, but the fact that 41 per cent of his parliamentary party voted no confidence in him came as a shock. He immediately welcomed the result as 'decisive and conclusive', but the prevailing view in Westminster was that his authority had been dealt a significant blow.

Former Conservative Party leader William Hague summed up that mood by writing the following day: 'If, with all the power of the party leadership, all the years of acquaintance with MPs, all the knowledge they have of your abilities and plans, you still cannot crush a vote of no confidence by a commanding margin, then not only is the writing on the wall but it is chiselled in stone and will not wash away.'

Hague pointed to the fact that the rebels did not constitute a faction who could be seen off but represented a widespread loss of faith in the leader that could not be repaired or reversed. 'For Johnson, continuing to lead the party after such a revolt will prove to be unsustainable,' he predicted in the London *Times*.

Alex Massie in the *Spectator* was even more brutal.

Despite what he may claim, Johnson is finished. The public know this and their sense of justice demands action. The precise moment of Johnson's demise may not yet be fixed but the gathering sense of inevitability means last night's vote was a shattering prime ministerial defeat in all but name. Tick tock. Tick tock. Time's up.

That is not the way Johnson saw the situation and he immediately embarked on a drive to shore up support from the Conservative Party and the public. His pitch to the voters was that he would take action to deal with the cost of living crisis sparked by the war in Ukraine. His pitch to his party's right wing was that he would act to override the Protocol.

The media reported that he would within days introduce a Bill that would unilaterally suspend parts of the Protocol. Micheál Martin appealed to Johnson to steady the ship and pull back from unilateral action. Addressing the European Parliament, the Taoiseach said the EU would respond in 'a calm and firm' manner to whatever decisions were taken by the British government and whatever legislation was published or enacted.

The President of the Parliament, Roberta Metsola, took a harder line that reflected the mood across the EU institutions. 'Renegotiating the Protocol on Northern Ireland is not an option. The European Parliament has reiterated its unwavering support for the Protocol on several occasions, and we remain fully committed to preserving peace on the island of Ireland.'

However, Johnson was not to be deterred. There was a tussle in the cabinet about how far the breach of the Protocol should go, but Johnson ultimately responded to pressure from Liz Truss and his old ERG allies and adopted a hard line, ignoring the concerns of Rishi Sunak and Michael Gove about the long-term impact on the struggling British economy.

The Northern Ireland Protocol Bill was finally published on 13 June. If passed into law it would give UK ministers the power to introduce a green channel with no checks for goods from Britain destined to remain in Northern Ireland; and a red channel applying EU checks to goods moving onwards across the border. A dual regulation system would allow goods in the North to comply with either EU or British regulations.

It would also give ministers the power to override almost every other part of the Protocol if they determined that they were causing political or economic disruption. The only elements that could not be changed were the Protocol's protection of the Common Travel Area, North–South co-operation and human rights in Northern Ireland. None of the changes will come into effect automatically if the Bill becomes law, and the Protocol will continue to be implemented as it is now until ministers choose to exercise their power to override it.

While Johnson maintained that the UK Bill was 'not a big deal', Micheál Martin was adamant that it was a very serious issue that went to the heart of the issue of trust. 'For a country like the United Kingdom to renege on an international treaty is something that does represent a new low point because the natural expectation of democratic countries, like ourselves, the UK, and all across Europe, is that we honour international agreements that we enter into,' he said.

The reaction in EU national capitals was similar. German Chancellor Olaf Scholz said the EU had its entire toolbox of trade retaliation measures at its disposal. His Foreign Minister, Annalena Baerbock, followed suit, saying that the EU 'cannot accept' the British government's unilateral moves. Italy's Europe Minister, Enzo Amendola, accused the UK of 'violating its international legal obligations'.

In his analysis of the move, *Irish Times* London editor Denis Staunton said the Bill was more extreme and far-reaching than had been anticipated, empowering British ministers to unilaterally scrap the Protocol almost in its entirety. 'But by leaving it up to ministers to decide if and when to override the Protocol, Boris Johnson has left open the possibility that nothing will happen at all.'

He made the point that the Bill offered no basis for negotiation with the EU, which has ruled out renegotiating the text of the Protocol and has no incentive to soften its position. 'The European Commission and the member-states know that Johnson's domestic position is too weak to allow him to make the necessary compromises so they will not squander concessions on what they see as a regime in its dying days.'

It was a repeat of the stalemate that marked the final months of Theresa May's time in office, when her position was so uncertain that the EU saw no point in making concessions she would not be able to deliver.

The European Commission formally responded to the British government's move by resuming the legal challenge it had put on hold in 2021 to the UK's unilateral extension of grace periods for the implementation of the Protocol. It also announced two new sets of legal proceedings over the failure to implement the Protocol as agreed. Announcing the moves, Šefčovič said the UK had no justification for unilaterally attempting to override an international agreement. 'Let's call a spade a spade. This is illegal,' he told a press conference, adding that it cast a shadow on relations at a time when international co-operation was even more important, a reference to the alliance against Russia's invasion of Ukraine.

What was striking was the low-key nature of the EU response. There was no talk of a trade war or other threats of strong action for the foreseeable future. It was clear that the decision had been taken in Brussels to wait and see whether the Northern Ireland Protocol Bill will become law.

When the Bill came before the House of Commons for its second reading on 27 June it came in for criticism from a number of Conservative MPs, including former Prime Minister Theresa May.

'This bill is not, in my view, legal in international law, it will not achieve its aims and it will diminish the standing of the United Kingdom in the eyes of the world, and I cannot support it,' she said, warning that unilateral action by the UK would not persuade the EU to change its negotiating stance.

> As I discovered after I had faced a no-confidence vote despite having won that no-confidence vote, they [the EU] then start to ask themselves, 'Well, is it really worth negotiating with these people in government because will they actually be there in any period of time?' ... Also, actually, I suspect they are saying to themselves why should they negotiate in detail with a government that shows itself willing to sign an agreement, claim it is a victory and then try to tear part of it up in less than three years' time.

The Bill was also criticised by Julian Smith, who called for fresh negotiations between Britain, the EU, Ireland and the parties in Northern Ireland. Simon Hoare, chairman of the Northern Ireland Affairs Committee, urged fellow Conservatives to oppose it. The second reading of the Bill passed by a comfortable majority but up to 40 Conservative MPs, including May, Smith and Hoare, abstained. British government hopes that the introduction of the Bill would persuade the DUP to participate in a power-sharing Executive were also dashed, with Jeffrey Donaldson saying his party would wait until the legislation was enacted before doing so.

18

The Downfall of Boris

'At some point we have to conclude that enough is enough. I believe that point is now.'

Sajid Javid, House of Commons, 7 July 2022

* * *

Boris Johnson's luck ran out in the early days of July 2022. His ability to dodge a succession of potentially fatal political and personal scandals had earned him the sobriquet of the 'greased piglet', but the tolerance of his party colleagues was tested once too often. Ernest Hemingway's famous line about two ways of going bankrupt, 'gradually, then suddenly,' aptly described Johnson's fate. It was no accident that his downfall happened after the disastrous loss of two by-elections in Tiverton and Honiton in the southwest of England, and Wakefield in the north in late June. The scale of the losses, one to the Liberal Democrats and the other to Labour, demonstrated beyond all doubt that Johnson had become an electoral liability for the Conservative Party.

The beginning of the end came on 30 June when the party deputy chief whip, Chris Pincher, resigned his position, saying that he had drunk far too much the night before at London's Carlton Club, a favourite haunt for Tory MPs, and had 'embarrassed myself and other people'. It soon emerged that he had allegedly groped two men while under the influence. Questions were immediately asked about how he could continue to remain a Conservative MP and, as pressure built, he resigned the party whip.

The floodgates then opened, with a string of allegations about Pincher's behaviour over the previous decade. There were complaints that he had made unwanted advances to other male MPs, one of them in a bar in the House of Commons and the other in his own office. As the media focused in on the story, Johnson was quoted as having privately referred to Pincher in the past as 'handsy' and on another occasion remaking that he was 'Pincher by name and pincher by nature'.

The immediate response of ministers was to say that Johnson was unaware of any specific complaints against Pincher when he was appointed as deputy chief whip in 2020. Later, Downing Street sources admitted that Johnson had been aware of general allegations but not of specific complaints. The BBC then reported that an official complaint and subsequent investigation into Pincher, while he was at the Foreign Office (July 2019 to February 2020), had confirmed his misconduct, and that Johnson had been made aware of the matter at that time.

The killer blow was delivered by the former civil service chief of the Foreign Office, Simon McDonald, who was appointed to the House of Lords in 2020. He sent an email to the parliamentary commissioner for standards, Kathryn Stone, early on 5 July stating unequivocally that Johnson's denials of knowledge about previous allegations against Pincher were simply untrue.

'Five days after Mr Pincher's resignation as deputy chief whip, there remains significant confusion surrounding complaints about his behaviour prior to the drunkenness he admits at the Carlton Club on 29 June,' wrote McDonald.

Inaccurate claims by 10 Downing Street continue to be repeated in the media. On 3 July, the BBC website reported: 'No official complaints against [Mr Pincher] were ever made.'

This is not true. In the summer of 2019, shortly after he was appointed minister of state at the Foreign Office, a group of officials complained to me about Mr Pincher's behaviour. I discussed the matter with the relevant official at the Cabinet Office. (In substance, the allegations were similar to those made about his behaviour at the Carlton Club.)

An investigation upheld the complaint; Mr Pincher apologised and promised not to repeat the inappropriate behaviour. There was no repetition at the FCO before he left seven months later.

McDonald then referred to the fact that the Prime Minister's official spokesman had claimed Johnson only knew of 'allegations that were either resolved or did not progress to a formal complaint', and had insisted that it was deemed not appropriate to stop an appointment simply because of unsubstantiated allegations.

> The original No 10 line is not true and the modification is still not accurate. Mr Johnson was briefed in person about the initiation and outcome of the investigation. There was a 'formal complaint'. Allegations were 'resolved' only in the sense that the investigation was completed; Mr Pincher was not exonerated. To characterise the allegations as 'unsubstantiated' is therefore wrong.

McDonald took the highly unusual step of releasing the contents of the email to the media. The impact was instantaneous and devastating for Johnson. It prompted Chancellor of the Exchequer Rishi Sunak and Health Secretary Sajid Javid to resign from the government within minutes of each other later that morning. They were followed by over 50 ministers, parliamentary private secretaries and other government figures over the following 48 hours.

In his resignation letter, Sunak referred to differences with the Prime Minister on economic policy but the main thrust of it was the issue of standards in government.

> The public rightly expect government to be conducted properly, competently and seriously. I recognise this may be my last ministerial job, but I believe these standards are worth fighting for and that is why I am resigning.

In his resignation speech in the House of Commons, Javid said he had given the benefit of the doubt to the Prime Minister on a series of issues, including the parties in Downing Street and the Sue Gray report.

And now this week again, we have had reason to question the truth and integrity of what we have been told. And at some point we have to conclude that enough is enough. I believe that point is now. … Last month I gave the benefit of doubt one last time. But I have concluded that the problem starts at the top and I believe that is not going to change. And that means that it is for those of us in a position who have responsibility to make that change.

The resignation of the two senior ministers started an avalanche of departures from office and it quickly became obvious to almost everybody except Johnson and his die-hard supporters that his time was up. Allies like Jacob Rees-Mogg and Nadine Dorries were loud in their support for the Prime Minister, denouncing the departing ministers, but it did nothing to stem the tide. Johnson filled the cabinet vacancies, quickly appointing Nadhim Zahawi as his new Chancellor. On the following day, as junior ministers continued to resign, the media reported that Michael Gove had told Johnson it was time to go. That evening Gove was sacked from the cabinet and Johnson vowed to fight on, continuing to appoint replacements. By the next morning, 7 July, he realised it was all over. After a little more than 24 hours as Chancellor, Zahawi called on the Prime Minister to go just as Johnson let it be known he was going to stand down.

Johnson appeared outside the door of 10 Downing Street at noon and delivered a defiant resignation speech which was totally in character.

I want to say to the millions of people who voted for us in 2019, many of them voting Conservative for the first time: Thank you for that incredible mandate. The biggest Conservative majority since 1987, the biggest share of the vote since 1979.

And the reason I have fought so hard in the last few days to continue to deliver that mandate in person was not just because I wanted to do so, but because I felt it was my job, my duty, my obligation to you to continue to do what we promised in 2019.

He claimed a list of achievements, the chief one being getting Brexit done and reclaiming the power for the UK to make its own laws in Parliament. 'Of course, it's painful not to be able to see through so many ideas and projects myself. But as we've seen at Westminster, the herd instinct is powerful. And when the herd moves, it moves.'

Opponents criticised Johnson for the tone of his speech and his failure to apologise for any of the events that had led to his resignation. There was also criticism of his announcement that he would stay in office until a new Conservative Party leader was elected in the autumn. However, it is the long-standing constitutional practice in the UK, and Ireland for that matter, that a prime minister who has lost an election or the confidence of Parliament remains in place until a successor is appointed.

In Dublin the response to Johnson's departure was generally one of relief. 'We won't know for a while whether the next prime minister will be any better but he or she simply cannot be worse,' said one senior official.

Taoiseach Micheál Martin deliberately avoided any personalised criticism. 'Prime Minister Johnson has led the British Government during an especially challenging period, including dealing with the impact of Covid-19 and the response to the war on Ukraine. From a personal perspective I am conscious that he has been through a difficult few weeks and I extend my best wishes to him and his family for the future, following the announcement of his resignation,' he said in a statement.

However, Martin did point up the strains in the Irish/British relationship.

Britain is Ireland's closest neighbour and the relationships between our two countries are long, deep and enduring. Our two governments working in close partnership is a key underpinning for peace and prosperity on these islands. While Prime Minister Johnson and I engaged actively together, we didn't always agree, and the relationship between our governments has been strained and challenged in recent times.

He referred to the fact that the two governments had joint responsibilities concerning stewardship of the Good Friday Agreement, as well as broader bilateral relations between them that required a spirit of respect, trust and partnership.

That is more important than ever today and I would once again urge a pulling back from unilateral action, whether that be on dealing with the legacy of the past, human rights, or the Northern Ireland Protocol. We have now an opportunity to return to the true spirit of partnership and mutual respect that is needed to underpin the gains of the Good Friday Agreement.

I welcome the fact that the United Kingdom and the European Union are working together closely in response to Russia's war of aggression on Ukraine. We need to see that approach extended to addressing other challenges, including the practical issues around implementation of the Northern Ireland Protocol that are of genuine concern to people and businesses in Northern Ireland.

I remain committed to working with the British Government and Prime Minister in that spirit in the times ahead.

The Taoiseach repeated the point in a number of media interviews, saying that he hoped for an opportunity to reset the relationship and insisting that the EU had been flexible in its approach to the Protocol. When pressed about what he thought of Johnson he insisted that he had 'never said anything negative' about the outgoing Prime Minister, despite their fundamental disagreements on Brexit, adding that Johnson was 'good company'.

Immediately after Johnson's resignation the EU architect of the Brexit deal, Michel Barnier, tweeted:

The departure of Boris Johnson opens a new page in relations with the UK. May it be more constructive, more respectful of commitments made, in particular regarding peace and stability in NI, and more friendly with partners in the EU. Because there's so much more to be done together.

US President Joe Biden also commented on the resignation, saying:

I look forward to continuing our close cooperation with the government of the United Kingdom, as well as our allies and partners around the world, on a range of important priorities. That includes maintaining a strong and united approach to supporting the people of Ukraine as they defend themselves against Putin's brutal war on their democracy, and holding Russia accountable for its actions.

What was noticeable and attracted a good deal of comment in the UK was that Biden made no personal reference at all to Johnson. The German Chancellor and French President made no comment at all on Johnson's resignation.

The clear message from Biden, Barnier and Martin was the wish that whoever succeeded Johnson would adopt a less aggressive posture towards the EU and would seek to make the Protocol work rather than pursuing the goal of scrapping it entirely and embarking on a trade war.

As the contest for the Conservative Party leadership got underway that seemed a forlorn hope. All of the initial eight candidates pledged to proceed with the Northern Ireland Protocol Bill, giving the British government the right to override the deal. There were significant differences of emphasis, with Rishi Sunak and Tom Tugendhat taking a less aggressive line and stressing the prospect of negotiating with the EU about the difficulties that have arisen. Sunak quickly emerged as the lead candidate and was widely regarded as the most competent of the contenders. However, opinion polls among Tory voters indicated that he could be beaten when it came to the run-off between the final two candidates left standing which would be decided by the vote of the entire party membership.

Foreign Secretary Liz Truss emerged the candidate of the hard-core Brexiteers, winning support from Rees-Mogg and Dorries, and by implication Johnson himself. The fact that she had actually supported Remain during the 2016 referendum and made passionate speeches about how damaging it would be for the British economy to leave the EU did not appear to dim the ardour of her backers.

Sunak appeared to be a better prospect for an improvement in British–Irish and EU–UK relations, if only on the basis that his experience as Chancellor might make him naturally reluctant to get dragged into a trade war with the EU over the Protocol. Truss's clear commitment to setting aside the Protocol and the enthusiastic backing of her candidature by the ERG made the prospects for a compromise on the issue under her leadership seem even more remote.

It is worth nothing, though, that it is not only the new Conservative Prime Minister who has serious issues with the EU over the Protocol. On 4 July, the day before the implosion of the Johnson premiership began, Labour leader Keir Starmer delivered a major speech setting out why he opposed the UK's return to the single market or the customs union, never mind the EU itself. Instead he promised to make Brexit work. 'We are going forwards not backwards, not reopening those divisions. I don't think reopening all the old wounds and going backwards is going to help us on that mission to drive the economy,' he told Sky News.

The leader of the Scottish National Party at Westminster, Ian Blackford, was scathing in his criticism.

Keir Starmer has strengthened the case for [Scottish] independence by embracing the Tories' hard Brexit. By running scared of the Tories and mutating into a pale imitation of Boris Johnson, Starmer is offering no real change at all.

While he may have departed office in disgrace, there is no escaping the profound impact Johnson had on his country; and it is one that looks likely to last for decades to come. On the purely political level his impact was huge. Over the course of six years he brought down three prime ministers: David Cameron, Theresa May and himself. However, his more significant impact was to alter radically the direction his country had taken for the previous half-century. His leadership of the Leave campaign was vital to the narrow victory in the 2016 referendum. Over the following three years he conspired with the ERG to bring down Theresa May in order to ensure that the UK would not simply leave the EU but the single market and customs union as well. The impact of that on the UK's economy and its place in the world will resonate for years and more likely decades to come.

As far as Ireland is concerned, Johnson's insistence on a hard Brexit made it inevitable that there would have to be a customs border either on the island itself or in the Irish Sea. Having assured the DUP that he would never agree to a border in the Irish Sea, to secure their support in the defenestration of May, he then reversed engines in October 2019 and struck a deal with Leo Varadkar to do precisely what he had promised to oppose.

That U-turn was a response to the steadfast opposition of the Irish government and the EU to a land border on the island of Ireland and it enabled him to find a way to avoid a no-deal Brexit and clear the path to a general election. His decisive victory in that election of December 2019 was based on the slogan 'Get Brexit Done' and he boasted that he had an 'oven-ready deal' to achieve it.

Writing on the day of Johnson's resignation, the respected *Financial Times* journalist Gideon Rachman pointed to the fact that Johnson had left Britain a troubled country in a dangerous time with the highest inflation rate of the G7 nations with the lowest growth prospects for 2023.

> To most foreign observers the root of all these troubles is obvious. The Brexit vote of 2016 destabilised Britain's politics, seriously damaged the economy and ruptured the country's trade and diplomatic relations with its European allies. Johnson, of course, led the Brexit campaign. The fact that he is now widely acknowledged to be a serial liar, deeply irresponsible and incapable of acknowledging hard choices might cast a shadow of a doubt over his signature 'achievement'. Could it perhaps be that his prolific dishonesty and refusal to look facts in the face extended to the way he campaigned for Brexit? But what is obvious overseas remains unsayable at home.

Far from Johnson's departure marking a change of course in relations with the EU, the battle between his potential successors to win the hearts and minds of the Tory faithful prompted them all to adopt his hardline stance. Despite the fact that Sunak was reported to have resisted the Protocol Bill when it was first mooted at cabinet, he fell into line with a series of anti-EU statements during the campaign. The sponsor of the Bill, Liz Truss, was even more hardline, launching bitter attacks on Sunak as the one most likely to betray the Johnson legacy.

In his final appearance at Prime Minister's Question Time on 20 July, Johnson defended his actions in office, declaring a 'mission largely accomplished for now', before signing-off by telling MPs, 'Hasta la vista, baby.' That was the catchphrase of the invincible character played by Arnold Schwarzenegger in *The Terminator* films. Its utterance by the departing Johnson as the final words of his premiership hinted at hopes of a return to Downing Street some day.

Conclusion

The deal concluded between Leo Varadkar and Boris Johnson in 2019 was a huge diplomatic victory for the Irish government as it succeeded in the core objective of avoiding a hard border on the island of Ireland. However, in the following years Johnson repeatedly attempted to override the arrangement he had not only signed but had touted in the subsequent British election as an 'oven-ready' deal that would get Brexit done.

Eventually, in June 2022, his government published a Bill that would override key elements of the Protocol. The move, which drew immediate condemnation from the European Commission and key member states, ensured that the Brexit process would continue to poison relations between the EU and the UK for some time and would also continue to destabilise the fragile political settlement in Northern Ireland. In the long run, the dispute could even undermine the entire Brexit settlement and lead to a trade war between the EU and the UK that would resurrect the prospect of a hard border in Ireland.

Nonetheless, the overriding Irish priority of avoiding a hard border remained intact in 2022, the Common Travel Area with the UK was preserved and the country remained firmly in the EU single market and customs union. At times during the negotiations it seemed inconceivable that all three ambitions could be realised and it was widely believed that one or other of them would have to be sacrificed. That this did not happen was due to a number of factors but the most important was that from the very beginning the Irish negotiators knew what they wanted and pursued a clearly defined strategy.

This was down to the political skills of Enda Kenny and Leo Varadkar who, in their very different ways, mobilised support from government leaders across the EU, particularly Germany. They were enabled to do this by strong team of officials in the Taoiseach's office and the Department of Foreign Affairs, who launched a sustained and successful diplomatic campaign to win support for Irish objectives.

That campaign only succeeded because of the backing it received from the Task Force established by the EU to negotiate the terms of Brexit with the UK. Michel Barnier's unwavering support for Ireland throughout the process was the essential ingredient that led to an acceptable outcome for the country. His determination to ensure that the interests of a small EU member state would not be sacrificed in the power struggle between London and Brussels stemmed from an emotional attachment to the Irish cause. Barnier's negotiating team, led by Sabine Weyand, provided the intellectual muscle and attention to detail that enabled him to deliver on that commitment.

On the other side of the equation the failure of the British stemmed largely from the fact that they did not have clear goals from the start because they were so divided about what they wanted to achieve. Those divisions had their roots in a deeply dishonest Leave campaign in 2016 which left the British public, the media and many politicians with delusions about the potential outcome. Theresa May started off by committing herself to a hard Brexit only to modify her position on a number of occasions as reality intruded. She was ultimately destroyed by her honest determination to ensure that Northern Ireland was treated in the same way as the rest of the UK in whatever settlement emerged.

Boris Johnson, who shamelessly used the DUP to help bring down May, ultimately agreed to the very border in the Irish Sea that the party had been determined to block. Gavin Barwell has noted that some people believed Johnson and his team didn't know what they were signing up to. 'The truth is that their initial plan was to prorogue parliament and leave without a deal. When that failed they switched to seeking an election. It would be easier to win an election with "an oven-ready Brexit deal" so the strategy switched to accepting whatever deal was on offer with a view to wriggling out of it subsequently.'

Dr Andrew McCormick, a senior Northern Ireland civil servant who was engaged in the Brexit negotiations, is adamant that Johnson and his ministers understood the full implications of the Protocol. 'There is little credibility in any argument that the UK government either did not anticipate the implications of what it had agreed, or was constrained and unable to choose any other option,' he wrote in an article for the Constitution Society in the UK in 2022. 'The facts and choices had been spelt out clearly over the whole period from 2016 onwards and the detail of the provisions (notably most of the applicable EU law contained in Annex 2 to the Protocol) were known at latest in autumn 2018.'

Having won the general election in December 2019, Johnson did not take long to start his campaign to override the key elements of the deal. After almost two years of wrangling about the implementation of the Protocol there was a glimmer of hope that the unified response of the EU, the UK and the USA to the Russian invasion of Ukraine in February 2022 might have made a settlement easier. Instead, with his leadership under pressure, Johnson moved to shore up support from the Brexiteer faction of the Conservative Party by taking an even harder line on the Protocol. The outcome was the publication of the Northern Ireland Protocol Bill in the summer of 2022. If that Bill becomes law in its present form the dispute will enter a new phase.

One positive from the Irish perspective in the summer of 2022 is that all the early predictions of an economic disaster flowing from Brexit did not materialise. The Trade and Cooperation Agreement facilitated the continuation of free trade between the EU and the UK, and that was crucial for Ireland. The country also benefited from the fact that to date the UK has not imposed costly customs formalities on Irish imports, as has happened the other way around. Even if they are ultimately applied, Irish exporters will have had ample time to prepare for the new regime.

There has been a significant shift in trading patterns, with a decline in the use of the UK land bridge for Irish trade with continental Europe. That process has been facilitated by a number of new direct shipping lines between Ireland and the Continent. Businesses in the Republic and Northern Ireland have also adapted to the opportunities provided by the Protocol to avoid much of the new bureaucracy, and trade between the two parts of the island has boomed.

By contrast, the UK's trade with the EU suffered a hit from Brexit, even if the impact was obscured by the Covid lockdowns, supply chain disruptions and a worryingly high level of inflation. The data on the negative impact of Brexit on UK exports is incontrovertible. The food and drink industry was probably the hardest hit by the post-Brexit border bureaucracy that arose from the absence of a veterinary agreement or standards alignment with the EU. The impact on British agriculture raised fears for national food security.

While Ireland has fared better on the economic front following Brexit, there have been significant downsides, not least the economic border in the Irish Sea and the resulting tension generated by the Protocol. Brian Murphy, one of the key people involved in the final stages of the process, is clear that the outcome is nothing to cheer about:

> I wouldn't want for a minute to suggest that the Brexit outcome was a success. We didn't want a border on the island or even in the Irish Sea. We got the best deal we could get in those terrible circumstances but it could have been so much better if any of those votes in the House of Commons had gone the other way and we didn't have any kind of border.

Brexit has inflamed the divide in Northern Ireland. Despite the heroic achievement of Julian Smith in getting the two sides to agree on a resumption of power sharing in January 2020, after three years of suspension, the turmoil in the DUP and the early collapse of the Executive has created serious doubts about its future. The outcome of the 5 May elections, which saw Sinn Féin emerge for the first time as the biggest party in Northern Ireland Assembly, winning 27 seats to the DUP's 25, has led to further political stalemate.

Having earlier pledged not to serve under a Sinn Féin First Minister, the DUP leader, Jeffrey Donaldson, changed tactics in the aftermath of the election and made the abolition of the Protocol the condition for participating in a new Executive. His approach tallied with that of Boris Johnson and Liz Truss, who used the DUP's position to justify their decision to override the Protocol.

Another negative impact of Brexit was to set back Irish–British relations in a fundamental way. Relations between the two countries had improved significantly in recent decades and common membership of the EU contributed greatly to that. Politicians and officials from both countries had grown increasingly close as they worked together in pursuit of common interests at EU level and that helped them to come together to work on common solutions to the problems in Northern Ireland.

Those close working relations have been badly damaged by Brexit and the inevitable tensions that developed between the two sides during the long-drawn-out process. It undermined the good relationships built up over decades between politicians and officials in Ireland and the UK. That fact that they will no longer be meeting at EU level to work out common positions means that the distance is likely to grow wider as times goes by.

At a popular level the entire Brexit process has also raised the ghost of troubles past. Brexit was a product of English nationalism and the tense and protracted negotiations with the UK inevitably generated the revival of a more aggressive form of Irish nationalist sentiment in the Republic. This was evidenced in opinion polls which showed the strongest public support for the Irish government at moments when it adopted a tough stance in opposition to the UK.

At a party political level, the nationalist rhetoric engendered by the Brexit process, when taken in tandem with the centenary commemorations of the 1916 Rising and the War of Independence, has helped to promote the rise of Sinn Féin. That party is committed to pursuing a united Ireland, with a border poll as its immediate objective. Ironically Sinn Féin was a strongly anti-European force in Ireland until the Brexit referendum prompted a sudden conversion.

The party condemned the EU/IMF bailout of the Irish economy during the financial crisis and is a member of the hard left group in the European Parliament composed mainly of communists and ex-communists. Sinn Féin supported Vladimir Putin right up to the invasion of Ukraine and opposes any Irish involvement in European defence. In the longer term the rise of the party has the capacity to create even greater tension with the UK and to fray Ireland's positive relationship with the EU, although the war in Ukraine may have changed the atmosphere in a significant fashion.

One big question is whether all of this could have been avoided if Ireland and the EU had been more willing to compromise with Theresa May. Gavin Barwell has suggested that if the consent mechanism in the Protocol given to Johnson had been offered to May she would have been able to get a deal through the Commons. Julian Smith takes a similar view, arguing that there was a moment when such an offer might have worked. Leo Varadkar has given this point a lot of thought but still thinks that May was so politically weak that even with a concession on a consent mechanism she would not have been able to deliver a deal. It will remain one of the 'what ifs' of history.

One way or another, the Irish state spent an enormous amount of political capital on getting the support of the EU institutions and the member states for its position on Brexit. After one late-night European Council session Angela Merkel warned Leo Varadkar that Ireland had better not come back looking for special concessions on anything else for a long time. Having benefited from such solidarity, the challenge facing Irish political leaders is how to show solidarity in return. The acceptance of the need to abandon the attachment to the 12.5 per cent corporation tax rate was an important step and was executed skilfully by Minister for Finance Paschal Donohoe.

The invasion of Ukraine raised the equally fundamental question of what Irish neutrality means in the modern world. Micheál Martin's unambiguous involvement in a common EU approach to sanctions on Russia signalled a shift away from prevarication on international conflict, but the question of common defence is going to become ever more important. Ireland will have to frame an approach that reflects its position as an EU state committed to common democratic values or face potential marginalisation in the decades ahead.

Sir Ivan Rogers, who served as Britain's ambassador to the EU until he quit over his government's approach to Brexit in 2017, forecast in June 2022 that the Protocol dispute would remain 'a crucial impediment to any improvement in the UK–EU relationship' for the rest of the British parliamentary and European Commission terms, which are both due to end in 2024. Following the publication of the Northern Ireland Bill it was clear that the consequences of Brexit will continue to be felt in a variety of ways for a long time.

Name Index